GLOBAL SECURITY CONCERNS

Anticipating the Twenty-First Century

Dr Karl P. Magyar
Editor

Lt Col Bradley S. Davis
Assistant to the Editor

Air University Press
Maxwell Air Force Base, Alabama

March 1996

Library of Congress Cataloging-In-Publication Data

Global security concerns: anticipating the twenty-first century / Karl P. Magyar.
p. cm.
Includes bibliographical references.
1. War—Forecasting. 2. Security International. 3. Twenty-first century—Forecasts. I. Magyar, K. P. (Karl P.)
U21.2.G53 1996
355.027'0905—dc20

96-12651
CIP

ISBN 1-58566-006-X

First Printing April 1999
Second Printing July 2000
Third Printing September 2001
Fourth Printing January 2003
Fifth Printing February 2004
Sixth Printing March 2006

Disclaimer

This publication was produced in the Department of Defense school environment in the interest of academic freedom and the advancement of national defense-related concepts. The views expressed in this publication are those of the authors and do not reflect the official policy or position of the Department of Defense or the United States government.

This publication has been reviewed by security and policy review authorities and is cleared for public release.

Air University Press
131 West Shumacher Avenue
Maxwell AFB AL 36112-6615
http://aupress.maxwell.af.mil

Dedicated to the students of the

Air Command and Staff College,

many of whom will soon make vital security-related

decisions concerning our future

Contents

PART III
Economic Issues

PART IV
Military-Strategic Issues

Illustrations

Tables *Page*

Preface

One of the most important and intellectually fascinating areas of investigation for the student of political affairs concerns the attempt to understand why man makes war. This ancient field of inquiry may be addressed at such various levels as the philosophical and psychological or the institutional and structural contexts of human behavior. For example, did the recent wars in Somalia, Rwanda, and Haiti result from clashing ideologies, tribalism, poverty and class warfare, the cold war, or distant ramifications of colonial history, or, as has been postulated, the trees of these countries having been cut down? These plausible sources of conflict offer insight into various dimensions of explanations for wars; however, the analysts in this volume focus on just one aspect of the inquiry. They were charged with the task of anticipating which specific contentious issues likely will propel large, organized political units to choose violent means of acquiring their sociopolitical objectives rather than attaining them peacefully. The units on which we focus have been traditionally identified as states, but we recognize that a host of new sub- and suprastate actors also will play major roles in such wars; hence, we also will allude to them.

The specific issues identified in the text are by no means completely new sources of contention. Indeed, we may easily argue that throughout history men have fought over the same objects and values—only the weapons, strategies, and tactics in their acquisition have changed. We concentrate on those issues that we believe will be prominent sources of contention at the dawn of the twenty-first century. We knowingly omitted some of the most pervasive and such well-articulated causes of wars as power-balancing initiatives or the quest for such natural resources as oil or strategic minerals. These causes no doubt will prevail as sources of violent conflict, but they will not likely assume new forms as will those issues which comprise our chapter topics.

Nor do we rank in order of importance a list of issues likely to lead to wars. We make no assumptions about the feasibility of such rankings as too many undetermined variables would enter into such an equation. We do offer a brief background on each topic; we attempt to assess the magnitude of them; we speculate on who the antagonists may be; and we attempt to project the disruptive potential of each topic under consideration and speculate on how it might impact the interests of the United States.

We also are sensitive to assumptions that the potential disputes we portray must lead to war. In our analyses we offer balance by exploring the prospect that our contentious issues also may be resolved peacefully. Currently, numerous available and prominent analyses caution us not to be overly sanguine about the end of war, and as analysts associated with the nation's military effort, we maintain a healthy respect for anticipating early the emerging challenges which counsel the timely formulation of appropriate responses.

We do not proffer the emergence of startling new world paradigms and, we avoid the "gloom-and-doom" approach in drawing attention to our investigations. In fact, most of the sources of instability identified in this volume have manifested themselves in modern-day conflicts, but we anticipate a larger role for them in the future. For example, it may seem innovative to identify international criminal activity as a future cause of armed hostilities between states, but we need only to recall our military operations in Panama and Haiti, which were motivated in part by our attempt to diminish the flow of narcotics into the United States. The US also has offered military support to the governments of several South American countries so they might curtail illicit drug production—ultimately headed for the US.

We may be struck by several observations in the following chapters. Foremost, in addressing prospective disruptive challenges emanating from the sources we identify, there will be little utility for addressing the challenges with nuclear weapons. Conventional military means, which address the issues while longer lasting political solutions are formulated, may address the host of conflicts having social and economic sources better than nuclear weapons. Another readily identifiable characteristic of many of the sources of conflict is the pervasiveness of economic bases. It may be the most overt reason on occasion, but many times economic foundations play an underlying role in support of other noneconomic causes. This requires that we analyze more than only the immediate, overt sources of instability but also the long-term perspective which may dictate a nonmilitary strategy for the ultimate resolution of those conflicts.

Not surprising, most, if not virtually all, armed conflicts in the near term will be experienced in the third world, although they will engage the interests—and involvement—of the developed world. While resource and ecological problems will underlie many conflicts as the third world attempts to come to term with its population growth in a constrained international environment, the developed world will not escape altogether these same concerns. That armed force has been implemented in recent years by several developed states to ensure access to food resources, namely in pursuit of established fishing rights and practices, has surprised many. Others have noted that in some regions of the world in the future water might be worth more than oil. And, a final suggestion cautions the reader to accept the complexity of causes of wars. Wars are rarely the product of a clearly defined object of contention between two rivals; instead, antagonists, as well as allied participants, pursue a combination of goals when the war allows them the opportunity to do so. What we present in these analyses are major, or precipitating, causes of potential conflicts. We do not present the myriad of underlying causes which ultimately will shape the passion and the final outcome of the wars.

The analysts have been requested to make only brief comments about the implications of their respective analyses for the interests of the United States. An elaboration of this subject will be a valuable addition to the text, but it goes beyond our modest undertaking in this present effort. There will emerge from our presentations several implications for adjusting the structure, capabilities, and mission of our military if we are to prevail. However, as noted, the defense capability of our country will realize inherent limitations in many of our projected conflicts, and often the defense establishment will have to augment sociopolitical initiatives, which will bear the brunt of conflict resolution. We offer no counsel on how to prepare our armed forces of the future; instead, our contribution identifies the sources of emerging security problems.

Finally, we must emphasize that we imposed no requirement on the authors to present a common view of the impact of future security instability. We encouraged each analyst to exercise personal judgment and the preferred analytic approach. Also, we all write in our private analytic capacities, and our views do not represent the official positions of the US Department of Defense nor of any US government agency.

As editor, I wish to thank Col John A. Warden III, USAF, Retired, who as commandant, Air Command and Staff College, was supportive of this undertaking. I am also grateful to Lt Col Bradley S. Davis for providing valuable, energetic, and competent service as editorial assistant. Ms Yuna Braswell offered excellent computer work for us—and I thank her. And, I am very pleased that my good friend, Dr Richard Bailey, with whom I have had the privilege of working on several earlier projects, was appointed by Air University Press to serve as our editor. Thank you all for a job well done.

Karl P. Magyar, PhD
Editor

PART I

INTRODUCTION
Anticipating the Sources of Future Conflicts

1

History, Culture, and Change

Foundations of Conflicts and Wars

Karl P. Magyar

A spate of cynical analytic literature has recently emerged about the "new world disorder." This spate is somewhat curious as global tensions during the cold war were certainly reason for cynicism, considering the destructive prospects of a nuclear exchange between the East and the West. In light of the evident cessation of tensions between the members of the former Warsaw Pact and the North Atlantic Treaty Organization (NATO), how can we explain the prevailing concern with the uncertainty of the post-cold-war era and the apprehension about the future?

The answer to this question is not elusive. As one of the two major powers in the cold war system, America realized that its entire security culture had centered on meeting the perceived challenge of an expansionist Soviet alliance. This challenge posed a real and an immediate threat to America's core security interests and to that of our allies. Furthermore, although numerous other conflicts and wars prevailed, those wars which mattered most to the West were perceived within the cold war context. This context applied especially to Korea, Hungary, Formosa, Cuba, Vietnam, Angola, Namibia, Ethiopia, and Afghanistan. Lurking on the other side was always the "Evil Empire"—the Soviets, Chinese, or other communists, which, for a long time, the West saw as a monolithic bloc.

However, in the midst of the cold war, much of the third world became independent, yet the West viewed their struggles not as liberation wars or as civil wars, but as part of a Soviet grand design for potential global revolution. The West simply ignored most of the lesser conflicts. In fact, countries which had their own agendas that generally remain unfulfilled to this day shaped most of these conflicts in the third world. The issue is not that such wars in the third world today are new conflicts or that significantly more of them have occurred than during the cold war, but the issue is that we have begun to recognize them for various reasons. They are becoming disturbingly destructive and tend towards prolongation.[1] These wars disrupt entire regions, potentially threaten global stability, and may disrupt the extensively intertwined global economic system. The collapse of the Soviet Union and Yugoslavia has brought these conflicts to the doorstep of Western Europe, America's trusted traditional allies, and members of NATO—who had banded together successfully to deter a nuclear threat only to now face the prospect of becoming engulfed in pre–World War II type conventional wars fueled by nationalism.

The end of the cold war has brought a welcome reprieve from a credible nuclear threat, but warriors and civilians dying in the steady stream of lesser conflicts have forged ahead unabated. The Stockholm International Peace Research Institute counted 30 major wars raging in 1991 and 34 in 1993.[2] From the perspective of the victims, the distinction between the catastrophe of a nuclear or a conventional war is illusory. We also may make a powerful case by arguing that the absence of the cold war will enhance hostilities as neither of the former Great Powers is available to repress the proclivity towards the use of force among their previous allies or among those over whom they previously had influence. Possibly, the Gulf War would not have occurred as it might have had to exact a commitment for alignment from the Soviets who might still have had their hands full in nearby Afghanistan. But certainly the Soviets would have taken an active involvement in the deteriorating situation in Yugoslavia and the threatened interests of the Serbs—their traditional allies. Nor would Chechnya's violent secession have been attempted under the authoritarian regime.

Yet another legacy of the cold war is the flood of arms which are dispersed throughout the world, as well as the transfer of technology for arms production. These weapons had been distributed liberally to allies and proxies, and today they proliferate throughout the third world. In Africa's Horn region, such arms have on several occasions been more available than bread. The use of these ubiquitous arms has fueled the prolonged wars in Sudan, Ethiopia, Djibouti, and Somalia in that conflict-prone region. Such arms abound in numerous global regions and are increasingly available to private terrorist and criminal groups.

The data and unfortunate impact of the post-cold war conflicts is evident, but can we not perceive any positive developments in the new era? The answer does offer encouraging signs, and an overall assessment requires a balanced analysis. The most significant accomplishment of the cold war was the fact that no nuclear war broke out—even in the face of many otherwise dire predictions. Furthermore, the nuclear control regimes have seen considerable progress in dampening the move towards nuclear proliferation.[3] Significant also is the demise of the Marxist Soviet state whose disintegration has led to some severe internal conflicts, but these conflicts have not spilled beyond the immediately affected region. The reluctance by some Russian military units to fight in Chechnya in December 1994 yielded a remarkable turnabout from the bellicose Soviet tendencies a few years before.[4] Czechoslovakia's "velvet revolution" led to the breakup of that country without an interfering Soviet Union. And, while Yugoslavia's disintegration has been an extremely violent affair, no Soviet Union intervened, and that conflict has not spilled into neighboring states. Around the world, numerous other conflicts ground to a halt or lost their significance in the absence of Soviet support. Except for the border skirmish between Peru and Ecuador in 1995, relatively weak internal insurgencies, and the waning stages of a few old internal conflicts, Latin America has rarely been as peaceful as it is now. Today, the area is dominated almost entirely by democratic governments. Similarly, the fortunes of southern Africa have quickly changed, and its conflicts have ceased or lost global importance through the departure of the Soviet/Cuban-sponsored offensive in Angola, their previous support of Mozambique, and the curtailment of Soviet support to South Africa's African National Congress, which led to a remarkably peaceful transition in that controversial country.

In the 1960s and 1970s, the US had been widely criticized for its aggressive "imperial" tendencies, but this impulse has not resulted in any permanent acquisitions or imposition of controls over new areas. Under US influence, democracy, human rights, and free markets have become the new standard; however, the realities vary considerably from the ideal. But this trend is a start. The United Nations has expanded its peacekeeping efforts enormously, with mixed results, but certainly as a commendable effort and indicator of the potential of cooperation. Other countries have begun to accept responsibilities for regional peace efforts, which portend another positive development. The efforts of West Africa's Economic Community of West African States (ECOWAS) force in Liberia, which, while not without controversy, is being examined for possible emulation in other regions. Yet another major realization is that extremist and doctrinaire cold war ideologies have not addressed fundamental problems in the third world and that they may do so sooner through liberal economic approaches than through mere ideological posturing.

These significant positive developments weigh heavily as a balance to the prevailing analytic literature which portrays a generally pessimistic view of the future. This situation is not entirely paradoxical as it may be explained by referring to the positive developments in much of the world. But for other substantial regions, these positive developments are not a reality, and continued conflicts may be a more apt characterization. The emerging pronounced division between two worlds is the general tenor of the analysis of Matthew Connelly and Paul Kennedy in their article, "Must it be the Rest Against the West?"[5] They argue that life is good for areas of the world that can compete, but the globe's growing noncompetitive sector, with its unmanageable population numbers, will soon swamp these areas. The evaluative balance must therefore be qualified within the "two worlds" context whose widening disparities between its two constituent parts may be the most important dynamic force and underlying source of conflicts in the future.

Global Perspectives

The demise of the second world—traditionally identified as the Soviet Union and its East European allies and characterized by their command economies—has produced the new two worlds division of states. The industrially developed democracies and their market economies comprise one world, with the rest comprising the other world. The latter comprises the numerous developing states, divided into several subcategories that depict their disparate economic status. Russia, the other new republics which emerged from the breakup of the Soviet Union, and the former East European states remain today in an analytic limbo. Max Singer and Aaron Wildavsky similarly recognize such a two-fold division of the "real world." They refer to its constituent parts as the zone of "peace, wealth, and democracy," and the zone of "turmoil, war, and development."[6] Their useful distinction suggests that more than only traditional criteria, which focused on the north-south division of the globe, must be considered and that economic status also coincides with security conditions.

The Demographic and Economic Context

The total global population is approaching 6 billion. Of this, fewer than 20 percent live in the first world, though by no means do all inhabitants of these countries live at typical first world standards. An analogy may be made with reference to the macro data for South Africa, where the country's entire economy masks the disparate distribution of wealth between whites and blacks. Collectively, the countries characterized as first world, dominate more than 80 percent of the globe's existing wealth and its economic transactions. Connelly and Kennedy point out that 95 percent of the total global population growth in the future will occur in the poor countries of the world. Despite economic growth in the third world, in terms of absolute numbers, there will be many more poor people than before. These people are rapidly migrating into the swelling shantytowns of third world cities, thus making the population numbers of these cities the size of some small countries. And, these populations will be predominately very young.[7]

Growing at an annual rate of 3 percent, the population of many of these countries will double in 24 years.[8] Many developing states exceed that rate today. Jessica Tuchman Mathews elaborates on the new concept of security which also must account for resource, environmental, and demographic issues and concludes, "Environmental decline occasionally leads directly to conflict."[9] However, observers must not view this phenomenon automatically as negative, according to Sheldon Richman. He points out that most of the world's population growth rate throughout history was exceeded by economic progress.[10] Observers must consider not only the raw aggregate data for the globe, but they also must identify the precise location of the growth to pinpoint the relationship between population growth, economic development, and conflict.

We may paint a generally rosy prospect for the peaceful first world—whose democracies make no war on each other. Also, there may be encouraging signs for the countries emerging out of the former Soviet Union, whose transformation, though volatile, has not been disruptive beyond their own regions. But vast parts of the third world are rapidly advancing towards greater uncertainty. They are doing so under conditions of utter deprivation and frustration, fueled by the technological advantages of the information age that depict the opulent and excessive splendors of the first world even to the most obscure inhabitant of the third world. Where in the past, rising expectations meant eventual ownership of a bicycle, now the standard expectation is a luxury automobile, house, electronic gadgetry, food, health care, education, vacations, and a splendid retirement. And the billions of poor demand it now. The economic strain on the world will be extremely great as the demand and increasingly illicit or unorthodox efforts to obtain such coveted lifestyles will outpace the political ability to ensure its lawful realization. At this matrix a new culture of conflict may explode in the world.

Where authoritarian governments are absent, third world democratic governments will have few resources to contain challenges to their rule. In the absence of immediate economic success, such frail democratic governments will lose the respect of their aggressive citizens or of ambitious or envious militaries, as occurred in Haiti. In the past, patience marked rising expectations, but since expectations tend to remain unfulfilled, the time allowed today for governments to produce results may be getting precariously short. The plight of the frustrated masses in Slovenia, Croatia, Bosnia, Chechnya, Eritrea, Somalia, Rwanda, and Liberia shows their impatience with the governments' hollow promises. The governments of such failing states amount to little more than small coteries of privileged elites, ensconced in embattled medieval-like fortifications, with their national armies constituting little more than paid mercenaries to protect, not the nation from neighboring predators, but the elite from the masses. Their citizens will judge such governments to be irrelevant as subnational units emerge in the vacuum, in effect, as warlords. These were in great evidence in Mozambique throughout its long civil war as its government exercised little authority outside of the capital, while the country's rebel force raped the scarce resources of the vast rural districts. The situation does not vary much in parts of Peru, Colombia, Burma, Cambodia, and Somalia and in numerous locations in Africa. Many who are able will flee; others will stay and fight. But the ensuing anarchy will depress the value of life greatly.

The economic and conflict data support such an assessment. At the crux is a question which has never been adequately answered: Why is it that much of the fighting in the world takes place in the poorest regions? At first sight, one is tempted to make a superficial judgment about the poor attacking the rich in pursuit of justice and redistribution, but this, of course, is not a valid assertion. The poor tend to fight other poor, mostly their neighbors with whom they have lived for centuries, or they fight among themselves. This phenomenon is explained by as many theories as there are analysts. Some analysts note that poor societies tend to be traditional societies that still view making war as a social necessity and cultural tradition.[11] Other explanations identify inequitable global economic relations which allegedly underlie and exacerbate hostile class relationships.[12] A third category of explanations argues that at an early stage of their development, virtually all states experience severe turmoil associated with their attempt to equilibrate internal legitimation forces; that is, poor states have governments which have never demonstrated their relevance to the masses, but only to a restricted elite.[13]

Whatever the precise or ultimate cause for such massive war-induced violence, one must understand that large-scale war atrocities are not abating in the post-cold war world and that such casualties in the half century since the end of World War II are occurring in the third world and not among industrially developed states—which had been the case prior to that war. This explanation does not suggest that the mostly colonized regions of the world have not experienced traditional conflicts on their own. However, because of the lack of modern armaments, absence of modern conceptions of nationalism, and lack of extensively intertwined external relations, it does suggest that their traditional conflicts were much more limited in scope—and in casualties. The existence of these factors today, however, suggests a much bleaker future for the third world.

The Conflict Context

When portraying the state of conflict of our contemporary period, a wide latitude of interpretation exists with regard to deducing trends or projecting future developments. Certainly, we may identify pessimistic and optimistic attitudes among analysts. Zbigniew Brzezinski offers a sober analysis of the twentieth century's record of war casualties. He notes that this is the century of "megadeaths."[14] Brzezinski identifies four individuals most directly responsible for the major war atrocities: Lenin, Stalin, Mao, and Hitler—who, incredibly, was a relatively minor offender compared to the other three. Other wars in the third world extinguished millions of additional lives. These wars included those in Paraguay, Ethiopia, India and Pakistan, Korea, Vietnam, Nigeria, and the war between Iran and Iraq. All told, Brzezinski calculates that "during the 20th century, no less than 167 million lives—and quite probably in excess of 175 million—were deliberately extinguished through politically motivated carnage." However, despite this grim assessment of the present century, the post-cold war era has allowed for renewed faith.

Two developments account for the current upbeat views regarding the cessation of major wars in which the US may become involved or attacks which may be launched against the US. The first emanates from the fact that despite the prevailing tensions of the cold war, neither a conventional nor a nuclear war broke out between NATO and the Warsaw Pact alliance. The gravity of those previous tensions is only now emerging from Soviet sources which note that it was not during the Cuban missile crisis that Soviets were prepared to utilize nuclear weaponry, but during the early 1980s, when top Soviet planners witnessed the shift in the "correlation of forces" which favored the West.[15] However, rational calculations projected that the risks and consequences of waging a nuclear war were simply unacceptable. The second development responsible for the currently more optimistic strategic assessment emerges from the stable and peaceful relations among the industrially developed states of the West. Democracies do fight, we are told, but not among each other. According to a report by Freedom House, this "rule" has held firmly in the 353 substantially sized wars fought since 1819, and from all appearances it promises to continue.[16] No doubt this reluctance to engage in global-level wars emanates from the hard lesson of twentieth century history; namely, that such wars cost too much and risk everything, while offering no certain commensurate gains. Regarding the eight-year war between Iran and Iraq in the 1980s, both sides had spent an estimated $416 billion up to 1985, which had exceeded the sum of $364 billion that they had earned from oil sales since they first started to export the mineral.[17] Accordingly, we have increasing reason to believe that because of the destructive potential of nuclear wars, and the excessive expenses associated with large-scale conventional wars, mature statesmanship will encourage the peaceful resolution of differences in conflicts involving major developed states. These statesmen will not base their decisions on great moral imperatives, but on pragmatic self-interests.

Nevertheless, as noted above, most analysts project the continuation of wars, but of a different nature, and believe that most will occur among or within third world societies—with frequent residual implications for the more peaceful world. The data regarding war casualties and destruction may well project exponential increases in the future, but it will not be generated among the developed states of the world. Since the war in Vietnam, US military involvements in such conflicts has been extraordinarily sensitive to body counts. US combat deaths in Grenada (1983) were 18; in Panama (1989), 23; in Somalia (1993), 29; and the Gulf War (1991), 182. These data contrast with the hundreds of thousands who lost their lives in the mostly civil wars which rage unabated especially in South and

Southeast Asia, Middle East, Africa, and Central America.[18] In some cases casualties approximated a million, and, indeed, the single largest killing war since World War II was the Biafran War in Nigeria during the late 1960s. It accounted for an estimated 2.5 million deaths. During 1993, of the 79 listed countries experiencing major conflicts and political violence, 65 were in the developing world.[19] Analysts widely agree that 90 percent of casualties in the third world's civil wars involved civilians caught in the battles from which they could not escape, or they were victims of ensuing starvation, dislocation, and disease.[20]

Another dimension of the new profile of wars concerns their prolongation. At the outset modern wars among the major powers generally were short affairs, with continuous actions marked by a series of related battles.[21] But modern insurgency warfare, expertly formalized in the writings of Mao Tse-tung, incorporates an element of protraction which deliberately capitalized on the time element as a strategic asset of the weaker-equipped insurgents. Unfortunately, this strategy also shifted the battlefield to population centers, thereby diminishing the difference between combatants and civilians. A prolonged war by contrast becomes bogged down beyond either side's original intentions. During the course of such prolonged wars, fundamental transformations take place in the purposes, methods, composition of combatants, and external support, with the main combatants rarely attaining their limited original objectives. The ongoing war in Angola offers a classic example. In this regard, the US learned a sobering lesson at a high price in Vietnam, and the Soviets received theirs in Afghanistan. Hence it is likely that capably equipped powers will shun such potential quagmires, but this will not be avoided by third world states where huge casualty rates in such prolonged wars will reflect their civil war nature.

The historical evidence regarding war casualties is not encouraging for the world, but for the stable, developed, democratic powers there is reason for optimism. In the third world, however, a much more pessimistic expectation is in order. This expectation reflects the volatile consolidative conditions of the third world and is exacerbated by the availability of modern arms. Analysts must also consider another dimension of third world conditions for a proper assessment of sociomilitary development. Dietrich Fischer reminds us that "the loss of lives caused by inequities in the global economy at present greatly exceeds that caused by wars."[22] His startling analysis argues that in 1965, 16 million lives might have been saved had per capita incomes been equalized across the world. He concludes that "structural violence exceeded direct violence by more than a factor of 100." His observation introduces an increasingly important element which is currently elevating economic well-being alongside military considerations as equally important measurements of security. Therefore, the true context of future security cannot neatly separate military from economic—and hence also political—affairs.

Changing Perceptions of Future Conflicts

The post-cold war era has introduced a plethora of projected conflicts. In 1994 President Bill Clinton introduced his administration's perception of the transformation of the security environment: "The end of the Cold War fundamentally changed America's security imperatives. The central security challenge of the past half century—the threat of communist expansion—is gone. The dangers we face are much more diverse."[23] Secretary of State Warren Christopher echoed this view: "The Soviet empire is gone. No great power views any other as an immediate military threat."[24] But Christopher elaborated on the new threats: "Aggression, tyranny, and intolerance still undermine political stability and economic development in vital regions of the world." Specifically, he singled out as most worrisome, proliferation of weapons of mass destruction, terrorism, international crime, and the relatively new problems associated with environmental degradation, unsustainable population growth, and mass movement of refugees.

The US Army's Special Operations Forces (SOF) *Posture Statement* offers another perception of important changes in today's complicated and unpredictable world. It identifies today's significant dangers as "regional conflicts, proliferation of weapons of mass destruction, failure of democratic reforms, economic concerns, and transnational threats."[25] It recognizes the diminished threat of global war, but suggests that a "torrent of previously repressed nationalism and religious and factional rivalries endangers world stability." These regional conflicts are "impelled by the proliferation of military technology, international drug trafficking, state-sponsored terrorism, subversion, insurgency, lawlessness, and famine." These conflicts force the US to rely on new security approaches overseas. This posture statement certainly recognizes fundamental changes taking place in the new global conflict culture and offers an excellent example of the departure from traditional perceptions of conventional threats which had characterized military thinking.

Analysts generally concur about the anticipated general diversification of conflicts in terms of causes, types, combatants, locations, and consequences. Yet they agree specifically on only a few concerns. As previously stated, few challenge the assertions that the US will not likely face a credible, massive nuclear threat, that the US will probably avoid involvement in a global-caliber conventional war, and that most of the fighting on a massive scale will occur in the developing states. Ingomar Hauchler and Paul M. Kennedy offer a concise summary of this latter third world focus in a chapter subheading: "A Third World Venue—but all the World Takes Part."[26] The chapter implies that the third world will be the battleground, but for diverse global interests. Beyond these broad characteristics, a wide variety of specific scenarios is offered.

Perhaps the best-known recent statement about future wars is that by Martin van Creveld. He argues that future wars "will not be waged by armies but by groups whom we today call terrorists, guerrillas, bandits, and robbers, but who will undoubtedly hit on more formal titles to describe themselves."[27] Van Creveld postulates that their organization will be based on charismatic lines and will be characterized by "fanatical, ideologically based, loyalties." This posture will blur traditional lines between leaders and their organization, between a specific population and its neighbors, some degree of territorial control but not necessarily within traditional national boundaries, and between soldiers and civilians. Today, these attributes are evident in the struggle between the Serbs, Croats, and Muslims in Bosnia—as well as in numerous other conflict zones around the world. Conventional wars, according to van Creveld "may be at its last gasp." He further suggests that "much of what has passed for strategy during the last two centuries will be proven useless." Accordingly, he expects today's most advanced and powerful weapons systems to lose their usefulness in future wars.

Richard Clutterbuck suggests a not-so-dissimilar view. He sees a "pattern of dissent, public disorder, crime and terrorism," which is to originate from the "pattern of work and living in the coming ten years."[28] Much of the disruptive activities will emerge in the third world with its "growing desperation and lawlessness amongst the sprawling urban populations" and the frustrations encountered by students in their failures to realize their rising expectations. The most threatening element, according to Clutterbuck, is the resurgence of Islamic fundamentalism in its appeal to the poorer sectors of Islamic societies. Within developed societies, he anticipates violent industrial conflict emerging in protest against "the sinews and symbols of the microelectronic era, notably the computer and communications networks." Echoing Georges Sorel of a century before, Clutterbuck expects an affluent workforce to lead industrial conflicts and educated participants in modern, affluent societies—"who prefer to reject its values for ideological and environmental reasons"—to lead political protests. He summarizes this disturbing perspective: "This rejection may take the form of disruption, sabotage, or malicious damage, perhaps escalating to bombing, personal attack, and other forms of terrorism."

Paul Rogers and Malcolm Dando also advance the third world focus. They note the global security shift from the cold war's East-West context to the North-South axis. The problem stems from the North, where one-fifth of the world's population lives, but where a disproportionate three-quarters of the world's wealth and resources is controlled. Combining global environmental constraints with the expected disparities in wealth places obvious constraints on the elevation of the entire world's population to the level of resource use, which the developed states enjoy today.[29] Rogers and Dando see the cold war's legacy remaining in terms of the formidable development of military technology, yet this technology has failed to address arms control. Also, "global environmental problems have proved to be peculiarly resistant to any effective international response." One likely consequence will be "militant migration," which was demonstrated in 1991 when thousands of Albanian men fled to Italy. However, in that instance, the emigration came more in response to socioeconomically induced turmoil than to environmental causes.

Hauchler and Kennedy note that the number of wars since the end of World War II has been increasing, and transformations in the type of wars are in evidence.[30] Some wars have atrophied due to the termination of the cold war, which had sustained them, while other wars were initiated because of the elimination of the cold war's dampening effects. These wars tend to be ethnonational, social, and religious in nature, and they result in civil wars. The development crisis in the third world and Eastern Europe's transition offer fertile fields for new conflicts. Since 1945, 174 of 186 rated wars have taken place in the third world. Hauchler and Kennedy also note the general lack of active hostilities between Western, industrially developed states. Facing the future, the authors write that "hopes for a more peaceful world have increasingly been melting away."[31] They identify as conflict sources "increasing predominance aspirations by regional powers," arms buildups, and proliferation of chemical and nuclear weapons.

For Robert L. Pfaltzgraff, Jr., the post-cold-war world is "in the midst of a process of disorderly transformation."[32] Nationalism has dominated most of the present century as the defining political-ideological force, but this domination has been replaced today with ethnosectarian conflict—which resembles its nationalist antecedents. For the present decade, there exists an intensification of "ethnicity with substantial ideological, nationalist, and religious fervor" as well as political fragmentation. Pfaltzgraff identifies a useful paradox represented in two coexistent trends. He notes the increasing penetration of civilizations by alien forces and the efforts of such civilizations to maintain their sense of identity. Joining other analysts, Pfaltzgraff anticipates the emergence of problems associated with weapons proliferation and various terrorist activities.

Writing about the overarching level of global change, Samuel P. Huntington inspires as many admirers as critics when he asserts:

> It is my hypothesis that the fundamental source of conflict in this new world will not be primarily ideological or primarily economic. The great divisions among humankind and the dominating source of conflict will be cultural. . . . The principal conflicts of global politics will occur between nations and groups of civilizations.[33]

According to Huntington, clashes between civilizations will dominate global politics, and "the fault lines between civilizations will be the battle lines of the future." Since the Peace of Westphalia, conflicts in the Western world had occurred largely between princes, and thereafter between nations, and subsequently between ideologies. Where these conflict sources had characterized global politics as reflections of Western influences, Huntington states that non-Western civilizations will "join the West as movers and shapers of history." He sees the identity of civilizations becoming increasingly important in the future with the most important conflicts occurring along the fault lines separating the seven or eight major civilizations. Each of the cultures holds different perceptions regarding religion, state, families, rights, responsibilities, liberty, authority, equality, and hierarchy. Traditionally, such civilizations have remained largely isolated from each other, but this case no longer exists in the modern world—hence the emergence of adversarial contacts.

Huntington's perspective is provocative but excessively alarming. His critics charge that the trend in the conflict environment weighs heavily towards civil wars which are fought among members within cultures. They also charge that much of the underlying sources of dissension is still based on economic foundations. But Huntington did well to identify the often-disregarded role of historically significant values and ideas as generators of conflict and to note the increasing complexity ensuing from the third world's emerging prominence in global security matters. However, Huntington's thrust suggests grand, conventional, and hostile encounters, which are not reflected in the analyses of the other writers in this survey. Many of these writers expect nonstate actors to initiate conflicts which will challenge the state with quasianarchic conditions. These divergent views buttress the contention of the anticipated diversification of actors, motives, and methods likely to be encountered in the future conflict environment.

Anticipating Twenty-First Century Conflicts

Waging wars has been a historically pervasive exercise, engaged in by all but a few societies. Generally, motives for conducting wars have not differed fundamentally throughout history if we include the categories of fear, pursuit of material gain, and the desire for power, influence, and control over the minds and actions of others. However, throughout history the specific manifestations of these motives, which are shaped by human nature, have reflected ever-changing demographic and technological forces. Ancient Sparta may have feared Athenian expansion much as Israel feared Iraq's nuclear weapons program in our own age. Both conflicts experienced the same genesis, namely fear, but the tactical response, and the weapons utilized, differed. Traditional societies have fought over rights to grazing, hunting, and croplands, or over control of oases in deserts, while modern societies pursue colonies, fertile lands, and *lebensraum* or oil and other scarce minerals. In both eras the core object of conflict was basic physical survival and once that was ensured, intermediate-level motives were expanded to include the retention or improvement of existing welfare levels. To emphasize, throughout history basic motives for conflict have not changed, but an evolutionary transition has occurred in the specific objects pursued and the weapons employed.

This present volume does not argue that human nature has changed and that we will experience fundamentally new sources of conflict. Indeed, Huntington argues persuasively the case for historical continuity—except for the interjection of modern demographic and technological variables. We seek to identify new manifestations of human desire that warrant war activities. We could identify such objects using scientific methodologies, but others may argue that the inherently subjective nature of such social phenomena will not necessarily add greater precision.

Projected conflicts in the near-term future already may be detected in nascent form by the attentive observer. Certainly war motives stemming from religious, economic, or security concerns are not new. Yet, as the various analyses in this book demonstrate, we may consider anticipated hostile confrontations over international criminal activities, population migrations, human rights violations, water and food access, land degradation, and terrorism as new conflict sources, but we have already experienced them earlier in history. The West does not conceive of overt transnational hostilities over food, yet the last several years have witnessed a dozen armed confrontations over fishing disputes on the high seas among developed countries. We may speculate that many existing tensions today may intensify to the point of overt conflicts in the future, but we must be mindful that such tensions will not represent sudden, completely unprecedented or unanticipatable causes of conflict.

Another dimension in these analyses should demonstrate that sources of conflicts are not singular but are invariably mixtures or combinations of motives. For example, wars over purely religious concerns have occurred in history, but despite public perceptions to the contrary, few wars are fought because of that cause today. Underneath the religious veneer, ethnic interests—or more than likely economic interests—may be in evidence. By way of example, one may argue that the conflict in Northern Ireland has more to do with class than it does with religion; that the Israeli-Arab differences stem not from religion but ethnicity, history, and territorial claims; that the widening large-scale civil disturbances in Algeria stem not so much from religious doctrinal sources as from the failures of economic development under the republican regime; and that the prolonged civil war in Sudan is not simply a conflict between Muslims and Christians, as often reported, but the conflict concerns race, ethnicity, history, poverty, oil, and water issues. Certainly in Bosnia, Western Christian states are not troubled by their support of the Muslim population against the Christian Orthodox Serbs. In this latter case, US economic concerns do not predominate as do humanitarian sentiments. In the same vein, the World Commission on Environment and Development recognized that "environmental stress is seldom the only cause of major conflicts within or among nations. Nevertheless, they can arise from the marginalization of sectors of the population and from ensuing violence."[34]

The search for motives of war represents the supreme analytic challenge for students of international relations. This search has produced historically the most engrossing literature on political discourse. Caution must be exercised that superficial assumptions about such motives are not made by the policymaker. Simplistic conclusions about most conflicts in Africa identify "tribalism" as the source of all conflicts, but this identification ignores the basic fact that tribal wars have been traditionally characterized by battles in pursuit of nonpolitical objectives.[35] Africa's wars are modern, but just what are the underlying motives? In Somalia clans have fought each other to the point of institutionalizing anarchy. Is this the legacy of history which resulted in a large population of Somalis residing within the borders of Ethiopia? Is it the same legacy which fueled war in the late 1970s and consequently led to stark poverty in the 1980s? Is it the consequence of the cold war which saw the US and the Soviet Union supplying vast quantities of arms to Somalia and Ethiopia respectively in their war—arms which feed today's anarchy? Or, is Somalia's devastating poverty, hunger, and civil conflict the product of a high population growth rate which had resulted in increased armed confrontations over diminishing arable lands—forcing the losers into hopeless urban ghettos? In a similar vein, is Haiti's problem one of corruption, military rule, lack of economic development, or economic ecology, wherein its trees were cut down, its soils leached, and its industrial base weakened by its rapidly expanding population?[36] And is Rwanda's primary problem simply tribal animosity, neighboring Uganda's interference, or the exhaustion of scarce arable lands in this impoverished country with Africa's highest population density? These current examples illustrate the complexity encountered when analyzing extant conflicts, which make the task of anticipating the future all the more precarious.

Huntington's observation about Western wars having encountered shifts in interests from princes, nations, ideologies, and now to civilizations suggests the continuity of predominantly political interests. Yet on close analysis, the potential conflict sources identified in this book reflect a remarkable degree of underlying socioeconomic foundations. Direct economic sources of conflict include the pursuit of strategic and mineral resources, industrial and agricultural water requirements, resource degradation problems, and standard requirements for food, transport rights, and unimpeded trade. Arguably, economic concerns were the most important factor in the breakup of Yugoslavia, Czechoslovakia, and the Soviet Union. Indirect economic influences are easily detected in such sociopolitical issues as religious conflicts, ethnicity and national fragmentation, population pressures, and transnational criminal activities. In addition, there exists a definite economic dimension to conflicts arising from human rights issues. Similarly, underlying economic bases may be detected in military security issues, especially in light of the diversification and intensification of hostilities in the third world being demonstrated in many poor regions. Are not hegemonial attempts, civil wars, and much of terrorism the product of economic ambition or dislocation? Indeed, the concept of security, which has traditionally implied military conceptions, has recently been widened to consider vital economic issues as well. The 1995 *Annual Report to the President and the Congress* by the secretary of defense expresses this dimension: "Economic security has become a vital issue for the Department in recognition that a strong military requires a robust commercial and defense industry."[37]

Reflecting the thrust of the projections made by some of the above analysts, the expected sources of future conflicts will mostly concern animosities within states or between neighboring states. This assumption implies that ensuing wars will be fought in unconventional style, by diverse forces, using conventional weaponry: often small arms, and possibly chemical and biological weapons. In the conflicts projected in this book, nuclear capabilities will not offer the same deterrent value as it did to the two dominant adversaries during the cold war. In fact, nuclear weapons will offer no decided advantage to adversaries in most cases. Wars arising from religious, ethnic, mass migration, or economic dislocation will not be capable of being countered by massive conventional armaments. Budding regional expansionists or terrorist cadres will value nuclear devices as novel offensive weapons. Such a regional power as

Iraq may be brought to heel with them, but the nuclear-equipped terrorist cannot be countered by such means. To be sure, analysts expect the continuation of traditional conventional wars between two or more national actors, and preparing to meet such familiar challenges will remain a valid defense exercise. But to meet the challenges posed by the projected diversification of conflict cultures, strategic planning by the major powers likewise will have to undertake commensurate response diversification. Much as a behemoth may be devoured by a new species of ants, against which it has no defenses, great powers will always face new uncertainties.

US or international responses to the anticipated diversification of conflicts will have to weigh the options of peaceful versus armed responses at all times. In illustrative terms, these options position tractors against tanks. If we are correct in postulating that most of the expected conflicts will have economic bases, the solutions to these conflicts may lie more often in economic formulations. And if we are correct in assuming that traditional forcible measures—short of indiscriminate nuclear usage—may simply offer inadequate or inappropriate responses, tractors may hold the only available means with which to address them. The costs of conducting war have become expensive, making the utilization of that ultimate tool for conflict resolution counterproductive. However, we must not assume that decisions for war will be based solely on dispassionate, quantified calculations.

The US Faces the Future Global Order

James B. Seaton offers a disturbing perspective on America's attitudes towards "low-level conflict." He finds American soldiers ill prepared for "missions that require them to work closely with people they will possibly help, and fight, simultaneously."[38] He charges that Americans "lack a unified mind-set and worldview to confront the changing political-military realities of international politics." America's military culture misunderstands and delegitimizes most forms of low-level conflict and prefers to emphasize firepower and mass when applying overwhelming force militarily. Seaton observes that this approach is limiting in contemporary, nontraditional "political-military" situations. Prospects for the occurrence of conventional wars will not dissipate. But if van Creveld's projections will be validated, Seaton's analysis points to the need for the American military to re-think its range of strategic responses. Seaton elaborates on most of the anticipated sources of conflicts, yet he makes it clear that our traditional military configurations or even our structural modernization through the application of the most advanced technology will not appropriately address them. The response options will therefore encounter the demand for greater sophistication by military planners who in the past have been noticeably uncomfortable with nuanced political dimensions of such third world, nontraditional conflicts in transition.

The single greatest factor which the US will face in the emerging order is its role as the greatest uncontested military power. Policy alternations will continuously shift between isolationists who will argue on behalf of a narrow, defensive posture and globalists, who will argue for our involvement in distant global conflicts. Essentially, that debate will occur between those whose only security concerns are core interests, which focus on immediate threats to our physical survival, and those who will argue that the US has a special responsibility in a variety of disturbing developments even if they are of peripheral concern to our strategic interests. This dilemma, of course, is not a new one, as it is a continuation of contrasting thought regarding our foreign policy posture. This posture has been debated throughout the present century.

However, muddying the debate are two considerations. First, responding to only threats to our core interests fails to recognize that the US is extensively locked into the expanding international economic infrastructure. The deterioration of this infrastructure can wreak havoc with our domestic—as well as international—stability as easily as a sizable war. Military involvement, accordingly, may not be avoidable on behalf of such intermediate-level economic security interests. And, certainly our economic relationships internationally will only become more extensive. Second, and this concern flows from the first consideration, the US no longer exists in isolation, hence the debate concerning our policy options is greatly proscribed at the outset. We cannot be extensively involved in the international economy, on the one hand, but isolationist in military security affairs, on the other. Our effective range of policy choices has, in fact, narrowed. The US will not design the nature of the conflict environment, instead it will respond to it. Therefore, waiting until someone threatens only our core security interests will be strategically inadequate, since it will be much more advantageous to address deteriorating security situations in their early stages.

If we are correct in assuming the validity of this projection (i.e., that extensive involvements in distant conflicts will be unavoidable), we still face the options of the implementation of peaceful as opposed to forceful measures (tractors versus tanks). The US must expend analytic energies on the true estimate of underlying economic factors that will drive conflicts, and we must address these factors appropriately. However, we also need to isolate those conflicts which historical hegemonic aspirations propel, those which countermilitary measures can neutralize, and those which will be value-driven, for which neither economic nor military responses will suffice. Yet each of these three types of conflicts could, if left unchecked, pose a resolute security challenge. Accordingly, peaceful diplomatic and economic measures must not be viewed only in humanitarian contexts, but within an expanding security perspective. This conclusion calls for the continuous development of our conventional and nuclear capabilities but also for the inclusion of politicoeconomic instruments in the military planning process.

In a speech at The Johns Hopkins University, former secretary of defense Les Aspin asked: "Should the United States use its soldiers to protect American values?"[39] Aspin reiterated the debate between realists and idealists, and he could not avoid pointing out that a nation can pursue idealistic, or humanitarian, objectives as an integral part of its security strategy. He also raised the prospect of US soldiers, though trained as military personnel, having to act in policemen's roles.

Therein we may identify another dilemma. Scarce reason exists to question the capability of the US military machine which had been finely honed during the cold war. However, will the implementation of that machine be the appropriate response in all future conflicts? We might be emphasizing too much our public concerns that our military is adequately prepared—at a time when the US defense budget dwarfs its nearest competitors. Perhaps we may argue, therefore, that the real challenge in the future will not be questions associated with military planning, but with analysis and policy formulation. Our interventions in conflicts since the demise of the cold war have certainly shown no weaknesses in our confrontation with Iraq during the Gulf War, but our involvements in Bosnia, Somalia, Rwanda, and Haiti have raised some important questions about the appropriateness of military responses and about the seemingly ad hoc nature of our involvements. As the world's most capable power, the US will face increasing demands to become more involved in distant and diverse conflicts. Our decision to do so cannot proceed situationally without perhaps unintentionally exacerbating global instability. As the sole superpower in the world, and if we agree that isolationism is not a realistic prospect, it is incumbent on the US to articulate its conception of a global security order encompassing, not only military, but also politicoeconomic security parameters. Doing so may not be an option, but a vital policy requirement.

Notes

1. This phenomenon is elaborated in Karl P. Magyar and Constantine P. Danopoulos, *Prolonged Wars: A Post-Nuclear Challenge* (Maxwell AFB, Ala.: Air University Press, 1994).

2. Michael Renner, "Budgeting for Disarmament," in Linda Starke, ed., *State of the World, 1995* (New York: W. W. Norton and Co., 1995), 151.

3. See Thomas J. Stark, "Changing Status of Nuclear Forces," in Karl P. Magyar, ed., *Challenge and Response: Anticipating US Military Security Concerns* (Maxwell AFB, Ala.: Air University Press, 1994), 387–89.

4. *Christian Science Monitor,* 20 December 1994 and 12 January 1995.

5. Matthew Connelly and Paul M. Kennedy, "Must It Be the Rest Against the West?" *Atlantic Monthly,* December 1994.

6. Max Singer and Aaron Wildavsky, *The Real World Order* (Chatham, N.J.: Chatham House Publishers, Inc., 1993), 3.

7. Connelly and Kennedy, 72–76.

8. Jessica Tuchman Mathews, "Redefining Security," *Foreign Affairs,* Spring 1989, 164.

9. Ibid., 166.

10. Sheldon Richman, "Cairo's Faulty Assumption," *Christian Science Monitor,* 23 September 1994.

11. Adda B. Bozeman, "War and the Clash of Ideas," *Orbis* 20, no. 1 (Spring 1976).

12. G. R. Berridge identifies a list of neo-Marxists who hold this view. See G. R. Berridge, *International Politics: States, Power and Conflict since 1945* (New York: Harvester Wheatsheaf, 1992), 62.

13. Karl P. Magyar elaborates on this idea. See Karl P. Magyar, "Culture and Conflict in Africa's History: The Transition to the Modern Era," in Stephen J. Blank et al., *Conflict, Culture, and History: Regional Dimensions* (Maxwell AFB, Ala.: Air University Press, 1993), 231–33.

14. Zbigniew Brzezinski, *Out of Control: Global Turmoil on the Eve of the 21st Century* (New York: Charles Scribner's Sons, 1994), chap. 1.

15. William T. Lee, "The nuclear brink that wasn't—and the one that was," *Washington Times*, 7 February 1995.

16. *Christian Science Monitor*, 15 December 1994.

17. Renner, 153.

18. Ruth Leger-Sivar, *World Military and Social Expenditures, 1991* (Washington, D.C.: World Priorities, 1991), 22ff.

19. United Nations Development Programme, *Human Development Report, 1994* (New York: Oxford University Press, 1994), 47.

20. Extensive research on such data has been conducted by Bill Eckhardt of the Lentz Peace Research Laboratory. See Karl Vick, "Civilians often bear war's brunt," *St. Petersburg Times*, 17 February 1981.

21. Karl P. Magyar, "Introduction: The Protraction and Prolongation of Wars," in Magyar and Danopoulos.

22. Dietrich Fischer, *Nonmilitary Aspects of Security: A Systems Approach* (Brookfield USA: Dartmouth, 1993), 7.

23. The White House, *A National Security Strategy of Engagement and Enlargement* (Washington, D.C.: Government Printing Office, 1994), i.

24. Warren Christopher, "American Foreign Policy: Principles and Opportunities," speech delivered at Harvard University, 20 January 1995.

25. United States Special Operations Forces, *Posture Statement*, 1994, 15.

26. Ingomar Hauchler and Paul M. Kennedy, *Global Trends: The World Almanac of Development and Peace* (New York: Continuum, 1994), 181.

27. Martin van Creveld, *The Transformation of War* (New York: Free Press, 1991), 197.

28. Richard Clutterbuck, *The Future of Political Violence: Destabilization, Disorder and Terrorism* (London: Macmillan, 1986), 10–11.

29. Paul Rogers and Malcolm Dando, *A Violent Peace: Global Security After the Cold War* (London: Brassey's, 1992), 153.

30. Hauchler and Kennedy, 177.

31. Ibid., 189.

32. Robert L. Pfaltzgraff, Jr., "Dimensions of the Post-Cold War World," in Robert L. Pfaltzgraff, Jr., and Richard H. Shultz, Jr., eds., *Ethnic Conflict and Regional Instability: Implications for U.S. Policy and Army Roles and Missions* (Carlisle Barracks, Pa.: Army War College, n.d.), 17–19.

33. Samuel P. Huntington, "The Clash of Civilizations?" *Foreign Affairs* 72, no. 3 (1993): 22.

34. The World Commission on Environment and Development, *Our Common Future* (Oxford: Oxford University Press, 1987), 291.

35. See Bozeman, "War and the Clash of Ideas."

36. Laurent Belsie, "Lack of Trees, Farmers' Groups Hinder Haiti," *Christian Science Monitor*, 25 October 1994.

37. William J. Perry, *Annual Report to the President and the Congress* (Washington, D.C.: Government Printing Office, February 1995), 93.

38. James B. Seaton, "Low-Level Conflict," *Society* 32, no. 1 (November 1994): 10.

39. Lisa Dicker, Dale Keiger, and Kevin Smokler, "Civil disobedience, etc.," *The Johns Hopkins Magazine*, April 1995, 30.

PART II

SOCIOPOLITICAL ISSUES

2

Religion—A Banner for Twenty-First Century Conflict

Paul J. Moscarelli

Religion is currently a major conduit of political change in the international arena. In a world of increasing complexity, believers are turning to their faiths in ever greater numbers for both moral guidance and group identification. In performing these key roles religion finds its place as a banner for political change or stagnation, and therefore a potential detractor, or contributor to global security.

Politically inspired religious movements are occurring throughout the world and are being initiated by groups as dissimilar as Buddhist revivalists in Thailand, Christian fundamentalists in America, Hindu nationalists in India, and militant Islamists in Tanzania. Some of these groups are pursuing their political agendas by way of peaceful, democratic means, while others have employed violence. In trying to assess the impact these movements will have on global security, we must recognize that each individual movement is unique. Nevertheless, fundamentalist movements share certain universal characteristics which analysts can use to measure the impact individual movements will have on global security.

This essay describes the universal political utility of religion and assesses some major trends and misconceptions regarding the anticipated impact of religiopolitical activism on the international environment. Finally, it offers policy responses that can enhance global peace in the twenty-first century.

Religion as a Political Instrument

Exploring religion's transnational conflict potential requires a clear understanding of religion and its role in individual societies. In *The Future of Religion*, Rodney Stark defines *religion* as "a system of thought embodied in social organizations that posits the existence of an active supernatural that can be influenced by human action."[1] Put more simply, he terms religion as a socially organized "belief in powers higher than man and an attempt to please them."[2] Human attempts to influence or "please" the supernatural are embodied somewhat in morality, that is, rules of right conduct prescribed by the particular religion. Morality is prescribed in some way by all major religions. Christianity, Islam, and Judaism provide laws, stories, and traditions which identify morally right behavior which is "the will of God." In Buddhism and Hinduism righteous behavior is considered as a step on the road to enlightenment.[3]

Much of religion's strength as a political rallying point comes from its moral foundation. Politics, in the purest sense of the word, concerns questions of power—Who shall have it? How shall it be applied? and Against whom shall it be applied? To these questions, religious and political leaders say that power should be used to promote good and to battle evil. Religion invariably distinguishes between good and evil. Anything that can be portrayed as evil can be righteously opposed and such opposition can be rationally defended with religious precepts. Religious concepts of justice are frequently reflected in local secular laws. This is as true of American laws with their Judeo-Christian grounding as it is of conservative Islamic legal systems in Iran and Saudi Arabia. Viewed in this light, the line between politics and religion becomes tenuously thin and in some cases disappears completely. Such is the case in Islam, no formal boundary between religion and politics is recognized.

As religious groups attempt to achieve a "greater good" through the acquisition of political power, they see few barriers to the use of violence. The violent struggle between good and evil holds a central place in the tradition of virtually every religion.[4] Any dispute effectively depicted as a "religious" conflict evokes enormous emotional response from the faithful. Righteous indignation, if generated in sufficient intensity, creates acceptance of self-sacrifice and a willingness to go to war. Provision of moral imperatives holds a key to religion's role as a banner for conflict.

In addition to morality, religion provides believers with a group identity and a sense of community. Indoctrination takes place at an early age, with family, friends, and neighbors usually sharing the same religious persuasion. A place of worship often connects friends, leisure activities, and business contacts. For many groups, religion is a part of everyday life, which is understood by all members of the group. It also provides a focal point for common commitment.

When religion does not function as a part of everyday life, it still serves as a source of group identity. In these instances there is no deep, underlying belief. Religion simply provides a basis for "us versus them." An example is Israel, a country built on the religious persuasion of citizens who proudly identify themselves as Jews. They have great national pride and have survived cohesively against enormous odds. Yet somewhat fewer than 20 percent of Israeli Jews describe themselves as religious.[5] The Protestants and Catholics of Northern Ireland fight not over religious values but over nationalism and economic matters. One needs not be an orthodox follower to rally with a group forged from religious identity.

Common identity and moral righteousness provided by religion offer an ideal rallying point for activism, which often takes on violent forms. Students of war understand that group identification and moral commitment of soldiers are essential to the successful prosecution of violent conflict. In a religious group, the essentials of an army are already present. The only additional requirement is a cause that can be justified religiously and portrayed as sufficiently important to fight for. Religion is not an "opiate of the masses" in the contemporary international environment. It is serving as an ideal rallying point for violent conflict which could be more accurately described as a "stimulant of the masses." This is the stimulant that is used by "fundamentalist" leaders to generate support for their programs.

Fundamentalism

Conceptions of fundamentalism are numerous. In *Fundamentalisms and the State*, Martin E. Marty and R. Scott Appleby define *fundamentalism*. They describe much of today's religiopolitical activism: "Fundamentalism is a strategy by which believers attempt to preserve their group identity. It involves revival of former beliefs which are modified by leaders in varying degrees to achieve political goals. The strategy is often innovative and rejects secular politics in charismatic fashion to renew group identity and expand popular support."[6] In effect, fundamentalist leaders mold religious doctrine as necessary to villainize their opponents, branding them as "immoral," while portraying themselves as good and doing the will of God. This battle between good and evil provides a sense of unity and purpose to followers and strengthens the group identity. Manifestations of fundamentalist groups in the contemporary international arena include political parties and movements, militant revolutionary groups, and established governments. They may be domestic or transnationally based.

A simple model of the forces influencing the changing thought processes of a group can help clarify this definition. Stark identifies three basic directions in which religious thinking can move:

- toward *secularization*—movement away from the spiritual and toward the temporal
- toward *revival*—return to the traditional ideas
- toward *innovation*—adoption of new ideas[7]

Figure 1, where extreme views on secularization, innovation, and revival are represented by the black circles, shows the aggregate thinking of a group of believers. A group which falls on the secularization circle is "religious" in name only. Secular concerns dominate decision making, while traditional religious ideas embody the thinking of a group which falls on the revival circle. A group that falls on the innovation circle is also governed by religious thought, but it has abandoned traditional ideas for a contemporary interpretation of a religion. Few if any religious groups take such an extreme attitude as to fall absolutely on one of the circles. All three factors influence most groups. A group in which religious considerations weigh more heavily in decision making would be located to the right, while one where secular concerns dominate (such as group G) would be positioned to the left. The Israeli Jews mentioned earlier could fall near group G, since religious leaders have influence, but on the whole, secular concerns dominate.

Figure 2 depicts the effect of a fundamentalist movement on group G. It may move to position C if fundamentalist leaders

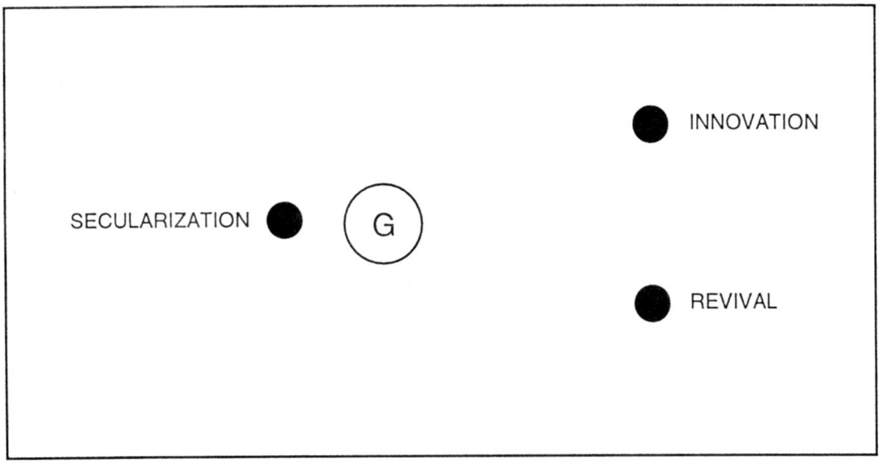

Figure 1. Continuum of Religious Thought

revive tradition, while it would move to position A if sweeping religious innovations are accepted by the group. A successful fundamentalist movement would move a group's thinking to position B if traditional ideas were revived partially intact and partially with innovation.

A good example of the impact of fundamentalist forces on a society is provided by Iranian Shi'ites (fig. 3). Many Iranian Shi'ites had accepted secular changes imposed by the Shah

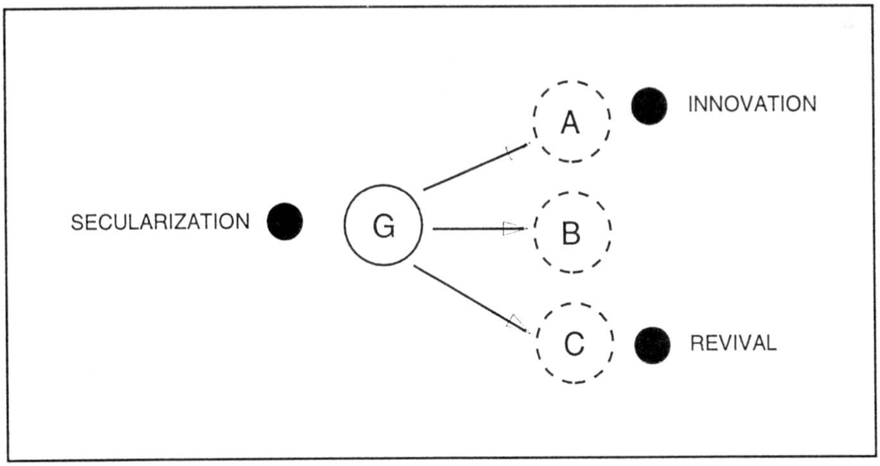

Figure 2. The Effect of a Fundamentalist Movement on Group B

prior to 1979. In 1979 the fundamentalist revolution of Ayatollah Khomeini pushed the country hard in the direction of traditional thinking. Starting in the mid-1980s, the realities of trying to govern a country suffering from high unemployment, high population growth, and a large debt from the war with Iraq forced the fundamentalist Iranian government to innovate and proclaim certain traditionally frowned upon practices to be in accordance with Islamic law. Iran's innovative 1995 version of Islam in many ways contains free-market reforms that have deviated from many of the traditional practices of Khomeini.

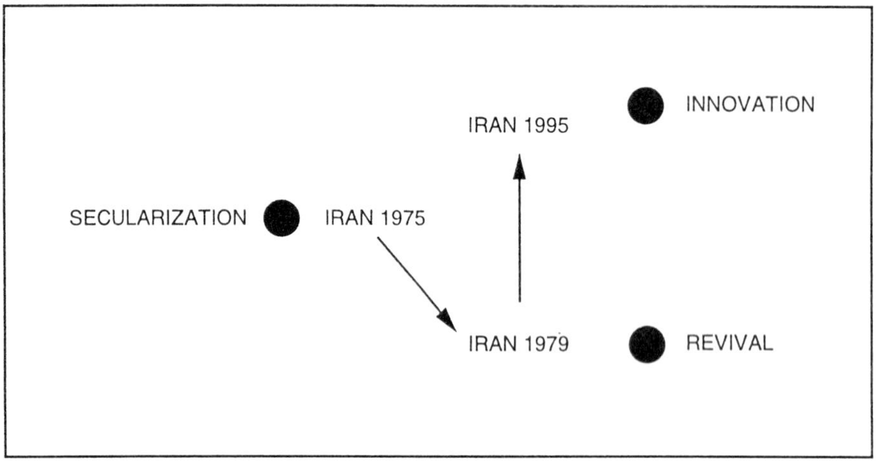

Figure 3. Impact of Iranian Fundamentalism

Major Trends in World Religious Activism

With an understanding of fundamentalism and an appreciation for the instrumentality of religion as a conduit for both violent and nonviolent political action, let us consider some of the major real-world possibilities for future religious conflict while we dispel some of the most popular fallacies.

Fundamentalists as Enemies of Global Peace

The word *fundamentalist* creates visions of New York World Trade Center bombers and airline hijackers in the minds of many Westerners. These actions, which are normally major media events, are symptomatic of a small number of radical fundamentalist elements and can mislead the observer as to the true nature of fundamentalism. It may be argued that fundamentalists are not always enemies of global peace but have in many cases pursued their goals peacefully and in some cases have exerted a positive influence on global security. The Afghan Mujahidin were a fundamentalist group who used US military aid to contain Soviet cold war expansionism. Such Christian fundamentalist groups as the Moral Majority peacefully pursue their religiopolitical goals within the borders of the United States. The views of the government of Saudi Arabia reflect fundamentalist thinking, yet it has allowed large numbers of United States military personnel to remain on its soil for more than four years after the Persian Gulf War to assure regional stability. Although religious fundamentalism is presently a conduit for political change in many places, it is misleading to stereotype such movements as threats to global security.

Fundamentalism as a Legacy of the Colonial and Cold War Periods

As European powers colonized Africa, the Middle East, and South Asia, they brought with them their secular institutions and governments. To Mark Juergensmeyer, secular nationalism "spread throughout the world with an almost missionary zeal and was shipped to the newly colonized areas of Asia, Africa, and Latin America. . . . [Colonial powers] provided their colonies with the political and economic infrastructures to turn territories into nation-states."[8] They established boundaries between modern-day states in these regions without regard for religious and cultural factors. A graphic example of this occurred in Nigeria, which the British created in 1914. The north is predominately Muslim, while the south is generally Christian and animist. Muslims comprise 55–60 percent of the population, while Christians make up approximately 30 percent. Also, numerous tribal divisions abound throughout the country. When the colonial powers departed after World War II, they left in their wake secular governments not compatible with the local religions, and political boundaries not representative of local cultures.[9] Since many indigenous peoples refused to embrace these divisions, the potential for conflict in these states was tremendous. That potential began to be realized in the late 1960s and is only now coming to fruition.

Jeff Haynes suggests that three events in the late 1970s signaled the birth of the current wave of religiopolitical activity. These included the deposing of the Shah of Iran in 1979, the war between the Soviets and the Afghani Mujahidin beginning in 1978, and the establishment of the Sandinista government in 1979.[10] These clashes were harbingers of the fundamentalist activity which has become endemic in the developing world.

One factor driving the increase in fundamentalist movements since the late 1970s is the attempts of secular governments to modernize their societies along Western lines. People fought to deal with sweeping economic and technological change. Haynes points out that they "struggled to make sense of what was happening to them. Not infrequently, in . . . the contemporary Third World, the explanations they came up with had a strongly religious form."[11] Third world peoples have increasingly turned to religion to provide a buffer between modernity and their inability to deal with economic and technological change.

Another factor which helps explain the acceleration of fundamentalist activity, particularly in the 1990s, is the onset of the information age. Though they may have bewildered the common man, information technologies aided potential fundamentalist leaders by providing a free flow of information and ideas. Information about a religious movement on one side of the world is instantly available to the potential fundamentalist leader on the other side courtesy of the electronic media. The Internet has facilitated a free exchange of ideas on the use of religion for instituting political change.

The final major factor responsible for the rising number of fundamentalist movements is the end of cold war competition between the superpowers. In many cases, post-colonial secular governments were propped up financially and militarily by the United States and the Soviet Union as they competed for allies in the third world. With the end of the cold war, the support for many of these regimes disappeared. This amplified the clarity of their failure to provide the freedoms and economic prosperity that had been advertised as a byproduct of secularism. A recent study offers this assessment: "'It is an economic, social, and moral failure' a Muslim leader in Egypt said, speaking of the policies of his nation's secular state."[12] Corruption and inequity have made post-cold-war governments of the developing world much more vulnerable to revolutionary activity and poured fuel on the flames of fundamentalism.

The colonial powers planted the seeds of revolutionary change by introducing secular ideas and creating ill-defined states in their colonies. The factors outlined in the preceding paragraphs caused those seeds to gradually grow into today's abundance of fundamentalist movements. The following paragraphs describe a number of current situations which hold promise for future religiopolitical conflict. Observers can directly or indirectly link to the current situation's legacy of the colonial era, the end of the cold war, failure of secular governments, and/or the onset of the information age.

- Secular Indian nationalists are clashing at the voting booth with the moderate Hindu nationalist Bharatiya Janata party while enduring terrorist attacks by extremist Hindu nationalists. Meanwhile, both Hindu and Indian nationalists continue to clash with Indian Muslims. Muslims in India make up approximately 11 percent of the population of the predominately Hindu state.
- In Algeria, when the Islamic Salvation Front (FIS) appeared to have won victory in the December 1991 elections, a military coup was staged to prevent them from taking power. The FIS was proscribed. This gave birth to a number of militant Islamic groups who presently operate in the country. As of this writing, over 30,000 deaths have been reported in this struggle.
- In Latin America, liberation theology (roughly speaking, a mix of Christianity and Marxism) was a strong contributor to the success of the Nicaraguan Sandinistas and was a rallying point for Peruvian Sendero Luminoso guerrillas. It is a factor in the ongoing peasant revolt in the Chiapas region of Mexico,

and continues to win support in many impoverished Latin American communities.

• In Pakistan, the Sunni fundamentalist Islamic Democratic Alliance is in power while the large Shi'ite minority, largely liberal and progressive, is bitterly opposed to fundamentalism. Violent clashes between the sects show no signs of abating.

• In Sudan, Lt Gen Omar Ahmed al-Bashir has declared *shari'a* (Islamic legal code) the supreme law of the land. His Islamic military regime has unified the northern Arabs in the civil war against the black Christians and animists in the south.

• The Sikh majority in the Indian state of Punjab view both Indian nationalists and Hindu nationalists as opponents of a separate Sikh state. The Indian government has effectively suppressed violence in Punjab, but the Sikh separatist movement remains fervent.

• In Saudi Arabia, the Gulf War partnership with the United States has sparked ongoing protests by Islamists against the monarchical, authoritarian, and nominally Islamic government, calling for further Islamic reforms. The Saudi government has responded by arresting large numbers of militants.

• The long-standing tension between Buddhist monks and the government of Vietnam is increasing. Twenty-three monks were arrested between October 1994 and February 1995. The Vietnamese government is now distrustful of the Buddhists who helped topple the regime of South Vietnamese president Ngo Dinh Diem in the 1960s.

• Egypt's secular government, although attuned to Islamic concerns, is challenged at the polls by members of the moderate Muslim Brotherhood. Such radical militant factions as the Gamaa al-Islamiya and the Islamic jihad are also at work. The efforts of the Muslim clergy in the huge Cairo slums remind observers of the situation in Iran prior to the downfall of the Shah.

• After decades of conflict between Sinhalese Buddhist nationalists and Tamils (Hindus), the Sri Lankan government has suppressed militant factions of the Sinhalese Buddhist nationalist movement. Many Sri Lankan observers believe the movement will reappear.

• In the Central Asian republics of Tajikistan, Uzbekistan, Turkmenistan, Kazakhstan, and Kyrgyzstan, Islamic movements of varying intensity have been met with fierce repression by secular government forces (most of them former communists). This repressive environment has set the stage for major confrontations in this region.

• Indonesia and Malaysia have Muslim majorities, and the governments are nominally Islamic. The actual tradeoff between Islam and secularism in government has varied over the years, and fundamentalist movements are active in both countries. The Malaysian government has banned the Al-Arqam Islamic sect, while Indonesian Muslims clash with Catholics on East Timor.

• The *tajdid* (Muslim reawakening) is having a profound impact on politics in Nigeria. Southern Christian elements insist on a separation of religion and government, while northern Muslims call for the introduction of *shari'a* law throughout the country.

• Turkey's 70-year-old secular government, a key stabilizing influence on the Middle East, the Caucasus, and the Balkans is experiencing increasing pressure from fundamentalist groups. Secularists have suffered attacks from Islamists, and the fundamentalist Welfare party won the March 1994 municipal elections in Turkey's largest cities.

Islam as a Global Threat

When the cold war ended, some Western observers suggested that aggressive Islamic fundamentalism would replace the Soviet threat. This view posits the rise of Islamic governments as a threat, perhaps even monolithic, where a "nation of Islam" will rival the threat formerly posed by the Soviet bloc. The evidence supports this view. Islam is presently the most active agent of violent and nonviolent political change among world religions. In addition to the prevalence of conflict involving Islamic groups, Islam has two salient characteristics that make it an extremely effective instrument of political transformation. The first is its overt rejection of secular government.

The idea of a non-Islamic government is inconsistent with the Islamic faith. The Koran specifies that the world will be at peace only when Islam becomes the world's religion.[13] Islamic tolerance is reserved for Jews and Christians only since Islam acknowledges the authenticity of such Jewish and Christian personages as Adam, Noah, Jesus, and others. This acknowledgment does not imply a right to equality or self-governance for these peoples.[14] The Koran allows no room for tolerance of non-Islamic political systems.

Islamic intolerance stems from the principle that Islam represents both the truth and the law to its followers. That is, when Muslims establish a government, they install the religion of Islam not just as a moral code but actually to identify laws that restrict the populace. In some Muslim countries, the government creates laws in accordance with Islamic principles. In Pakistan, Iran, Saudi Arabia, and Sudan *shari'a* has been proclaimed the law of the land. It is based directly on the Koran, Islam's holy book, as well as Islamic traditions. It encompasses aspects of life from personal finance to table manners. Islamic use of religion as a legal system could be contrasted to Western Christianity, where biblical stories sketch a moral code that Christian fundamentalists promote as a guide for secular lawmakers. For secular lawmakers, religious exhortations are only one voice taken into account as laws are created. In Islam, religion is in theory the only voice.

The impact of this aspect of Islam is that the only acceptable government to a fundamentalist-minded Muslim is one adhering strictly to Islamic principles. In their most extreme form, these ideas negate the need for modern state boundaries and governments. Since Islam is the law, what need is there for lawmakers? The ideal world would be one where the planet is unified as a single Islamic nation in which all peoples adhere to Islamic principles. Whether the goal is a unified Islamic nation or a world of separate Islamic states, the prescribed method of attainment is known as jihad (holy war).

The concept of jihad is the second characteristic that makes Islam an extremely effective instrument of political transformation. Lewis B. Ware offers the following definition of jihad: "Conceived broadly, jihad signifies the obligation of every Muslim to strive for both the physical and spiritual defense of the ummah" (the ummah being the entire community of Muslims).[15] The practical application of jihad has changed over the years depending on the prevailing circumstances of the time. In the seventh and eighth centuries jihad was clearly interpreted as a requirement to take control of societies and govern them in accordance with the principles of Islam. During this period, Islam spread from its roots on the Arabian peninsula to as far west as Spain and as far east as India. However, in the face of Western dominance during the nineteenth and early twentieth centuries, Sunni Muslim modernists viewed jihad as an individual act "of the heart and mind, which, through reflection, would defend and strengthen Islamic values under the assault of Western belief systems and lead eventually to the West's acceptance of the self-evident truth of Islam."[16] Current Islamist movements adopt a more traditional view of jihad as they attempt to gain power and transform societies into ones that adhere to the principles of Islam. Jihad is being pursued in some areas by way of democratic means while in others, Islamists are attempting to gain power by way of revolutionary violence.

The evidence seems to support the view that Islam can pose a monolithic threat to the West. Many Muslim activists avoid speaking of national interests and prefer to call for the realization of a pan-Islamic vision as evidenced by Mark Juergensmeyer's observation: "On the wall of one of the Palestinian leaders in Gaza is a map of the world on which is superimposed the Koran drawn as if it had hands extending from Morocco to Indonesia."[17] However, despite such ominous symbolism, no substantive signs exists that such a dream may come to fruition. Today, no large popular rallies occur in the streets calling for pan-Islam under the leadership of a new caliph, nor are secular state boundaries being erased between Muslim states.

Nonetheless, several glaring reasons indicate that Islam will not soon become a monolithic threat: religious incongruence, secular incongruence, and pragmatism. Islam is rife with major doctrinal divisions, the most pronounced incongruence exists between the Sunni and Shi'ite sects. Evidence of the incompatibility between these sects could be seen in the Iran-Iraq war (1980–89) and the current dispute between Sunni and Shi'ite groups in Pakistan. Within the Sunni sect itself enormous differences exist where Islam is practiced in various regions. Islam in Nigeria, Indonesia, and Saudi Arabia has developed very differently, with each country influenced significantly by local cultures and local secular considerations.

Although in theory there is one "nation of Islam" with no recognition of modern state boundaries, in reality, enormous secular barriers exist to the notion of pan-Islam. Revolutionaries have concerned themselves with national as well as religious causes. There exists an Egyptian identity, a Palestinian identity, an Iranian identity, and so on.[18] Among national leaders there is no clamoring to give up power to a modern-day transnational religious authority.

Finally, pragmatic considerations keep pan-Islam from becoming a reality. Although some Westerners view Muslims as religious fanatics, in reality the average Muslim is not strictly a religious individual, but rather a composite of religious and rational person. The average Muslim has a family, a job, and holds membership in groups other than the ummah. If he is educated, he is familiar with the story of Islam's Khawarij sect, which adopted a strict doctrine of offensive jihad and was intolerant of any established political authority. This sect, not well known in the West, was nearly exterminated in the eighth century. The fate of the Khawarij has tended to temper Islamist movements over the centuries. Today, it is widely agreed that a conventional war—for whatever reason—with the militarily superior West is not a practical undertaking. Leaders of today's Islamist movements and Islamic countries are well aware that it would be imprudent of the ummah to go to war with an enemy that possesses vastly superior military technology and resources. For pragmatic as well as religious and secular reasons Muslims—at least as a unified group—will not pose a threat to global security.

The preceding argument that Islam will not likely become a monolithic threat was not meant to belittle its importance to future global security. It will remain the single most powerful agent of change in the third world and will threaten lesser interests of the US. Civil wars will occur, blood will spill, human rights will be violated, oil flows may be disrupted, and some foreign investors will lose money. Islam's overall impact on global security will not weigh on a collectivist movement but on the actions individual Islamic fundamentalists take in their attempts to gain and exercise political power. This is particularly true for fundamentalist governments as they face real-world problems in the information age.

Fundamentalism versus Modernization

After discussing the relationship between religion and development, Douglas Eugene Smith concludes that "it is widely, and correctly assumed that religion is in general an obstacle to modernization."[19] A recent study of modernization in Pakistan, Egypt, and Turkey concluded that Islam impedes economic and technological advancements in those countries.[20] Everett Mendelsohn sums up the problem:

> Fundamentalists seek influence and control of political decisions, including the extent and direction of funding for scientific research. . . . They also attempt to shape the discussion of science in the educational process. But fundamentalists face a vexing problem in this ambition. There is evidence to suggest that religious fundamentalism and the power to govern a modern nation state effectively represent deeply conflicting forces. . . . When once-radical or militant fundamentalists in the developing world find themselves faced with the concrete problems of health care, population growth, adequate useable water, food production, modern industries, participation in international trade, or the requirement of securing borders and maintaining modern armed forces, then science and technology become proximate means by which social problems may be effectively addressed.[21]

Fundamentalists argue vehemently and effectively that progress causes moral decay; but when they attempt to govern, they find themselves drawn to progressive solutions offered by the secular world out of practical necessity. Modern-day Iran offers such an example. In Iran, the Islamic government has been forced to make accommodations as the country attempts to attract foreign trade and investment to recover from the debt accumulated during its war with Iraq.

Fundamentalists in power face an interesting paradox. The more they lean toward secular answers to social problems, the more their policies resemble those of the government they ousted. The more they try to resist secular solutions, the more they resemble their former opponents in the sense of failing to provide economic prosperity. This no-win situation keeps the door open for new fundamentalist or secular movements to surface and challenge the old.

Modern-day Iran also exemplifies this paradox.[22] Adherence to religious dogma caused the government to mismanage the economy badly. With the economy in shambles, the government is attempting free market reforms to alleviate the problem. These reforms are being met with violent protest from peasant and merchant classes—the same groups whose support was key to the success of the revolution.

Perhaps over time fundamentalist movements will arise and adopt religious innovations to allow for modernization. Until that time, fundamentalist resistance to modernization will inhibit their ability to stabilize their countries. From an international perspective, in an information era where rapid change is the key to success, it will lead to increasing first world technological/economic superiority over developing nations.

Implications for US Policy

Realize that when examining religious conflict in the contemporary international environment, we seldom see crusades; that is, situations where religious conversion is a primary motivating force. No significant evidence suggests that religious conflict at the global level is probable. A continued strong US military posture will likely help to deter such an eventuality. Although the prospect for large-scale transnational conventional religious conflict is low, the prospect for religiopolitical conflict within state boundaries is high and will remain so in the foreseeable future.

Revolution in the third world will continue to affect nonvital Western interests as investors lose money and individual foreign citizens are placed in harm's way. Nevertheless, US policy must seek restraint regarding the use of force. To oppose a religious movement, particularly with the use of force, is to align oneself with the "forces of evil." The decision to oppose and especially to intervene militarily against a fundamentalist movement may be to invite terrorist retaliation. In a world which features an increasing threat of nuclear, biological, and chemical terrorism, such a prospect is a grave one indeed.

An example of the importance of nonintervention in the affairs of religious groups can be seen in the state of current US-Iranian relations. Note that Iran's disagreement with the US stems not from Iran being ruled by an Islamic government while the US remains a secular state. Japan, Italy, Germany, and France would not be among Iran's major trading partners if current animosity were based simply on religion. Iranian animosity toward the US is grounded in historical (and they believe ongoing) US intervention in Iranian affairs. US opposition to the Iranian revolution in the late 1970s has left it today at odds with a country that is known to sponsor terrorism and to develop weapons of mass destruction.

If a country decides to intervene in a religious conflict, it must make the decision with the realization that from Northern Ireland to Lebanon to Nicaragua such a conflict has been fought for a variety of both religious *and* nonreligious motives. Policy crafted to bring peace to areas where religious conflict is prevalent must focus on finding and addressing the nonreligious motives. Since many of the underlying problems are economic, the answer will not rely on the use of military force. Whether diplomatic and economic initiatives offered by secular governments can help bring peace to areas suffering from religiopolitical conflict, however, is unclear in the case of fundamentalists, as their ideas are opposed to secular modernization.

Perhaps the answer to increasing instability in affected regions lies in the informational instrument of national power. If fundamentalists can agree that their religious movements must consider the realities of international free market competition in the information age, they can make progress toward a more peaceful world. As noted in the discussion of jihad, religions have historically adapted themselves to suit the circumstances of the age in which they exist. Out of practical necessity religions will at some future point be forced to alter their dogmas. They must come to accommodate international economics and the free flow of information and ideas which are so critical to success in today's world. The question is how much destruction and loss of life will be required to bring about the realization.

Notes

1. Rodney Stark, *The Future of Religion* (Berkeley: University of California Press, 1985), 3.
2. Ibid., 5.
3. Lynn G. Stephens, *Seven Dilemmas in World Religions* (New York: Paragon House, 1994), 140–41.
4. Mark Juergensmeyer, *The New Cold War? Religious Nationalism Confronts the Secular State* (Berkeley: University of California Press, 1993), 153–55.
5. Charles S. Liebman, "Jewish Fundamentalism and Israeli Policy," in *Fundamentalisms and the State*, ed. Martin E. Marty and R. Scott Appleby (Chicago: University of Chicago Press, 1993), 68.
6. Martin E. Marty and R. Scott Appleby, eds., *Fundamentalisms and the State* (Chicago: University of Chicago Press, 1993), 3.
7. Stark, 2.
8. Juergensmeyer, 28.
9. Jeff Haynes, *Religion in Third World Politics* (Boulder, Colo.: Lynne Rienner Publishers, 1994), 29.
10. Ibid., 1.
11. Haynes, 2.
12. Juergensmeyer, 23.
13. Lewis B. Ware, "An Islamic Concept of Conflict in its Historical Concept," Stephen Blank et al., *Conflict, Culture, and History: Regional Dimensions* (Maxwell AFB, Ala.: Air University Press, 1993), 62. His chapter contains a concise discussion of the evolution of the concept of jihad from the Sunni and the Shi'ite perspectives.
14. Ibid., 63.
15. Ibid., 62.
16. Ibid., 68.
17. Juergensmeyer, 47.
18. Ibid.
19. Douglas Eugene Smith, *Religion and Political Development* (Boston: Little, Brown and Co., 1970), xi.
20. Javaid Saeed, *Islam and Modernization: A Comparative Analysis of Pakistan, Egypt, and Turkey* (Westport, Conn.: Praeger Publishers, 1994), 197.
21. Everett Mendelsohn, "Religious Fundamentalism and the Sciences," in Marty and Appleby, 25.
22. Lamis Andoni, "Second Revolution Brews in Iran," *Christian Science Monitor*, 12 April 1995, 6.

3

National Fragmentation, Ethnicity, and the New World Order

Vicki J. Rast

Nationalism is anything but a thing of the past, thus, and even the newest claims to nationalism are often rooted in a rhetoric of pre-existing ethnicity.

—Craig Calhoun
Nationalism and Ethnicity

Bosnia . . . Chechnya . . . Rwanda . . . Sudan . . . Liberia . . . Tibet . . . Sri Lanka. Thoughts of the conflictive situations represented by these names represent but a few of the many ethnic conflicts raging today. While the world attempts to find solutions to these current-day manifestations of disharmony, the question of the true roots of the problem remains unanswered. Indeed, it may be unanswerable! Yet, analysts must determine the roots of ethnic conflict if we are to reduce the frequency of wars based upon this source as we witness the ascendancy of a more peaceful environment within a new world order.

The dismantling of the Soviet Union presents interesting challenges to the rest of the world. The escalating bloodshed amongst African nations continues to permeate the consciousness of developed societies. As newly liberated states and other states around the world struggle to determine the complexion of their futures, one issue will emerge somewhat unassumingly. It will structure the nature of their very existence. Will these states form their sovereignties based upon nationalism or ethnicity? If they choose nationalism, will they sow the seeds of future conflict? If they choose ethnicity, will they have the ability to sustain future onslaughts of "tribal" domination as stronger clans exert their will upon those deemed incapable of fending off their acts of aggression? These questions seem rhetorical in one sense, yet they hold the key to the future viability of these infant nations and their more developed supporters around the world.

This essay identifies the bases of nationalism and ethnicity and shows the inseparable relationship between them. By presenting a brief history of the relationship between these two concepts, this analysis shows why ethnicity may lead to future conflicts. It focuses on those geographic locations of critical importance and discusses the conditions which create an atmosphere predisposed to ethnic conflict. In looking at the impact of both of these aspects of the problem, this essay anticipates the global impact of these forces, the projected security implications, the prospects for peaceful resolution, and United States' interests. To frame that peaceful resolution, we must first understand the roots of the problem.

Nationalism and Ethnicity

The relationship between nationalism and ethnicity is neither clearly identifiable nor universally distinguishable. Many scholars do however make an academic distinction between these two concepts. These concepts are distinct, yet undeniably interrelated.

Nationalism

Within the historical context, the idea of nationalism is associated with flag-waving, popular anthems, and unquestioning allegiance to "the state." Nationalism is that entity for which people are willing to die, and perhaps more importantly, for which they are willing to kill. While they may not have "exact" knowledge of the national disagreement upon which their particular conflict is based, they may instead be inundated with the images depicted by the media (in modern societies) or their communal leaders (in traditional societies). Nevertheless, people will go forth to conquer in the name of nationalism. This sense of nationalism emanated from the Renaissance and Reformation.[1]

The broad social and political developments during the 1500s parallel those in developing states today. Then, as now, education, commerce, and the "information superhighway" are bringing diverse peoples closer together; missionaries are traveling to areas never before explored by modern cultures; and the world is growing increasingly smaller as time progresses. As a result, indigenous populations in various countries are being influenced in ways they never deemed imaginable. While the result of this increased contact is multifaceted, one of the most important outcomes is the desire of these peoples to retain their individual, communal, historical, or ethnic identities. As such, their desire to retain their specific identity, and thereby prevent the elimination of their basic culture, has led many to stand together under the umbrella of nationalism. Even this collective action has not gone without controversy, as debate surrounds the conceptualization of nationalism. Paul A. Gobel, executive director of the Carnegie Institute for Peace, points out ironically that the idea of nationalism presents beliefs that coexist as polar opposites: one is the idea that nationalism "stressed that the state had a responsibility to make the population homogeneous; another, stressed that the state must reflect the culture and beliefs of the community to be legitimate."[2] Still another view asserted that nationalism is the accumulation of three ideals: "collective self-determination of the people, the expression of national character and individuality, and finally the vertical division of the world into unique nations each contributing its special genius to the common fund of humanity."[3] While both perspectives have merit, this present analysis uses the framework espoused by Anthony D. Smith in *Nationalism in the Twentieth Century* (1979).

> Nationalism, therefore, involves four elements: a vision, a culture, a solidarity and a policy. It answers the ideological, cultural, social and political aspirations and needs. Its success over two centuries is partly attributable to the range of needs that it satisfies. But equally important is the manner in which nationalists can adapt the vision, the culture, the solidarity and the programme to diverse situations and interests. It is this flexibility that has allowed nationalism continually to reemerge and spread, at the cost of its ideological rivals.[4]

From this latter perspective, nationalism enjoys a broad-based foundation. Its roots are diverse, having substance in ideology, culture, human relations, and political organizations. However, of these four elements, "culture" represents the entity most closely associated with the identity of a people. Consequently, it tends to overshadow the remaining factors. This determining characteristic of nationalism is closely related to, and sometimes used as a synonym for, the concept of ethnicity.

Ethnicity

Not unlike the concept of nationalism, conceptions of ethnicity have taken many forms throughout history. Yet, most have remained a variation of Max Weber's original idea that "an ethnic group is a human collectivity based on an assumption of common origin, real or imaginary."[5] Andrew H. Greeley expands this definition to include the notion that these groups function as conduits to carry forward the cultural traits of a people, and further, they serve as a metric for evaluating the "self-definition" of a person.[6] These cultural traits include language, physical appearance, religious affiliation, and those "other" individual attributes that apply to a section of society's population as an entity. This statement is not meant to suggest that these "other" traits cannot be shared by neighboring populations, only that they apply universally to the group claiming to separate themselves from those people who do not exhibit the particular trait in question.

Problems arise when the members of these ethnic groups feel threatened by external forces. These external forces pressure ethnic groups into adopting changes with which they may not agree. Recognize that these external forces take the form of three major actors, each with independent goals. The first actor may represent such international organizations as the United Nations and its subordinate agencies. They intend no harm to the people. Here, their goals usually seek short-term stability and long-term peace and prosperity for the region. Closely related to this positive end, the second group of actors is comprised of nongovernmental or private voluntary organizations. These groups also wish to promote the humanitarian well-being of the people, regardless of their political affiliation. No governmental agency controls them, and usually they do not have a strategic vision for the long-term welfare of the people. Finally, the third actor that pressures an ethnic group is the government that controls that ethnic group as part of its authority. This may include a desire to conquer a weaker nation to expand the aggressor's realm of influence and thus its own culture, or efforts to prevent a smaller nation from breaking away from the motherland. Since nations have a dominant say in the movements of the first two actors, indigenous populations usually allow those two actors to intrude on their sovereignty (if only temporarily). With the third actor, however, we must be concerned.

Whether trying to override the autonomy of an ethnic group or prevent it from seceding, government actions are likely to spark conflict and bring international attention to the region. The first situation—attempting to override the sovereignty of an ethnic group—was commonly observed during the periods of imperialism and national expansion from the 1500s until the mid-1950s. Because the government hopes to fully integrate new ethnic groups into its sovereignty, it will openly attempt to change the traditions, language, and other characteristics which have defined ethnic groups. The Soviets exercised this tactic extensively. If it cannot achieve this goal forcibly, the stronger nation will use more subtle means, including education and training, to indoctrinate and to convert the outlier and bring it into the fold. As acts of open aggression against another sovereignty are met with worldwide reproof, their occurrences will continue to decline. Yet, it is the second case—preventing internal secession—that is becoming more prominent today. Separatism by way of secession presents another problem altogether: because societies are beginning to recognize the strength of their ethnic identities, they are attempting to break away from their mother countries and define their own systems of government. Known historically as self-determination, these attempts at nationhood are making quite a wave in what once was a sea of domestic tranquillity (and relative international stability).

Separatism

Separatism is not new to the international stage. It is found worldwide, and Europe has witnessed a historical ethnic renaissance over the past 50 years. In *Nationalism*, Anthony D.

Smith argues that Britain, France, Spain, Holland, and Italy and North America (Canada, specifically) have all faced separatist challenges.[7] Ethnic groups have attempted to define their own boundaries and government institutions for centuries, but the movement has never been stronger than at present. These movements may have different bases, but Smith illuminates their commonalities: "These autonomous movements have arisen this century in their political form, in well-established, often ancient states, with clear and recognized national boundaries, and with a relatively prosperous economy. . . . All these states are fairly industrialized, and much of the population is literate and even quite well educated."[8] In *Nationalism*, Smith concentrates on the more modernized societies when he scripted his thoughts in 1979. A follow-on work published in 1983, *State and Nation in the Third World*, outlined his thoughts on the five phases of African nationalism: "primary resistance movements to European incursion; so-called millennial protest movements against colonial rule; the period of gestation, and 'adaptation,' of new local strata; the phase of nationalist agitation for self-rule; and the adoption of social programmes for the masses by nationalism."[9] While analysts may base the context of separatist feelings upon a conglomerate of motives, this analysis concentrates on the economic and sociocultural reasons, since they broadly characterize the two extremes of peaceful and conflictive separatist movements.

Peaceful, separatist movements are becoming prominent within democracies where ethnic groups exhibit a strong desire to separate themselves from a confederation of states. One of the strongest movements in this regard is Quebec's attempted breakaway from 127 years of centralized, national government control. Ongoing for decades, only in 1994 did separatists see their first real chance of seceding. While many in Quebec insisted they did not want to be a separate nation from Canada, voters elected hard-line separatist Jacques Parizeau as premier.[10] Based upon economic as well as cultural issues, they voiced their concern about remaining under the control of a national government who did not fully recognize or act on their desires as an ethnic people. Undoubtedly an important issue for the US and international trade markets, the premier made clear his desire that the American government should "stay out of the process."[11] To date, the US has honored that request, even though separatist actions could have adverse economic effects on the North American Free Trade Agreement and negatively impact the global economy.[12] And while we only see economic impacts at this point, we would have to ask ourselves if we would sit on the sidelines if, in a violent separation, human lives were at risk. This scenario leads to a discussion of the second category encompassing conflictive separatist movements, those based upon sociocultural issues.

Conflictive separatist movements occur when ethnic groups try to detach themselves legally and politically as an entity from their *sovereign* governments using force or being prepared to do so. Chechnya's attempted secession reveals a current example. The Russian government's attempts to "put down the rebellion" as the West watched, waited pensively, and prayed for the immediate cessation of hostilities. Unfortunately for the Chechnyans, they were caught in a situation which allowed for only one winner. This zero-sum game is important for both sides, as the Chechnyans wish to govern themselves. The Russians, in the face of the Soviet erosion, cannot sustain yet another group's disengagement: it may set a precedent which could lead to the further disintegration of Russia.

Is the conflict between Serbia, Croatia, and Bosnia any different from that between the Tutsi and Hutu in Rwanda and Burundi? and Southern and Northern Sudan? These examples are only a few of the conflicts exhibiting an ethnic dimension, yet they continue today. We must determine the root causes of these conflicts to anticipate their evolution and disruptive potential.

Toward the Twenty-First Century

Ethnic conflict will continue well into the next century. As a result, the relationship between ethnicity, separatism, and nationalism becomes one of logical progression. As people continue to look inward to retain their cultural foundations, they will work to separate themselves from external influences. For many, this will result in attempts to separate from their sovereign nation since they no longer accept as valid another culture's domination. Accordingly, these ethnic groups will be fighting for their individual nationalism and separatism. This attempt to exercise self-determination also will serve to legitimize their actions on the world stage. In the words of Anthony D. Smith,

> The national ideal leads inevitably to "nationalism," a programme of action to achieve and sustain the national ideal. . . . The homeland must be free. It cannot be ruled by others of a different historical culture. The nationalist therefore is drawn into politics, into the struggle for self-government and sovereignty in his homeland.[13]

Thus, the differences between ethnicity, separatism, and nationalism are becoming blurred. However, it is important to recognize that ethnicity will catalyze these factors. As ethnic groups look to separate themselves from their current locus of control, they will incite conflict within those governing nations (or clans) who have a strong desire to prevent their separation.

Contemporary authors like Max Singer and Aaron Wildavsky cogently identify those regions which have the greatest potential for future ethnic conflict. Singer and Wildavsky's *The Real World Order* points out that only 15 percent of the world exists in what they term "zones of peace"; the remaining 85 percent live in "zones of turmoil."[14] We may debate their figures, but these authors highlight the reality of the world in which we live today and forecast the nature of the one in which we'll reside in the future. They believe the nations identified as those in the zones of peace will continue to interact and resolve differences by peaceful means.[15] Only these nations represent the new world order; thus, their behavior will mark a distinct passage away from concentrating their interests on fundamental national security threats. Since the nations listed in the zones of peace are democracies, Singer and Wildavsky insist they will influence one another by means other than force and will thus work diligently to minimize internal and external conflict to prevent escalation.

Conversely, the nations included in the zones of turmoil will continue to exhibit traditional nineteenth century behavior.[16] Forceful engagement will continue to characterize their actions as attempts to preempt escalation fail. These nations "can expect not only violent and deadly turbulence but also difficulties in the processes of economic and political development."[17] In part, this turbulence will be the result of continuing ethnic strife. For example, we may refer to the African nations of Rwanda and Burundi. Third parties planted the seeds of ethnic conflict for these peoples in the 1800s, when they determined which cultural, economic, political, and religious characteristics would identify these peoples as distinct groups. Referring to Africa, Alex De Waal, co-director of African Rights (a newly established human rights organization) points with disbelief to the actions of outside groups in drawing ethnic lines throughout the continent. With respect to Rwanda and Burundi, he states that in the 1930s the Belgians conducted a census and issued identity cards for three clans: Tutsi, Hutu, and Twa. Determinants of personal identity included the number of cows an individual owned: "Those with ten or more were Tutsi, those with less were Hutu, in perpetuity."[18] During the early stages of Burundi's civil war (April 1972–February 1973), more than 250 thousand people were killed because of these ethnic lines. Despite decades of United Nations intervention, the Tutsi and Hutu continue to fight today because of ethnic differences, and we have no grounds to believe this conflict will end in the near future.

Africa, as Singer and Wildavsky point out, does not stand alone in the zones of turmoil. The Bosnia-Herzegovina conflict continues to take the lives of innocent civilians in the name of ethnicity. Many believed the Yugoslavs, including the Serbs, had progressed too far as a modern society to revert to wasteful, tribal hatred. The events of 1991 through today have proven this assumption faulty.

Regional Perspectives

Can we be certain of the future hot spots? Aside from Singer and Wildavsky's "blanket statement" regarding the zones of turmoil, researchers have attempted to specify future regions of ethnic conflict. One source document is the 1994 *ACCESS Guide to Ethnic Conflicts in Europe and the Former Soviet Union.* This report provided a disturbing listing of ethnic (and religious) conflicts that are projected to continue throughout Europe, the former Yugoslavia region, and the lands of the former Soviet Union. Additionally, the media paints a vivid picture of numerous areas and peoples, for which bloodshed and dying continue as a part of everyday life.

Europe

ACCESS identified 18 potential hot spots in Europe. The list began with Albania (Serbian repression of Albanian minority in Yugoslavia; Greek minority in southern half of Albania believe they are being treated as "second class citizens" by Albania).[19] Divided attention between Kosovo in Yugoslavia and southern Albania could enable a Greek population in Albania that has been calling for greater autonomy the opportunity to join with Greece (i.e., change the border as it now exists to expand the national boundary of Greece).

Belgium presents a substantial problem as well. The country consists of two major ethnic groups, the Dutch-speaking Flemings in the north and the French-speaking Walloons in the south. While these two groups formed Belgium, the Flemings now feel they are paying a regressive tax to aid the Walloons. Since these groups coexist more as neighbors than a united country (due to increased regional autonomy), they could separate in the near future.[20]

The European list of potential struggles continues with the nations of Basques, Brittany, Bulgaria, Catalonia, Corsica, Cyprus, Northern Ireland, Poland, Romania, Saami, Scotland, Slovakia (which has already separated from the Czech Republic), South Tyrol, and Wales.[21] Although the reasons for continued conflict range from pure ethnic unrest to economic dislocation, the underlying ethnic strife which prompted these conflicts will not be easily mitigated.

Former Yugoslavia Region

While all the contests within this region do not receive widespread publicity, this area currently concerns five major conflicts: Bosnia-Herzegovina, Croatia, Kosovo, Macedonia, and Vojvodina. Most notable among these is the struggle in Bosnia-Herzegovina. It continues to take lives in the name of ethnic cleansing. A people steeped in the tradition of fighting to establish their own political identity, their Bosnian government is acting to maintain Bosnia as a unified multiethnic state.[22] However, each faction among Bosnia's three main ethnic groups—the Muslims, Croats, and Serbs—has a much different political arrangement in mind.

To halt the bloodshed, the United Nations formulated a plan to redraw the geographic boundaries of the region, giving each group a region to govern independently. While this arrangement suited the dissident Croats and Serbs, the Bosnian government withheld agreement. And, while the United Nations is working to broker a cease-fire agreement, the future is uncertain as each group works to amass as much territory as possible before a final peace agreement is signed. As a result, these three ethnic groups continue to wage war to make their individual regions of control ethnically homogeneous, no doubt, with a view towards joining them to Croatia and Serbia or to remain independent.

Former Soviet Union

The countries identified as potential war zones continue to encompass those areas where ethnic strife forms the foundation of the disputes. Georgia emerges as an area with excessive ethnic instability. It has many regions of conflict, including Abkhazia. Georgia subsumed Abkhazia as part of its sovereign territory in 1921. However, when Georgia declared its independence from the Soviet Union in March 1990, Abkhazia followed suit, declaring its independence from Georgia in August. When Georgia refused to recognize this declaration, full-scale war erupted (summer of 1992). With this separatist movement the future of Georgia is now in question. Analysts are concerned that this may be the first of many such actions, since ethnic conflict exists in other regions of Georgia as well (including the region of South Ossetia which has strong desires to unite with North Ossetia, in Russia).[23]

Another area within the bounds of the former Soviet Union that bears close watching is Crimea. Here, a resurgence of Crimean nationalism is serving as the basis for a future conflict. With population lines drawn at 66 percent ethnic Russians, 26 percent Ukrainians, and 8 percent Crimean Tatars, this last group may reestablish the dominance of their historical culture. The Crimean Tatars' opposition to the decision to restore the region to an autonomous state following the transfer of Crimea from the Soviet Union to the Ukraine in August 1991 confirmed these fears. As its indigenous people, and in spite of the fact they only represent 8 percent of the total population, the Crimean Tatars alone feel they should decide the future of the nation.[24]

The potential for ethnic conflicts in other areas of the former Soviet Union is widespread. The *ACCESS* report identifies other potential ethnic-based conflict areas: the Baltic States of Estonia, Latvia, and Lithuania, Chechen-Ingushetia, Dniester Region, Gaguzia, Nagorno-Karabakh, North Ossetia-Ingushetia, South Ossetia, Tajikistan, and Tatarstan.[25]

Africa

Potential war zones exist worldwide, but none is as preeminent as is Africa's. Over the course of the last two decades, civil wars and protracted struggles in "Chad, Somalia, the Saharan area, southern Africa, and elsewhere" promoted a chaotic, destabilized atmosphere.[26] During this period, economic progress, the strengthening of the political infrastructure, and the promotion of human health and welfare were brought to a halt. Like the regions previously discussed, Africa is not immune to separatists movements. Upon bringing the Ethiopian civil war to a close in 1991, another separatist action ensued: The government established in Eritrea as part of the cessation of hostilities declared that region's independence in 1993.[27] Elsewhere, ethnic cleansing in the process of political competition continues on this turbulent continent. One such example is the ongoing bloodshed between Rwanda's and Burundi's two major ethnic groups, the Hutu and the Tutsi.

The world's most recent experience in Somalia demonstrated that the cry for help may indeed secure an international response. Here, while the main issue for international onlookers concerned feeding a hungry nation, internal struggles for political dominance continue along subethnic, clan lines. An endeavor lasting two years, claiming the lives of 42 Americans and more than 100 peacekeepers from a 21-nation force and costing almost $2 billion, has produced little. Indeed, in the wake of the March 1995 United Nations withdrawal, Somalia, according to one contemporary report, "has no government, and warring clans are preparing to battle for the city's spoils—the air and sea ports—once the U.N. withdrawal is complete."[28]

The former discussion highlighted a few of the conditions which may lead to future ethnic conflict. Among them are an innate desire to preserve one's culture, economic instability, religious fundamentalism, misrepresentation or corruption, and perceived fiscal mismanagement. While these by no means exhaust the list of potential reasons, they indicate that the "aims and specific context of each of [the potential conflicts] naturally varies as much as their scope and intensity."[29] We must examine the global implications of these conditions to evaluate the potential impact on global security.

Global Impact

By examining the nature of the ethnic conflicts around the world today, we see that immediate and long-range implications for a peaceful world order are not promising. Most assuredly, increased ethnic nationalism which manifests itself in separatist wars will lead to increased instability throughout our world. Jacques Attali et al. asserts that the world is viewed from a backward perspective. Instead of attempting to identify conditions wherein more Yugoslavs will create themselves, we should be asking "[w]hy should they not happen?"[30] These authors declare that "the ingredients are all in place: the collapse of a strong central authority; economic dislocation; historical grievances; injustices of many types, both ancient and modern, burgeoning ethnic rivalries; disagreements over minority rights; border disputes; limited experience of the democratic ordering of political questions."[31] With the growing ability of the media to bring the atrocities of "ethnic cleansing" and related activities into the living rooms of those in the "realm of peace," pressure for interventionist activity from special interest groups will continue to mount. And, while the United States has held off such pressures for direct, unilateral intervention in Bosnia, the same cannot be said for other humanitarian operations where human lives are at stake, such as in Somalia.

Perhaps more important than the adverse effects of direct intervention is the unseen cost these situations have on the world economy and overall global stability. If left unchecked, these movements may slowly erode our international relationships to the point where we can never maintain stability. Additionally, the ever-shrinking global economy will make separation of economic and political convictions increasingly more difficult. As linkages between nations progress toward more complex interdependencies, the actions of one nation will influence others. This is not to say that we'll soon reach the point where nations decide allegiance based upon a single issue, but the probability exists that the connections between issues will exert additional pressures on nations to act. For as much as Clausewitz said that war is an extension of politics, economic war has moved into a position of coequal status in the latter half of the twentieth century. From this point forward, politics and economics will be inextricably linked. While we must consider the battle before us, the economic instrument of national power certainly has the potential to replace the military as the politician's weapon of choice.

Security Implications

As the democratic nation which is intended to serve as the world leader, the United States faces a complex future. While these ethnic conflicts, separatist movements, and civil wars in the third world pose no immediate or direct threat to our vital interests, they have the potential to force the United States into a position where it once again is serving as the "world's policeman." Pursuit of this role's objectives by the employment of military force could ultimately overextend the United States fiscally and could require us to take a position behind the growing economic prowess of our competitors. As a result, the United States would no longer stand out as the dominant player on the world stage. Does this present a real security threat? The answer lies in the freedom of the United States to choose whether she will become involved in one of these conflicts and whether she has the authority to dictate the parameters of her involvement. If the answer to either of these questions is in the negative, the ideology upon which the United States is founded is at stake.

Zones of Turmoil

The above discussion makes clear that a vast majority of the ethnic conflicts will occur within the zones of turmoil. Even though actions within those regions may not be of vital, national importance to the United States, we must recognize them and prepare to react to the broader regional instabilities these conflicts may create. As with any system, instability emerges from change. While change can be good in some respects, it frequently creates a more stressful environment for international relations.

A more serious security threat is the one being discussed throughout our armed forces and in Congress today. It is the drain, whether perceived or real, that humanitarian and peacekeeping operations are having on our forces' ability to train, equip, and prepare to defend the nation against threats to its vital national interests (including allies). As these ethnic conflicts continue to create conditions wherein our military services will become physically involved, our armed forces may be spread across too many borders. Questions regarding the armed forces' ability to conduct wartime operations while continuing to feel the drain from humanitarian operations are creating concern amongst our nation's leadership, both civilian and military.

Does a Peaceful Resolution Exist?

As a result of this potential drain, the United States and its allies should actively seek to develop the infrastructure of third world (or the Tofflers' "first wave") nations today to prevent another Somalia tomorrow. Implied herein is the notion of involvement on a proactive, as opposed to reactive, basis. While the prospect of this type of commitment does not seem likely, the issue rests with the fundamental position of taking the steps now (which obviously include a financial price tag) to avert a potential moral, economic, and political disaster in the future. This concern should prompt the United States (and its allies) to diligently seek peaceful solutions to these increasingly complex problems of ethnic nationalism.

How then are we to deal with these situations? Gobel discusses the three most prominent options. First, he believes we should support self-determination regardless of its implications. In the second option, conversely, he insists we should never support self-determination regardless of its implications. Third, Gobel insists that we support self-determination in almost all cases.[32] Admitting this is a "convenient out" for those nations who have already experienced self-determination, Gobel feels each case must be examined on an individual basis. The consequences of such actions must be fully considered before the United States decides to support antinationalist actions against a sovereign nation.

Gobel's preference that we support self-determination in almost all cases is somewhat paralleled by the words of Graham E. Fuller. In "Neonationalism and Global Politics," Fuller submits that nations may encounter ethnic strife in the form of "ethnic self-determination" as a normal phase of the national maturation process, especially in those regions where an ethnic group has historically felt oppressed.[33] In essence, Fuller believes that only after these diverse groups have been given an opportunity to self-identify, both culturally and politically, will they be willing to submit themselves to the authority of an externally imposed authority. With this idea in mind, we must formulate a strategy to achieve our national goals.

Singer and Wildavsky provide such a framework for our national strategy through suggestions to achieve future national goals. These analysts insist the United States must first and foremost remain focused upon our essential foreign policy goals: the continued protection of American freedom and peace. First, because we exist within a zone of peace and because third world ethnic strife poses no direct threat to our vital national interests, they believe we will continue to meet this superordinate goal without taking any action. Second, these analysts posit that our "twin goals must be to try to keep international trade as open as possible and to protect ourselves against other countries' efforts to give their citizens special advantages at the expense of our citizens."[34] While we may continue to keep international trade open, should we fall behind such other nations as Japan as a result of continuing to become involved in third world and other ethnic conflicts, we may become ill equipped to pursue these economic goals. Actions which provide the necessary flexibility to "implement sensible negotiating tactics and strategies that reflect our genuine national and political interests" must be pursued.[35] Therein lies the crux of this issue for the United States: How are "genuine national and political interests" differentiated from those that are nonvital? Who makes this determination? The answers to these questions represent the focus of our nation and they will continue to define our international involvement worldwide.

Finally, Singer and Wildavsky indicate that the United States should, in conjunction with other democracies, participate in efforts to minimize violence and encourage democracy within the zones of turmoil. Through this effort, we should gradually build an international set of principles regarding future interventionist activity.[36] These principles should guide our behavior and should ultimately lead to the advancement of stable democracies throughout the world. The result of which, according to these two authors, should be the extension of the zones of peace. In the final analysis, this strategy will secure the future of generations to come.

Singer and Wildavsky cogently argue that "wealth, peace, and democracy eliminate what have been the biggest killers: poverty, disease, war, and government murder."[37] The latter presents the greatest security concern for the United States and the remaining democracies; ethnic conflict, as evidenced in Bosnia-Herzegovina and Rwanda, encompasses all four of these debilitating conditions. Consequently, we should construct and implement a national strategy to minimize ethnic conflict and, in turn, minimize its hazards to global democracy.

Conclusion

The concepts of nationalism and ethnicity are not new. However, in today's increasingly complex and interdependent world they take on new dimensions. As a result, we see ethnic nationalism serving as the catalyst for emerging separatist movements. This trend will likely continue well into the future. While ethnic conflicts will occur primarily in the zones of turmoil, and as a result pose no direct threat to our national security, the implications for the world remain severe. For the United States, a major concern is the potential economic drain these conflicts have on the US economy. Currently supporting 31 percent of the United Nation's peacekeeping tab, the US president and Congress are moving to decrease our support to 25 percent. The rationale is simple: Competing US domestic interests have prompted our national leadership to lessen its financial support for this international organization. Coupled with the economic drain is the fear that our fighting forces will not be prepared to defend an attack against what the United States deems as its, or its allies', vital national interests.

As a world leader and a nation built upon the foundation of fundamental human rights, the US must recognize these conflicts early on and prepare to help the vanquished wherever possible. In the words of Singer and Wildavsky, "Unless we are able to be serious about our foreign policy, the practical result is likely to be that the press will determine when there will be intervention."[38] While it is widely known that the press does not establish the fundamental beliefs of the United States, the presentation of news can have a significant impact on public opinion through the shaping of issues with which the nation must deal. If the United States must focus primarily upon self-preservation, it must also take steps, in accord with the other democracies, to minimize ethnic tension and extend the zones of peace. However, only through the development of a foreign policy based upon moral principles, coupled with those which promote our strategic interests, will our increasingly complex and interdependent world continue to grow peacefully.

Notes

1. Paul A. Gobel, "A New Age of Nationalism," in *The ACCESS Guide to Ethnic Conflicts in Europe and the Former Soviet Union* (Washington, D.C.: ACCESS, 1994), 2.

2. Ibid.

3. Anthony D. Smith, *Theories of Nationalism* (New York: Harper and Row Publishers, Inc., 1971), 23.

4. Anthony D. Smith, *Nationalism in the Twentieth Century* (New York: New York University Press, 1979), 4.

5. Andrew M. Greeley, *Why Can't They Be Like Us?* (New York: E. P. Dutton and Co., Inc., 1971), 41.

6. Andrew M. Greeley and William C. McCready, *Ethnicity in the United States: A Preliminary Reconnaissance* (New York: John Wiley and Sons, Inc., 1974), 91.

7. Smith, *Nationalism*, 153.

8. Ibid.

9. Anthony D. Smith, *State and Nation in the Third World: The Western State and the African Nationalism* (New York: St. Martin's Press, 1983), 39.

10. Mark Clayton, "Separatist Party in Quebec Rolls Toward Ballot Victory," *Christian Science Monitor*, 27 July 1994, 2.

11. Adam Tanner, "Independence Efforts of Quebec Separatists Make Wall Street Jittery," *Christian Science Monitor*, 14 December 1994, 3.

12. Ibid. The US will have to help the Mexican government overcome the instability of the pesos to the current tune of $9 billion, yet the effects of the instability which could occur from a separate Quebec have not yet been determined. It is enough to say at this point, however, that such a move could hold drastic repercussions for foreign investments. To date, foreigners hold almost 40 percent of Quebec's $45.2 billion in direct [*sic*] debt.

13. Smith, *Nationalism*, 3.

14. Max Singer and Aaron Wildavsky, *The Real World Order: Zones of Peace/Zones of Turmoil* (Chatham, N.J.: Chatham House Publishers, Inc., 1993), 3.

15. Ibid. According to Singer and Wildavsky, these nations include Western Europe, the United States, Canada, Japan, and the antipodes.

16. Ibid. To Singer and Wildavsky, these nations include Eastern and Southeastern Europe, the territory of the former Soviet Union, and most of Africa, Asia, and Latin America.

17. Ibid., 7.

18. Alex De Waal, "The genocidal state: Hutu extremism and the origins of the 'final solution' in Rwanda," *Times Literary Supplement*, 1 July 1994.

19. *ACCESS*, 17.

20. Ibid.

21. For a complete discussion of the reasons for continuing and future ethnic conflict in this region, see *ACCESS*, 17–20.

22. *ACCESS*, 30.

23. Ibid.

24. Ibid., 51.

25. Ibid., 21–22.

26. "Africa," Microsoft (R) Encarta. Copyright 1994 Microsoft Corporation.

27. Ibid.

28. Reid G. Miller, "U.N. force pulling out of Somalia," *Montgomery Advertiser*, 28 February 1995.

29. While Smith uses these words to discuss the nature of nationalism, the concept applies to the relationship between ethnicity and nationalism, the resulting effects of which we can no longer separate. See Smith, *Nationalism*, 153.

30. Jacques Attali et al., "After the Nation-State: Rekindling Tribalism," *New Perspectives Quarterly*, Fall 1992, 38–40.

31. Attali et al., 38.

32. *ACCESS*, 7.

33. Graham E. Fuller, "Neonationalism and Global Politics: An Era of Separatism," *Current*, July/August 1992, 17–22.

34. Singer and Wildavsky, 197.

35. Ibid.

36. Ibid., 198.

37. Ibid., 203.

38. Ibid., 199.

4

Population Pressures, Migration, and Refugees

Wayne D. Davidson and Bradley S. Davis

The dawn of the twenty-first century will present us with unique security challenges. Many of these challenges will not provide any historical precedent in dealing with them. The term *security* may well encompass a set of issues and circumstances that we simply do not yet understand. One of these new challenges may deal with population pressures and the associated disruptive problems of immigration, refugees, and conflict. The world is entering an era of exponential change in the number and distribution of people over the globe whose negative impacts we cannot anticipate today based only on our historical and current experiences. This chapter addresses these changes, how they might impact international tensions, and what might be done about them, if anything, to mitigate the worst of the consequences.

When anticipating the global security concerns of the early twenty-first century, one must consider the issues of overall population pressures, migration of peoples, refugees, and conflict. When referring to population pressures, we mean the total number of people in the world at any given time. While the total number is important, a related and an equally important issue is the distribution of the total number of people over the planet. Traditionally, the migration of people between states has a primary impact on international politics. Local population pressures often create such situations as inadequate economic opportunities, which push people from an area over time. Likewise, other areas can pull people towards new opportunities. Migration implies a sense of permanency in the shift of people from one location to another. The related issue of refugees refers to displaced peoples who, at least initially, hope to return to their own homeland. The United Nations High Commissioner for Refugees defines refugees as "people who flee their homeland because of fear of political, religious, or ethnic persecution or of war."[1] While these issues and problems have always been factors in international life in the past, current trends indicate they will carry much more impact for international security and stability than before.

The Problem Defined

To best appreciate the potential problems and concerns of population pressures for the future, one needs only to look briefly into the past. One way to place a perspective on the problem is to examine the number of years it takes to produce another one billion people. The one billion population mark was reached around 1830. In other words, it took from two to five million years for the human race to reproduce to the one billion mark. From 1830 it took only a mere 100 years to reach the two billion mark. It required only another 30 years to hit the three billion level in 1960. The four billion mark was reached in 1975, and in 1987 the five billion level was topped.[2] Currently, the world population stands at around 5.6 billion with a fairly steady annual global population growth rate of 1.56 percent.[3]

The general migration of peoples has been prevalent throughout history. Through the 1800s and early 1900s, many people left Europe for the New World, which was happy to receive them. The early 1990s saw a significant migration of peoples from the former communist countries to Western Europe. Given this large flow of people over a relatively short period of time, Western Europe would like to close the flood gates somewhat to control the large influx of people. At one time, most of the Americas and considerable portions of Africa were open to immigrants, but today, only three other principal recipients exists besides Western Europe: the United States, Canada, and Australia.[4] These countries are now seriously rethinking their immigration policy.

For much of the world, the problem is not one of legal or illegal immigration, it is one of refugees. The plight of refugees has been a steadily growing issue considering the increasing number of people involved. In 1960 there were about 1.4 million refugees. The number hit the 10 million mark in 1982 and now includes from 17 to 23 million refugees who have crossed international borders and at least some 25 million more who are displaced within their own countries.[5] Refugee numbers often serve as an imprecise barometer for other factors that are extremely difficult to measure including political stability, human rights, justice, and order. Ethnic upheavals, civil wars, or such resource shortages as food are quite often the root cause of refugee movements. The United Nations High Commissioner for Refugees coordinates relief efforts for some of the refugees, but it is not staffed, equipped, or funded to help in all refugee situations. Most refugees must rely on the generosity of neighboring countries or other tolerant states.[6] Unfortunately, as the pressures to help resettle refugees (and immigrants) have grown, the global willingness to accept them has declined.

The problems of population pressure will continue for the foreseeable future. Although the rate of population growth has actually declined over the past several years, it is declining at a slower rate than originally anticipated. In 1982 United Nations data projected the world population would continue to grow at increasingly lower rates until around the year 2100, when the population would stabilize around the 10.2 billion mark. Now the United Nations expects the world population to continue to grow until the year 2200, with the total population mark leveling off at about 11.6 billion people.[7] A brief look into some of these overall trends reveals some interesting points.

A millennium ago the global population was a fraction of what it is today. High birthrates were required to offset the prevailingly high mortality rates, as well as to provide for a modest growth rate in total numbers of people. The mortality rates began to decline in Europe because of initial advances in agricultural technology, sanitation, health care, and transportation of commodities. The decline in mortality rates was not followed immediately by a concomitant decline in fertility rates. For example, there was a period of surplus births relative to deaths in most of Europe and North America. However, today mortality and fertility rates have essentially equaled-out in these regions as they have transitioned from high mortality and fertility populations to low mortality and fertility populations.[8]

The non-European areas of the world have undergone a somewhat different demographic experience with dramatically different results. The demographic changes in these areas of the world did not begin until the twentieth century and were much more compressed and dramatic. The transfer of modern medical and associated technologies from Europe and North America to the non-European areas occurred much quicker than it took to develop in the West. The immediate result was the significant decline in mortality rates, certainly far more rapid than the decline experienced in Europe. Just as in Europe earlier, the decreased mortality rate was not immediately offset by a decrease in fertility rates. As a result, a significant gap opened between mortality and fertility rates, and population growth in these areas accelerated. The gap continued to widen between mortality and fertility rates to about 2 percent growth annually until around 1960, when the gap finally began to shrink. While this gap is still slowly shrinking, the non-European areas of the world continue to grow at a far greater rate than the European areas of the world, thereby creating an increasingly unequal population distribution.[9]

Even though the world's annual population growth rate is getting smaller, this growth rate is applied to an ever-increasing total population, which still means ever-increasing numbers of people. The overwhelming portion of the growth is in the non-European or nondeveloped areas of the world. In 1993, 94 percent of the world's population growth occurred in the developing world. Currently, 4.3 billion of the 5.6 billion of the world population (78 percent) reside in the developing world.[10] Additional challenges are imbedded in the age distribution in these regions. In African and Central American countries 45 percent of the population is under the age of 15. This percent jumps from 47 to 49 in Iraq, Iran, and Syria. These large populations of young people who lack employment, homes, medical attention, or even clean drinking water have explosive needs but dim futures.[11] In the near and medium future, these areas will be hard pressed to lower or stabilize population growth while having an unprecedentedly high number of people in child-bearing ages.

With increases in population come increased demands on the environment in several ways. First, larger numbers of people place greater demands on the environment for food, energy, and other raw materials. Second, the increase in economic activity as a result of more people produces outputs that affect soil erosion, deforestation, air and water pollution, and other environmental factors.[12] In fact, every year an area of agricultural land almost the size of Ireland is lost to various forms of degradation.[13] With more and more people placing greater demands on and having a greater impact on their local environment and that environment becoming less able to support those people, one of the logical results is the migration of large numbers of people from one area to another.

Migration is, in part, a by-product of increasing population pressure. Although not the only cause for migration, population pressures tend to balance themselves through migration. As of this writing, about 123 million displaced people are looking for a better life or simply trying to escape with their lives. Of these, approximately 100 million are living in countries in which they are not citizens, and the remaining 23 million are displaced within their own countries. Taken together, these people represent about 2 percent of the world's population, and the numbers grow annually.[14] As the developing world continues to swell in population, and the developed world population remains fairly stable or in some places is actually decreasing, migration from the developing world to the developed world can be expected to continue. The influx of immigrants to new locations, mostly urban areas, often create tinder boxes of conflict.

So far, we have identified and discussed the problem from a macro perspective. We've offered a brief history of the current state and size of the problem. We also have shown that population pressures, migration, and refugee problems will be with us into the next century. Let us now examine the regions where these problems most likely will occur.

Regional Perspectives

Population pressures will strain most areas of the developing world. Asia, including the Middle East, is already home to 3.4 billion people, about 60 percent of the world's current population. Within Asia are the world's two demographic giants, China and India. China's 1.2 billion people, about one-fifth of the world's total number, make it the most populous country in the world today.[15] While its population pressures are significant, current trends show that China's fertility rate is declining. From 1991 to 1993 China's total fertility rate dropped significantly from 2.3 to 1.9 percent. Government officials attribute the decline to the "one-couple, one-child" policy, improvements to birth control services, and an improved standard of living. While China has been a demographic concern in the past, it appears that population pressure may be an issue that is under reasonable control for the near-term future.[16]

The other demographic giant is India, currently with 900 million people. Unlike China, India has not controlled its population growth. For example, in 1993 India's population increase was almost 17 million, surpassing the combined population increases in the United States, Europe, Latin America, and the former Soviet Union. No evidence supports a slowdown in the population increase in the near future. The recent "Second India Study" estimated that a baseline 1971 population of 548 million will double by 2007 and that the population will double again before it levels out. The report further indicated that India's environment is rapidly decaying. Extensive deforestation is further causing the rapid siltation of dams which has led to one million acres of land being waterlogged or salinized. Among other concerns, agriculture is severely affected.[17] Social problems are being magnified with nearly 40 percent of the population living below the official poverty level. There is a rapidly growing backlog of low-skilled, low-productivity jobs, and the problems are mounting.[18] Someone should ask if the Indian government can withstand the weight of its own population, coupled with many of the deleterious collateral environmental and social effects of its huge population growth. Is it possible that India could collapse under the weight of its population numbers?

A neighbor and potential rival to India is Pakistan. Currently at 130 million people, it is the seventh most populated country in the world. Like most developing nations, Pakistan's population growth soared following World War II due to improvements in sanitation and other health-care measures. To date Pakistan has not mounted any effective population control measures. Pakistani women average 6.7 children, twice the global average, and Pakistan's population total is expected to double within the next 23 years.[19] Until now, it has sustained an economic growth rate of between 5 and 6 percent each year, which almost matched the enviable economic performance of such Asian countries as Singapore and South Korea. However, the tremendous increase in population has more than offset the large economic strides Pakistan has made. Despite the economic successes, the per capita gross domestic product stands among the world's lowest at around $350.[20] As with India, Pakistan has felt the problems associated with population strains in both the physical and social environments. Should sustained economic performance slow down, Pakistan could possibly buckle under the strain of its population numbers and associated burdens, adding more fuel to an already politically volatile subregion of the world.

Of the world's regions, Africa has the bleakest prospects in terms of population numbers and associated problems. Africa's overall population growth rate is 2.9 percent, the highest of any region in the world.[21] There are currently 719 million people in Africa, comprising 13 percent of the world's total population; in 1950 it comprised only 9 percent. By the year 2015, Africa is projected to contain 19 percent of the total population.[22] Fertility rates are staggering in comparison to Western trends. For example, northern Africa's fertility rate stands at 4.5 percent, western Africa at 6.6 percent, central Africa at 6.6 percent, eastern Africa at 6.5 percent, and southern Africa at 4.5 percent. By comparison, western Europe's fertility rate currently stands at 1.4 percent, North America's and northern Europe's at 1.8 percent, and eastern Europe's at 1.6 percent.[23] Of the world's fastest growing countries in terms of population increases, three of the top five are located in Africa. Over the next 35 years Nigeria's population is projected to increase by 198 percent, Ethiopia's by 180 percent, and Angola's by 175 percent.[24]

Being faced with the highest rate of population growth in the world, Africa is arguably the region least capable of sustaining or supporting that growth. In the past 10 years, the world's food production has increased by 24 percent, outpacing the world's population increase. However, this is not the case in

Africa. The continent's food production during this same period decreased by 5 percent, while the population increased by 34 percent. On the entire African continent only about 7 percent of the land is arable.[25] Scenes of starvation and privation, reminiscent of Ethiopia, Somalia, Sudan, and other African countries, which the West has become accustomed to viewing since the 1980s, are likely to be repeated in the near future. Africa will be the scene of terrible suffering in the next decade with no prospect for improvement on the horizon. Many governments could collapse under the sheer burden of their own human weight. The huge population explosions will likely fuel ethnic problems already present on the continent and fan the flames of long-standing and current conflicts. Africa possibly could enter a tighter and tighter death spiral, which will require help from the rest of the world.

Growing population pressures also exist in the Americas, primarily in Latin America. Although they might be serious, they are not nearly as severe as they are in Africa or Asia. The relative population giants in Latin America are Mexico and Brazil, with total populations of 83 million and 151 million, respectively. As of this writing, Mexico's population doubling time is 27 years, and Brazil's is 38 years. Additionally, seven other Latin American countries have populations exceeding 10 million and have population doubling times ranging from 25 to 63 years. While these statistics have implications for the medium and long term, they do not present the ominous near-term catastrophic situations that exist in other regions.

One of the major repercussions of the growing population pressures experienced in the developing world is migration. Population density increases place greater stress on the local territory to support increasing numbers of people. If a certain territory exceeds its natural-carrying capacity, then at least some people will have to migrate to lower the overall population density so that the remaining inhabitants will have the bare necessities of life. It is incorrect to blame the problem of population growth as the only root cause for external migration, since the cause cannot be analyzed in isolation from a country's economy, environment, politics, and culture. For whatever reason or combination of reasons, today and for the foreseeable future, the unprecedented current rate of migration will continue and create serious challenges for both the developing and developed world. The majority of migration flows first from one developing country to another more economically sound developing country within the same region or second to a more distant developed country.[26]

In Asia over the last three to four years, large numbers of people have migrated from the south and southeast areas to Japan, Hong Kong, and South Korea. Africa has three general migration patterns. Ivory Coast and Nigeria are the primary destinations in western Africa. In southern Africa the flow is predominantly from such countries as Mozambique, Botswana, Lesotho, and Swaziland into South Africa. The flow from northern Africa is mainly into western Europe. In the Americas, the movement from or through Mexico to the United States dominates the migration pattern. Brazil and Venezuela also have attracted increasing numbers of migrants. Western Europe absorbed over eight million people between 1980 and 1992, half of them from north Africa, Turkey, and Yugoslavia. Since 1989 a migratory surge from eastern Europe and the former Soviet Union has occurred.[27] Most migrants flock to the larger cities, which migrants have overburdened with their ever-increasing influx. High-fertility rates, coupled with increasing rural poverty and environmental degradation, will serve only to increase the flow of people into urban areas in the immediate future. The world's six largest cities (or urban agglomerations) are Mexico City, Tokyo, Sao Paulo, New York, Shanghai, and Los Angeles.[28] Many other cities in the developing world and to a lesser extent in the developed world have come under the siege of migration. However, within the next 10 to 15 years there will occur into the developed countries and their cities an increased flow above the present rates.

The problems of migration due in part by billowing population pressures is challenging enough by themselves. However, once placed in the real-world context of conflicts, wars, and other human interactions, the problems become murkier. One of the major products of the various ethnic conflicts and civil wars raging throughout the developing world centers around refugees' attempt to escape with their lives and what little they can carry. The plight of Rwandan refugees over the past year illustrates this phenomenon. The deadly ethnic turmoil between the Tutsis and Hutus has killed between 500,000 to one million people. More than 250,000 refugees currently survive in Rwanda and up to two million live in surrounding countries, though each of these countries are barely able to sustain their own populations. Even with UN humanitarian relief, much of which is flown in by US and European military units, the overflow of these refugees makes their new camps ripe for conflict.[29]

With mushrooming population and emigration, Africa leads as a source of refugees. Of the current top 10 refugee-producing countries, nine are located in Africa: Sudan, Liberia, Guinea, Zaire, Angola, Rwanda, Tanzania, Somalia, and Eritrea. The countries taking in most of the world's refugees are also among the world's poorest. Ethiopia, the east African nation that is now home to almost 500,000 refugees, has one of the world's lowest per capita annual incomes, a meager $100. Zaire, with one and one-half million refugees, more than 10 times the number in the US, has only 1/30 of the US's per capita income.[30] The United Nations High Commissioner for Refugees has stated that the United Nations is facing the most difficult and demanding refugee situation since the organization's inception. As long as nationalistic, ethnic, or communal conflicts and tensions continue to rise, so will the growing throngs of refugees.[31]

Projected Impact

The impact of the combined aspects of overpopulation, migration, and refugees will continue to be felt in the developing world, most notably in Africa. As people swarm to the larger cities in these developing areas, the supporting infrastructures will run serious risk of collapse. The rule of law will flounder, and the snowballing of failed states will gain momentum. Existence in these countries will resemble man in the Hobbesian state of nature, where life will become increasingly solitary, poor, nasty, brutish, and short.

The developed states also will feel the impact of population pressures, migration, and refugees. People will see more and more the developed world as their only hope for salvation and attempt to enter legally, illegally, or any other way they can. At the same time, the developed countries will resist more and more the attempts of migrants and refugees to enter. The resistance already has started and will become more strident. The United States, western Europe, northern Europe, and Japan are starting to close their doors to this apparently endless flood of humanity seeking relief from their nightmare. "Given the general tenor of the times, it's going to be a lot tougher than before for refugees to make their way into the US," says Joel Kotkin, a writer and a senior fellow at the Center for the New West in Denver. "We have become . . . far less likely to want to make exceptions for people."

A basic fact of overpopulation in the world is that eventually a portion of the overpopulation is pressured by economics, politics, or unavailable resources to migrate to what it considers a better place to live. In doing so they take their cultural and environmental heritage with them. In the past, the relatively small sizes of the various immigrant groups arriving in a new homeland like the US were assimilated easily. Nowadays, this human flow is dramatically larger and new homelands are simply finding it harder to assimilate the new cultures quickly. This trend has and will continue to lead to conflict.

The exodus of the Mariel boat people of Cuba to the US was at first an emotional roller coaster for Americans. We watched in horrified fascination the pitiful collection of makeshift boats and floats, not fit enough to cross an Olympic-size pool, yet miraculously crossing the 90 miles between their old and new homes. The sheer size of the migration overwhelmed the Coast Guard and Florida officials. Camps were established to handle the huge influx. More importantly, the demographics of those arriving began a negative whiplash within the US. Fidel Castro, in what many would consider a political masterstroke against the US, simply emptied his prisons and pointed the way north. While awaiting disposition of their pleas for asylum, fighting within the camps erupted into full-scale riots, necessitating the call-up of US military units.

This nightmare began once again in 1993–94 as Haitians went to sea in search of better lives and to leave behind the repressive military-led government which had ousted President Jean Bertrand Aristide. The reaction in the US was obviously hardened by our recent memories of the Cubans, and we established camps for the Haitians at our military facility at Guantanamo Bay, Cuba (a small irony there), and several locations in Panama. The rioting did not occur as much this time, because the US ensured large contingents of military for guard duty.

Is this the portent to the future? It could be according to Jean Raspail's haunting novel of the future, *The Camp of the Saints*. He paints a chilling scenario of one million Indians who were so desperate to flee the inhuman conditions of Calcutta that they begin a startling odyssey by sea (reminiscent of the Cubans and Haitians) around the Horn of Africa, through the Strait of Gibraltar, and to the south of France, in search of a better way of life. Albeit a moving description of their travels, it is the debate within France, within the government, and by the common Frenchman that is so chilling. A review of the book highlights the "crumbling away of resolve by French sailors and soldiers when they are given the order to repel physically by shooting or torpedoing, the armada of helpless, yet menacing people. The denouement, with the French population fleeing their southern regions and army units deserting in droves, is especially dramatic."[32]

A modern-day example of this is occurring in Albania. As this country emerged from its communist veil of secrecy, the wonders of the West flooded into this country. What ensued was nothing more than a human wave of over 40,000 people destined for the near shores of Italy. Hijacking a boat and sailing into the Italian harbor of Bari, Albanians jumped ship and swam ashore, only to be caught by the awaiting Italian riot squads. They were herded unceremoniously into the local stadium. When a helicopter attempted to drop food and water to the Albanians, it was attacked and flew off, and all signs of control left the jailed Albanians. They were eventually flown home, but the aftermath and horror felt by the Italians cost the mayor his job and a standing policy to return future Albanians to the boats on which they arrived was instituted.[33]

The prospects for a comprehensive solution to these problems is at present remote. While some steps are planned to alleviate the worst of the problems, the vastness of them defies a universal solution. An agenda for action was established during the Cairo Conference in September 1994. The plan called for nations to provide universal access to a full range of safe and reliable family planning methods and related reproductive health services by the year 2015. The conference also focused on the status of women worldwide. The key concern was to improve the economic status of women through better education so that they will have an "alternative to perpetual motherhood."[34] While these goals certainly have an admirable quality, it remains to be seen if the world will be willing to pay for these programs, which no doubt will be seen by some as a pure wealth transfer with little or no result in the long term. The most common area of agreement is that if nothing is done, present tendencies eventually will result in more drastic conditions.

The impact on the United States will be felt more and more. First, the United States will be more active in protecting its southern border from illegal immigrants and refugees. The borders already are being tightened, as evidenced in the 1994 California proposition to restrict immigration and the withdrawal of financial state support for those already living illegally in the state. Yet more migration can be expected. Second, there will be a louder cry from the United Nations and the developing world for the United States to do more. The problem for the US will be to choose where and when it should help out or intervene. Pictures of suffering will only become more commonplace, and an infinite number of opportunities will present themselves. The risk to America in these circumstances will be spreading its finite resources and national treasure too thinly. However, continued active United States involvement in international population, migration, and refugee problems is likely, and is consistent with the new national security strategy of engagement and enlargement. Most of its involvement will come in terms of humanitarian and economic assistance, with the inevitable associated peaceful military operations involved.

The United States military response largely will fall into nontraditional roles. Given its unique strategic airlift capability, the Air Force will be called on increasingly to deliver humanitarian relief. Peace operations will continue to increase in number, and will consume more relative shares of national and military money, resources, and personnel. The military also will begin to work closer with civil authorities from the federal level on down to help monitor and tighten our borders to the south. The potential problem is that the military may be parceled out in the numerous variety of nontraditional tasks, so that it will end up being spread too thinly and become unprepared to do its traditional warrior roles adequately.

Throughout the world the mass displacements of people challenge the sanctity of national borders and national identities, and they may be thought to impact the disintegration of nations. They have recently become a challenge to a nation's traditional concepts of its own policies on security and foreign relations. It is quite easy to discern why mass movements of migrants or refugees contribute to internal or interstate conflict and regional and international instability. The recent and repetitive attacks in Germany by roving gangs of skinheads upon Turkish immigrants exemplify the growing frustration, usually misplaced, towards the flood of immigrants.

Migrants also have become instruments of warfare and military strategy. Numerous incidents on every continent show where armed exiles have been used as freedom fighters and guerrillas to wage war. The assistance provided by the Pakistani government to the Afghan rebels (Mujahedin) against the Soviet invasion and the help by the Honduran government to the Contras in Nicaragua are clear examples. South Africa, Israel, and Vietnam have all been accused of making multiple attacks upon refugee camps in neighboring countries, claiming these camps were hotbeds of radical resistance fighters.

These examples of conflicts involving population overpressures pale in comparison to some solutions advanced for the control of migrants and refugees, especially those towards the developed countries. A Finnish philosopher has become the author of a best-selling book by arguing the world can continue to be habitable only if a few billion human beings are eliminated; another world war therefore would be a happy occasion for the planet.[35] But one senior UN diplomat argues against this view (and is somewhat reminiscent of Raspail's story). Kishone Mahbubani feels that "superior Western military technology will be useless against the mass migrations from the third world. These invading armies will arrive as poor and defenseless individuals and families, moving without commanders or orders, and seeping slowly through porous borders."[36]

Certain possible implications and consequences exist for international relations at the beginning of the twenty-first century due to these population pressures. Some analysts have predicted an increase in interstate wars with the developing regions to acquire resources to support their own people. However, other analysts have argued that during famines and other hardships, people are too weak or preoccupied with day-to-day survival concerns to take on military expeditions without the preparation and diversion of human and material resources that they require. Analysts also have hinted at a war of redistribution between the developed states (the "haves") and the developing states (the "have-nots"), especially considering the clear numerical advantage of the developing world. However, this course is not a likely one since, for one, too much is made of the possibility that the developing states could unite and remain united for an extended period of time. A more likely possibility holds that some developing states, perhaps just one, would resort to extortion by threatening to detonate a nuclear device, employing terrorist hijacking, or relying on kidnapping to obtain scarce survival resources.[37] While each of these tactics is a conceivable possibility, any of them probably would work one time, but would result in retaliation by the developed states. One can easily find optimists concerning this subject. The well-respected author, Max Singer, in his book, *Passage to a Human World,* argues that "we need to be, and can be, so confident that we have enough space and raw materials for ten billion people that we do not need to fear twenty billion." In any case, the magnitude of the problems of population, migration, and refugees is potentially large and will aggravate existing political, social, and economic problems as well as potentially create new threats in a new-world environment.

Conclusion

This chapter addressed the growing trends and dangers of population pressures, migration, and refugees for the near-term future. These topics are interrelated. Also, while the subject was treated in relative isolation to other problems of economics and politics, it cannot, in reality, be separated.

These concerns affect other pressing issues which make the future even more difficult to decipher. The bleakest observation holds that the regions with the fastest growth are the same regions that have the least natural support capacity, least infrastructure, and least expertise to treat the problems. As people flee to avoid their fate, they find they are not wanted elsewhere. The situation already may have too much momentum for a near- to mid-term solution, despite great interest and involvement from the developed world. However, in the long term, the most draconian of solutions to the problem of overpopulation may be enforced by Mother Nature (widespread famine) or man himself (full-scale war) if we do not find the answers ourselves—and soon.

Notes

1. Hal Kane, Lester R. Brown, and David Malin Roodman, "Refugee Flows Swelling," in Linda Starke, ed., *Vital Signs 94: The Trends That Are Shaping Our Future* (New York: W. W. Norton & Co., 1994), 106.
2. John Spanier, *Games Nations Play*, 8th ed. (Washington, D.C.: Congressional Quarterly, Inc., 1993), 271.
3. Aaron Sachs, "Population Increase Drops Slightly," in Starke, 98.
4. Barry B. Hughes, *Continuity and Change in World Politics: A Clash of Perspectives*, 2d ed. (Englewood Cliffs, N.J.: Prentice-Hall, Inc., 1994), 439.
5. Amy Kaslow and George Moffett, "Refugees Without a Refuge: US Starts to Pull Up the Drawbridge," *Christian Science Monitor*, 1 March 1995, 1,10.
6. Hughes, 441.
7. Sachs, 99.
8. Ibid.
9. Hughes, 4.
10. Ibid., 4–5.
11. Kane, 106.
12. Hughes, 6.
13. Ibid., 437–38.
14. Kane, 106.
15. Bob Sutcliff, "The Tides of Humanity," *World Press Review*, October 1994, 8.
16. Boyce Rensberger, "Damping the World's Population," *Washington Post National Weekly Edition*, 12–14 September 1994, 10.
17. Sachs, 98.
18. Brad Knickerbocker, "Population Doubling Strains India's Environment, People," *Christian Science Monitor*, 11 August 1994, 11.

19. George Moffett, "Pakistan's Population Growth Saps Economic Prosperity," *Christian Science Monitor*, 6 September 1994, 7.

20. Ibid.

21. Rensberger, 10.

22. Guy Arnold, "Tackling the Population Explosion," *New African Market*, October 1994, 24.

23. Ibid.

24. Rensberger, 10.

25. Arnold, 24.

26. John Pomfret, "Europe's Rio Grande Floods with Refugees," *Washington Post*, 11 July 1993, A1.

27. Ibid.

28. Ibid.

29. Joyce Hackel, "Reconciliation in Torn Rwanda Set Back After Camp Massacre," *Christian Science Monitor*, 3 May 1995, 7.

30. Kaslow and Moffett.

31. "Fighting the Odds," *The UN Chronicle*, December 1993, 89.

32. Matthew Connelly and Paul M. Kennedy, "Must it be the Rest Against the West?" *Atlantic Monthly*, December 1994, 62.

33. Nils Kongshaug, "A Thousand Secret Paths Lead from Albania," *Christian Science Monitor*, 20 March 1995, 7.

34. Arnold, 24.

35. Connelly and Kennedy, 79.

36. Kishore Mahbubani, "The West and the Rest," *The National Interest*, Summer 1992, 3.

37. David W. Ziegler, *War, Peace, and International Politics*, 6th ed. (New York: HarperCollins, 1993), 436.

5

Transnational Crime

Its Effect and Implications for International Stability

Richard W. Chavis

Transnational crime poisons the business climate, corrupts political leaders and undermines human rights. It weakens the effectiveness and credibility of institutions and thus undermines democratic life.

—Boutros Boutros-Ghali
Secretary-General, United Nations

Crime is increasing worldwide, and all signs indicate it will continue to do so. Many observers consider this type of civil disorder an internal, domestic problem that must be solved by indigenous governments, thereby overlooking the security implications caused by crime involving the international community. Article 2 of the United Nations Charter reflects this attitude which bars the organization from involvement in activities which are essentially within the domestic jurisdiction of states. This traditional and limited approach fails to sufficiently explain our new international order and the possible effects of crime on national and international societies. For example, crime in emerging nations may inhibit the advancement of democratic processes and limit political and economic development. In addition to such detrimental internal effects, organized crime creates direct international implications as its nature becomes more transnational and its effect more widespread. Regional and international organized criminal activities increasingly influence the stability, effectiveness, and reliability of foreign regimes and institutions and thereby comprise a significant challenge to international stability.

Shifting Basis of Power

Traditionally, most conventional discussions of international relations invariably focused exclusively on official relationships between states. In the past, such relatively simplistic discussions may have provided some insight and possibly a predictive model for the actions of governments in the international arena and, more importantly, the coalitions they formed. For example, during the cold war blocs of states—and the impact, reaction, and influence one bloc or coalition had on the other—defined international relations. During this same period, the only relevance of nonaligned nations centered around the influence the blocs had on them.

The end of the cold war signaled a drastic revolution in the international order. As Professor Donald Snow relates in his book, *The Shape of the Future: The Post-Cold War World*, "Infrequently, a dramatic event or series of events occurs that results in a basic change in the way the international system works and that requires us to alter how we look at that system."[1] Like the events following the end of World War II, Snow identifies the events of 1989 as just such a dramatic occurrence. However, many political scientists believe the nature of change in the international political environment may run much deeper than those encountered because of the events following 1945. Instead of looking to the 1940s for a similar change or historical benchmark, some observers reach back three centuries. They contend the impact of change emanating from the cold war compares favorably with the rise of the state system following the Peace of Westphalia.[2] This period in the seventeenth century witnessed the emergence of the dominant features of modern international relations. These features included the principles of territorial integrity and self-determination. Regardless of the specific magnitude of the current change, which is largely an academic debate, it suffices for this discussion to understand that the international order is significantly different from what it was before the fall of the Berlin Wall.

Accepting the reality of things being different since the breakup of the Soviet Union, analysts have scrambled to redefine the world in the terms which made them comfortable for

50 years. Generally, they have based these terms on descriptive relationships between states. One thing remains certain, we can no longer realistically view the world in terms of first, second, and third world countries or even in terms of coalitions. Arguably the world is now divided into relevant and irrelevant states. This notion postulates that the industrialized states of the world really matter, and they should therefore be concerned mostly with their economic and political security. The industrialized states have some obvious economic incentives to encourage members of the second and third worlds to join them. However, the social, political, and economic problems of these less-developed countries are, for the most part, relatively insignificant to the industrialized states. Some notable exceptions to this view exist. For example, analysts cannot view the countries of the Persian Gulf as irrelevant to the industrialized nations of the world as their oil reserves are far too valuable, and therefore their stability is important to the industrialized states. This conceptualization is not dissimilar from perceptions by Max Singer and Aaron Wildavsky as outlined in their book, *The Real World Order*, where they describe the international arena as zones of peace and a zone of turmoil.[3] In the past, this kind of grouping may have been useful when attempting to draw conclusions concerning similarities and differences to understand and predict behavior.

However, in light of the radical change in the political landscape of the world, a more appropriate approach to grouping states views relations among peoples in the international community in terms of forces or power that give rise to cultural, religious, and economic movements. The dictionary defines *power* as "a person, group, or nation having great influence or control over others."[4] Through power the irrelevant becomes relevant, or the zones of conflict affect the zones of peace. Even with the changes in international relations, one undeniable truth exists—power dictates relationships in the world. Historically, central institutions of the state embodied power in the international arena. With the decrease in the relative power of states today, such other sources of power as ethnic, religious, and economic factions may reveal increasingly greater power to influence international affairs and dictate agendas. For example, today's multinational corporations often possess more power than many states. Power continues to dictate relationships in the new world order; however, some sources of power are now shifting to nonstate institutions and actors. One of these nonstate actors with increasing power and significance is organized criminal groups. These groups have undoubtedly become more powerful and will emerge as a major force in the new international system.

Significance of Organized Crime

Ample evidence abounds in contemporary literature, and sufficient quantitative data, to validate the spread of crime worldwide. A corresponding increase in organized crime groups and the amount of crime attributed to them accompanies this rise in criminal activity. These groups are becoming very powerful and a potent force in the international arena. Roy Godson, of Washington's National Strategy Information Center, estimates the "annual worldwide profits for all organized crime activities at $1 trillion, almost the size of the United States federal budget."[5] Organized crime, long the plague of industrialized societies, has begun to impact areas where it had traditionally been restricted. For example, organized crime as a growing enterprise now operates in Russia and throughout Eastern Europe, as well as in South Asia, Africa, Central and South America, and the countries of the Pacific rim.

In Russia crime has spun out of control since the Soviet Union's demise in 1991. According to an estimate by the Federal Bureau of Investigation, at least 100,000 Russians are now members of mafia-style organized criminal gangs.[6] These people comprise nearly 5,700 organized crime groups operating in Russia.[7] The majority of them are small groups averaging around 20 members. Most of these small groups are involved only in local rackets like protection schemes, prostitution, and surreptitious marketing activities. However, analysts contend that approximately 160 of these are powerful enough to operate internationally in more than 30 countries.[8] The disruptive influences of these Russian gangs have spread throughout the countries of the former Soviet bloc and into Western Europe. Several reports clearly show that gang activity has spread beyond Russian borders into various criminal enterprises ranging from drugs, prostitution, and money laundering. Some observers postulate that some of these Russian gangs have close ties with narcotraffickers in South America.

Russian criminals are also profiting from the Balkan war. They are thriving on smuggling and surreptitious market activities throughout the war zone. Also, observers believe Russian crime groups to be the prime source of the women who work the brothels in Zagreb and Belgrade.[9] But the Russians are not responsible for all the crime that has occurred in the Balkan war. Indeed, Russian crime groups operating in Belgrade must compete with local crime groups. The number of organized crime groups in Belgrade is swelling under its current conditions of war and poverty. Teenagers there have succumbed to organized crime in large numbers.[10] The number of crimes committed by minors doubled in 1994 alone. Observers credit the increasing involvement of minors in criminal activity to the growing number of organized crime groups and their demand for assassins. Belgrade is experiencing "around one hundred" underworld killings a year, a 100 percent increase from the prewar rate.[11]

Around the globe, drug production and smuggling activities are two of the more common activities of organized crime and are best characterized by the drug cartels of Central and South America. While these are the most notorious, many similar operations, rivaling the cartels in various parts of the world exist. For example, Albanian mafia barons have created transportation networks that move illegal drugs from Turkey through Bulgaria, Romania, Hungary, Slovakia, and the Czech Republic.[12] According to the East European office of the Brussels-based Customs Cooperation Council, one-quarter of the heroin sold in west Europe passes through east Europe.[13] Additionally, South Africa has experienced drug smuggling by Nigerian drug syndicates. These organizations employ South Africans to carry drugs from Thailand to South Africa, where drugs are transshipped to other major consumption countries in Europe and to the United States.[14] A US State Department report attributes almost 45 percent of the heroin seizures made at US ports in 1990 to Nigerian couriers.[15]

Another specific transnational crime problem holds that organized crime around the world is contributing to the explosion of international smuggling of humans. These organizations earn billions of dollars each year by violating immigration laws and feeding on the innocent, who only want to improve their lives. In the United States, which is a primary destination of many smuggling operations, law enforcement officials have disrupted $1 million rings that attempt to smuggle Indian, Pakistani, Albanian, and Chinese nationals into the country. These operations compound the illegal immigration business established by long-standing and continuing criminal operations originating in Central and South America and the Caribbean Basin.

Human smuggling is not unique to the United States. Austrian officials have recently discovered that their country was the destination for Asians smuggled through Russia and Eastern Europe. Spanish officials have discovered a scheme to use credentials of deceased citizens to smuggle Chinese nationals into their country. Further, Swedish officials are continuing to crack down on a Baltic Sea smuggling route that reportedly delivers Iranian and Iraqi immigrants through Moscow to Latvia, Estonia, or Lithuania before finally reaching Sweden. Finally, the Japanese recently exposed a smuggling ring that transports Chinese citizens through Thailand and then to Japan. This boom in international smuggling of humans reaps huge profits because of the effect of the changes in the international environment since the fall of the Soviet Union. The emergence of weak states, the decline of civil authority, and the rise of organized crime complicate the problem.[16] These are only examples; analysts have found organized criminal activity flourishing practically everywhere in the world and, more importantly, it is becoming transnational in nature.

Domestic Effects of Organized Crime

Without the support of the coalitions of the cold war world which provided a stable power base, many states no longer influence events in their own country, much less their region. Rather than fill the vacuum of power left by the fall of the communist coalition and East-West disengagement, these governments have been unable to respond to the demands of the new international environment and therefore have given way to other bases of power located internal and external to their borders. This vacuum is allowing organized crime to become a powerful force in the internal affairs of many countries.

Crime is accelerating far beyond the ability of current institutions to deal with it. In some societies, crime threatens to undermine the fabric of political stability. "Organized crime," says Sen John Kerry (D-Mass.), "is the new communism, the new monolithic threat."[17] Lawlessness and organized crime, at least to some extent, can provide an alternative means of support and a seductive source of personal and criminal profit that may subvert ideological or political fervor.[18] To counter its effects, fragile governments will have to wage a new kind of war. They must wage this war against crime, which may delay progressive reforms. Eduardo Vetere, chief of the UN crime and criminal justice branch of the United Nations office at Vienna, stated, "Crime is undermining the foundation of trust upon which government is based, by eroding its authority and legitimacy."[19]

The adverse effects of crime hampers the general shift of political systems from communism, dictatorships, and other repressive regimes toward more progressive systems. Specifically, internal crime in Russia is trying to make the political and economic systems more difficult to reform. A 1994 opinion poll published in a Russian newspaper revealed that nearly one-third of ordinary citizens believed organized criminals controlled the government, almost twice as many as believed Boris N. Yeltsin controlled the government.[20] To counter the growing crime problem, President Yeltsin issued a decree on 14 June 1994 to give police broad new powers to crack down on suspected organized crime members. The disputed decree allows police to hold suspects for 30 days without charge and to investigate their finances.[21]

Another example of the effect of crime on the internal, domestic processes and state development focuses on South Africa. Since the recent elections, which installed a majority democratic government and led to the lifting of international sanctions, officials in the country have expected a return of external business investment and growth. Neither has been forthcoming. The most plausible explanation for this absence is the skyrocketing incidence of crime. Drugs are flowing into the country over South Africa's borders along with Zimbabwe, Mozambique, and Botswana.[22] Additionally, South Africa's murder rate is three times that of the United States. Experts predict that if the crime rate continues, corporations in South Africa will do what corporations in Angola did—set up their own townships for their own employees, with sophisticated security systems walling them off from the increasingly lawless population which is controlled by organized crime.[23] Crime invariably dictates the agenda for many such states and complicates their efforts to steer their country to more pluralistic, market-oriented societies.

Many may consider the current challenges to states posed by organized crime not unlike the historical challenges to the United States from the Italian mafioso. This particular crime organization originated in Italy as a subcultural phenomenon which was borne of an intricate history of injustice and a questionable application of the law, misgovernment, and mismanagement.[24] Like the American experiences with the Mafia, other states have long had to deal with individuals or groups who violate standards of conduct or restrictions on personal activities which are designed to protect the states' internal social structure. While the relative power of the criminal element or enterprise does not compete with the legitimate power of a stable state, organized criminal activity throughout the world causes concern because many of the involved states cannot effectively combat it. These states do not have adequate resources or social structures to attack and mitigate organized crime without consequential detrimental effects on their stability.

Martin van Creveld cautions, "Once the legal monopoly of armed force, long claimed by the state, is wrested out of its hands, existing distinctions between war and crime will break down."[25] Organized crime threatens "war" within the societies in which it exists. Even though this war may be an unorthodox one, it is nonetheless a battle of survival among factions of a society. Van Creveld contends that the nature of war is transforming. He predicts that future wars will no longer be waged by states but by factions spurred to violence by scarcity.[26] Just as the shifting of power occurs from state to nonstate actors, so too does the ability to wage war shift in the same direction. If van Creveld's predictions hold true, this shift will be accompanied by a propensity for violent conflict. Whether this shift is permanent or transitory is not yet certain.

Robert Kaplan predicts that as crime rates continue to rise and the ability of states and their criminal justice systems to protect their citizens diminishes, states will lose the power to control events within their borders. He adds that when this happens, power may be wrested from the state and placed into the hands of powerful private security organizations like those we have seen jeopardize Mozambique and Angola and threaten parts of South Africa. Worse than these private security companies is the possibility of mafioso, who may be better equipped to protect citizens than indigenous police forces: "To the average person, political values will mean less, personal security more."[27] Organized crime has adversely affected the state, threatening political and economic reform, undermining the very basis of the state's legitimacy, and threatening warfare within the society.

International Effects of Organized Crime

In addition to internal, domestic effects, organized crime can influence states throughout a region or worldwide. States concerned with economic growth and enlarging markets will find that organized crime can dissuade international economic relations by restricting entry and border requirements to reduce criminal activities across the states' borders. But such rising trends as new technologies and expanding transnational aspects of economics are making borders meaningless, and the inabilities of existing law enforcement agencies to mitigate the effects on these borders are becoming abundantly apparent. States will find it exceedingly difficult to isolate themselves from transnational criminal activities. These activities will challenge them to respond to organized criminal activities that transcend international boundaries and will necessarily cause them to dedicate an increasing amount of their resources to combat them.

Drugs, acts of terrorism, and problems concerning the smuggling of humans provide a glimpse of the significance of the transnational implications of organized criminal activity which threaten to draw states into conflict. For example, consider the United States' efforts to curb the smuggling of narcotics from Central and South America. These experiences indicate the complexities and threat of conflict posed by transnational criminal activities. Recall the efforts to bring to justice the president of Panama, Manuel Noriega, who was indicted at the peak of the drug war hysteria and had been portrayed as a "drug lord" and "poisoner of American children."[28] Determined to show his resolve against the domestic threat posed by the transnational nature of the illicit coca trade, then-President George Bush initiated Operation Just Cause. This military operation included an invasion of Panama by 23,000 United States troops whose primary goal was to capture Noriega for trial in a United States court. The ensuing guilty verdict against Noriega may have been the costliest criminal conviction in history, coming at a cost of $164 million and the lives of 23 United States soldiers.[29]

In 1992, the United States spent 93.6 percent of the $11.9 billion of its drug control budget on domestic enforcement, demand reduction, and border control.[30] These border controls have included the gradual and increasing involvement of the United States military. What originally began as the use of military equipment to monitor land, sea, and air lanes used by traffickers now involves an active counterdrug program—which includes United States military personnel participating in foreign counterdrug operations. Their participation includes training foreign personnel in counterdrug operations and operating bases and training facilities in foreign countries. The United States Department of Defense now provides nation-building assistance, training and operational support, technical assistance, intelligence support, and other direct and indirect support to foreign governments cooperating with our counterdrug effort.[31] Such high-profile operations as these could draw the United States into disputes with other state and nonstate actors in the region. For example, the 1995 border war between Peru and Ecuador included an allegation by the Ecuadorian leadership that the Peruvian armed forces used helicopters, provided by the United States for drug suppression operations, to ferry troops to battle areas in the disputed territory.[32]

Finally, consider Colombian drug lord Pablo Escobar as an early prototype of the new international gangster. He was a billionaire whose drug wealth bought him a mansion in Miami, as well as other prime pieces of real estate around the world. More dangerous than his products and their ultimate damage to the individuals and societies around the world was the power he possessed. He was a political force, capable of intimidating weak governments and defying strong ones for years until his death in 1993.[33] Media and United States Drug Enforcement Administration reports substantiate Escobar's complicity with Panama's Manuel Noriega, as well as with the Nicaraguan Sandinistas in the trafficking of illegal drugs. Escobar allied himself with Noriega and the Sandinistas in exchange for transshipment locations, money laundering, and safe haven.[34] Noriega and the Sandinistas profited monetarily from their relationship with Escobar. Both used the money to keep themselves in power. Then-President Ronald Reagan used Escobar's relationship with the Sandinistas as part of his justification for aid to their opponents, the Contras. Also, Escobar's illegal business arrangements with Noriega provided evidence that ultimately prompted United States military action against him. These relationships portend the conflict potential of powerful criminal organizations and their transnational activities.

In addition to the threat of drug traffickers, the impact of terrorism is well documented and commonly understood throughout the world. In terms of effect, analysts find it exceedingly difficult to separate criminal activity strictly for economic gain from criminal activity designed to support political objectives. The former is criminal, antisocial behavior; the latter is terrorism. For example, the daily death toll from murder in Algeria in 1994 was around 50.[35] Analysts attribute most of these murders to Islamic fundamentalist groups who used terrorist tactics to further their political cause. But these groups are not the only ones responsible for the violence in Algeria. As in any society where political murder is commonplace, others, including criminals, will soon become involved for economic gain. Killing of any kind lowers the threshold for violence and perpetuates it. Ironically, when responding to terrorism, security or law enforcement forces must increase the level of violence and restrict individual liberty to thwart illegal violent activity. Organized crime, like its counterpart, terrorism, has a transnational nature that affects many nations in the international community and serves as an increasingly significant source of potential conflict.

From Russia to Thailand, the export of precious raw materials is falling into the hands of organized crime. In Central America and Asia, the political control of small nations or weak governments is falling into criminal hands.[36] The most obvious concern among the industrialized nations of the world about Russia's organized crime involves the chances of nuclear components being sold surreptitiously. Some nations harbor a legitimate fear that nuclear materials from the former Soviet Union could fall into terrorist hands. The arrests of several persons attempting to smuggle or sell weapons-grade plutonium have justified these fears. In August 1994 German police arrested a man after he had allegedly tried to sell 70 grams of plutonium 239 to undercover police. This was the fourth such incident in as many months. Also, a week after this arrest, Bavarian police reportedly seized three to 10 ounces of plutonium 239 in the luggage of three men aboard a Lufthansa airliner arriving from Moscow.[37] These and other actual cases cause concern because their quality and quantity of fissile material has reached the threshold of what it takes to make nuclear weapons.[38] These incidents were the impetus behind the cooperative agreement between the United States' Federal Bureau of Investigation (FBI) and Russia's interior ministry to combat organized crime. This agreement included unprecedented mutual law enforcement cooperation as well as the opening of an FBI office in Moscow.

Relations between states have sometimes been strained because of the actions of individuals of one country who violate the law in other countries. Without culpability of their own governments, home nations generally hold individuals liable for their actions in another country, and the international community accepts the right of the host state to punish criminal law violators regardless of citizenship. For example, the investigation from the crash of Pan Am flight 103 resulted in the indictment of two Libyan intelligence agents but stopped short of implicating Muammar Kaddafi himself or the Libyan government.[39] Without the existence of a "smoking gun," responsible states in the international community generally hold individuals personally accountable for their actions rather than the governments of the countries in which they hold citizenship. On the other hand, evidence acquired as the result of the 1987 discotheque bombing in West Berlin clearly implicated the Libyan government in the killing of three people and wounding of others. The killed and injured included United States servicemen and German citizens. The international community generally supported the subsequent United States punitive military airstrikes against targets in Libya. Both incidents further demonstrate the potential for conflict and effects of transnational criminal activity. Furthermore, the lack of standard, recognized "rules" for dealing with international criminality increases the potential for conflict.

Causes of the Rise in Crime

Crime, like other darker aspects of human existence, thrives on hopelessness, greed, and despair in an environment of ineffective governmental institutions. Many places in the world today are mired in confusion and consumed by the change caused by the transition from the cold war era. Organized transnational crime takes advantage of the weakness of such states and their institutions.[40] The collapse of communism weakened the social and political institutions of the former Soviet bloc countries. Additionally, other countries in the world are experiencing an unraveling of their social fabric and an erosion of their moral values because of the challenges posed to them by rapid change. Transnational organized crime results therefore as a natural consequence of the events of our time.

Crime rates have been high in such multicultural, industrialized, democratic societies as the United States. However, the rapid rise of crime in other locations of the world where previously there had been low crime reflects a much greater problem which will have implications for the economic and political security of the industrialized nations of the world. Analysts attribute rising crime rates to such conditions as increasing heterogeneity, greater cultural pluralism, immigration, realignment of national borders, economic deterioration, and the lack of accepted national social norms. Evidence of these conditions occur in many places throughout the world.

Two factors—technology and the evolving nature of our economic system—spur this trend. Information and communications availability are enlarging the playing fields and opportunities for organized crime. Criminals now launder money electronically. Their illegal transactions use cellular phones, fax machines, and on-line communications. These technologies make illegal transactions easier to conduct and difficult to investigate and control. For example, Russian criminals swindled more than $40 million from the Russian banking system in 1993 through modern technology and by exploiting Russia's antiquated bank transfer system.[41] Also, through sham companies Russian-organized crime elements cheated the United States government of $14.6 million between October 1991 and December 1992.[42] They accomplished this maniacal feat by establishing dummy companies to sell gasoline without paying taxes. The companies submitted records indicating that taxes had been paid and were therefore due a refund. In reality, no company existed nor had any taxes been paid.

In addition to the opportunities provided by technology, part of the blame rests with our free market economic system. Since the fall of communism and its command economies, some former communist countries view capitalism as "good" and worthy of attainment. But misunderstanding capitalism as only the pursuit of wealth fails to emphasize social conduct free of crime and corruption. The revolutionary changes in our international system diminishes state sovereignty over many economic issues as multinational corporations operate increasingly outside the purview of a specific state. Therefore, as the economies of the industrialized world become transnational, a logical consequence of this action produces a similar transnational criminal activity.

Conclusion

The post-cold-war world differs from its better understood predecessor. During the cold war, the world needed the United

States to balance the influence of the Soviet Union, and other states joined blocs to protect their interests. Even with the elimination of this reason to remain engaged internationally, sufficient reasons to preclude isolationism on the part of states in the international community still exists. The transnational nature of illegal behavior, whether it is strictly criminal or conducted with some political motive as in the case of terrorism, adversely affects industrialized and developing states. For example, the United States offers an especially lucrative target and cannot isolate itself from transnational criminal activities. The US cannot depend on isolationism to protect its citizens' interests in its political and economic development.[43] The United States, as the remaining superpower, is too engaged and has too much at stake to withdraw from world affairs. In addition to this fundamental reason, the United States also has displayed a 200-year preference for showing a genuine and humane face to the world.

No grand conspiracy is using organized crime to disrupt human society and corrupt international relationships. Instead organized crime is taking advantage of the failures of weak governmental institutions and is thriving on the change in the international system. As organized crime thrives, like other expanding economic enterprises, it is becoming transnational.

Transnational criminal activity can adversely impact specific national interests of states. A necessary cooperative strategy to counter the effects of organized crime requires a strong union of democratic alliances. This cooperative strategy must include a role for the United Nations and regional security alliances in cooperative international law enforcement efforts. However, United Nations involvement does not offer a panacea for global problems. Standard peacekeeping measures cannot be applied to transnational organized crime activities. A monitoring agency must apply international peacekeeping efforts judiciously rather than in blanket fashion.[44]

Traditional collective security arrangements do not offer adequate measures to tackle the global challenge of transnational criminal activity unless we broaden the functions of collective security arrangements to include the protection of citizens from the threat of organized international crime. To effectively combat the problem, we must attack the causes. This step requires a collaborative application of peaceful and forceful instruments, including political, economic, military, and informational resources. Success will depend more on cooperation than competition and reconciliation more than retribution. Regardless of our specific response, this phenomenon has created a much more complex international environment which will challenge existing state structures and relations among states around the world.[45]

Notes

1. Donald M. Snow, *The Shape of the Future: Post-Cold War World* (New York: M. E. Sharpe, 1991), 3.

2. James B. Steinburg, "Sources of Conflict and Tools for Stability: Planning for the 21st Century," *Dispatch* 5, issue 28 (11 July 1994): 464.

3. Max Singer and Aaron Wildavsky, *The Real World Order: Zones of Peace, Zone of Turmoil* (Chatham, N.J.: Chatham House, 1993).

4. *Webster's II New Riverside University Dictionary* (Boston: Riverside Publishing Co., 1988).

5. Michael Elliott and Douglas Waller et al., "Global Mafia," *Newsweek* 122, issue 24 (13 December 1993): 22.

6. Adam Tanner et al., "Russia's Notorious Mafia Spreads Tentacles of Crime Around the Globe," *Christian Science Monitor*, 11 January 1995, 1.

7. Wendy Sloane, "FBI's Moscow Mission: The Mob, Nuclear Theft," *Christian Science Monitor*, 5 July 1994, 6.

8. Louis Freeh-Journeys, *Facts on File* 54, issue 2797 (7 July 1994): 479.

9. Tanner et al., 1.

10. Yigal Chazan, "Baby-Faced Hitmen Add to Rising Crime in Troubled Serbia," *Christian Science Monitor*, 22 November 1994, 4.

11. Ibid.

12. Yigal Chazan, "Albanian Mafias Find New Drug Routes Around Yugoslavia," *Christian Science Monitor*, 20 October 1994, 6.

13. Ibid.

14. Maj Gen Julian Thompson, "Drugs and the Constraint on Commerce in a New Democracy," *INTERSEC: The Journal of International Security* 4, nos. 11/12 (November/December 1994): 403.

15. US Department of State, Bureau of International Narcotics Matters, "International Narcotics Control Strategy Report," March 1991, 325.

16. Paul J. Smith, "The Rising Tide of Human Smuggling," *Christian Science Monitor*, 30 November 1994, 19.

17. Elliott and Waller et al., 22.

18. Graham H. Turbiville, Jr., "The Organized Crime Dimension of Regional Conflict and Operations Other Than War," in *Ethnic Conflict and Regional*

Instability (Strategic Studies Institute, Carlisle Barracks, Pa.: US Army War College, 1994), 126.

19. "Regions Prepare for 1995 Congress," *UN Chronicle*, June 1994, 69.

20. Freeh-Journeys, 479.

21. Sloane, 6.

22. Thompson, 403.

23. Ibid.

24. Gaia Servadio, *Mafioso: A History of the Mafia from its Origins to the Present Day* (New York: Stein and Day Publishers, 1976), xvii.

25. Robert D. Kaplan, "The Coming Anarchy," *Atlantic Monthly*, February 1994, 74.

26. Martin van Creveld, *The Transformation of War* (New York: Free Press, 1991), 197.

27. Kaplan, 74.

28. Michael Isikoff, "The Case Against the General: Manuel Noriega and the Politics of American Justice," *Washington Monthly*, December 1993, 53.

29. Bob Cohn, "Noriega: How the Feds Got Their Man," *Newsweek* 119, issue 16 (20 April 1992): 37.

30. "An Analysis of DOD Counterdrug Efforts," unpublished Research Report (Maxwell AFB, Ala.: Air Command and Staff College, April 1994), 9.

31. Joint Publication 3-07, *Doctrine for Joint Operations in Low Intensity Conflict*, chapter 5.

32. Andrew Selsky, "Helicopters Downed in Border War," *Montgomery Advertiser*, 30 January 1995, 1.

33. Russell Watson and Peter Katel et al., "Death on the Spot," *Newsweek* 122, issue 24 (13 December 1993): 18.

34. Kevin Buckley, *Panama: The Whole Story* (New York: Simon and Schuster, 1991), 59.

35. Maj Gen Julian Thompson, "Islamic Fundamentalism and Western Society," *INTERSEC: The Journal of International Security* 5, no. 1 (January 1995).

36. Elliott and Waller et al., 22.

37. Wendy Sloane, "With Plutonium Arrests, Accusations Fly Between Russia and Germany," *Christian Science Monitor*, 18 August 1994, 6.

38. Peter Grier, "Nuclear Heists Show Thieves' Sophistication," *Christian Science Monitor*, 19 August 1994, 6.

39. Eloise Salholz, "Who Paid for the Bullet?" *Newsweek*, 25 November 1991, 28.

40. Boutros Boutros-Ghali, "Transnational Crime," *Vital Speeches of the Day* 41, no. 5 (15 December 1994): 130–32.

41. Elliot and Waller et al., 22.

42. Tanner et al., 2.

43. Lincoln P. Bloomfield, "The Premature Burial of Global Law and Order: Looking Beyond the Three Cases from Hell," *Washington Quarterly*, Summer 1994, 145–62.

44. Paul F. Diehl, *International Peacekeeping* (Baltimore: Johns Hopkins University Press, 1993), 165.
45. Ibid., 125.

6

Human Rights and Humanitarian Concerns

Gregory T. Frost

The prisoners in the Government jail in Kibungo, Rwanda, will tell you how they killed their Tutsi neighbors and burned their houses, but they deny they did it willingly. Their testimony has a chilling similarity: not just their repeated invocations of "orders from above" or their matter of fact delivery, but their depiction of the massacres as a military operation, a matter of guns and grenades. The duty of the civilian conscripts, they say, was nettoyage, "cleaning up"—killing the survivors.

—Andrew Jay Cohen

Introduction

Over the last two decades, human rights and humanitarian concerns have become an enduring facet of US foreign policy and have earned a permanent place on the international agenda. American concern for human rights and humanitarian conditions throughout the world is longstanding and reflects the fundamental values of our society. Any effort to predict and analyze future global security trends must reckon with this reality. As it is beyond the scope of this essay to address the broad subject of human rights and humanitarian concerns in its global breadth and depth, it considers human rights issues insofar as they provoke a US or international military response, and it also discusses the likely implications for US national security policy and military strategy.

This essay further defines human rights abuses as large-scale, high-profile crises and includes widespread massacres and other forms of ethnically, religiously, and politically motivated violence and mistreatment directed against civilians. This essay limits humanitarian concerns to such major cases of general and severe material deprivation as famine, caused principally by the activities of man, which results in widespread death and destruction.

A Whole New World

During the cold war period, US treatment of human rights and humanitarian concerns was substantially determined by the larger context of the West's global struggle with the Soviet Union and its allies. The enormous resources the two superpowers devoted to nuclear and conventional military forces tended to limit their spending on secondary concerns, and both were generally wary of military involvement not easily linked to the global struggle between them, given the ultimate risk of provoking a global nuclear war which both feared. The collapse of the Union of Soviet Socialist Republics (USSR), the sharply decreased threat of nuclear holocaust, and the demise of the old bipolar power structure have combined to remove this focus. This collapse has vitiated many of the constraints which had previously limited and circumscribed US and allied freedom of action in the human rights sphere. At the same time, the end of the stable two-superpower equilibrium, which often served to check conflicts which could generate new humanitarian crises, seems to have removed the lid from numerous simmering conflicts, many of them having a distinctly humanitarian dimension.

In contrast to the previous four decades, the immediate post-cold-war years already have witnessed relatively large-scale US and international military interventions in direct response to human rights abuses and humanitarian crises, most notably in Bosnia, Somalia, Rwanda, and Haiti. A key challenge to American and allied policymakers in the next decade will be to determine the wisdom and necessity of further interventions of this sort. The obvious fact of America's unparalleled and virtually unchallenged global reach and power will combine with instantaneous and graphic televised images of humanitarian tragedies (the so-called Cable News Network factor) to generate pressure on the US to assume the role of the world's social worker and policeman.

Zone of Turmoil

Most of the human rights abuses and humanitarian disasters likely to attract international attention, resulting in calls from some quarters for unilateral or multilateral military intervention, will occur in what Max Singer and Aaron Wildavsky have termed the *zone of turmoil.*[1] A vast area comprising the bulk of the third world plus the constituent republics of the former Soviet Union, the zone of turmoil is characterized by political units whose political, economic, and social development have either never risen above the formative or early consolidative stages of state evolution[2] (e.g., Somalia) or have reverted to these levels due to the disintegration of the existing polity (e.g., former Yugoslavia). It seems probable that the less-than-viable first wave[3] countries in sub-Saharan Africa and South Asia, still mired at the consolidative level or below after several decades of political independence and formal nationhood (e.g., Rwanda) in the foreseeable future will provide the venue for most human rights/humanitarian crises catastrophic enough to warrant a major US or international response. While the impact of such crises will assuredly not be global, the prospect of a regional ripple or domino effect, as the problem expands and spreads to neighboring states, is much greater. This scenario has been the case with the refugee crisis generated by the Liberian civil war, which has spilled over into the contiguous countries of Sierra Leone, Guinea, and the Ivory Coast, with adverse consequences to the stability of the entire region.

The Coming Anarchy

Given the shifting and uncertain post-cold-war international environment now commonly referred to as the "New World Disorder," the long-term growth potential for humanitarian disasters can appear limitless, particularly if one accepts the pessimistic futurism of Robert Kaplan[4] and Martin van Creveld.[5] It is unlikely that the immediate future will witness a great explosion of conflict-driven human misery. However, it does seem quite probable that we will confront a number of perplexing, heartrending, and sometimes unanticipated humanitarian tragedies which will defy easy solutions yet provide a persistent impetus for outside intervention.

The ostensible causes of the humanitarian crises of the coming years will vary. They will include repressive or totalitarian regimes, intrastate or civil wars, internal or transnational ethnic conflicts, the socioeconomic collapse of states, extreme migration and population pressures, epidemics, and natural and ecological catastrophes. These factors can lead to the demise of fragile states and governments and the breakdown of public order, creating a downward slide from mere poverty into abject deprivation. Those human rights abuses and humanitarian disasters, which constitute both intended and unintended consequences of war and conflict will pose an especially difficult challenge.

The US military is virtually the only standing organization capable of responding quickly and successfully to major humanitarian crises and disasters worldwide. It possesses not only the equipment, personnel, and logistical base to undertake and sustain large-scale relief operations but also the all-important capability to provide security for unilateral and bilateral humanitarian efforts through the threat or application of its combat power. Therefore, the simple fact is that any call for significant US or international assistance inevitably will imply consideration of a supporting part, and, possibly, a leading role, for US military forces.

Problems and Pitfalls

Human rights abuses and humanitarian concerns constitute a phenomenon which one should not view in isolation. In considering human rights abuses as a source of conflict, note that the humanitarian dimension is usually more effectual than causal. That is, human rights abuses and humanitarian crises serve as symptoms or outgrowths of an underlying conflict which cannot, for long, be successfully treated without addressing their root causes. In many situations, human rights problems are natural and predictable consequences of ongoing or recently terminated civil or intrastate wars. In other scenarios, however, humanitarian tragedies represent deliberate war-fighting strategies and tactics employed by combatants to achieve political or military objectives. As the US contemplates intervention to remedy a humanitarian crisis, it should realize that its efforts may be short-lived, unsuccessful, or even counterproductive, absent the ability and willingness to address the cause of the crisis. In situations where the underlying conflict has yet to erupt, is momentarily quiescent, or has reached its termination phase, care must be taken lest the mere prospect of outside intervention upset the equilibrium and provoke or intensify the conflict.

Peripheral Interests, Peripheral Involvement

The US should cautiously approach humanitarian crises which are only of peripheral interest to our own national security and be honest with ourselves when we contemplate an intervention unrelated or marginal to our self-interest. When a US objective is an altruistic one, the commitment of resources and effort might be inadequate. This possibility is especially true when the parties in the underlying conflict are relentlessly pursuing clearly defined political and military objectives flowing directly from what they perceive as their own core national or group interests, if not their fundamental survival. The parties to such conflicts perceive the human rights issues on which we focus as secondary concerns at best. While the combatants themselves may well regret and deplore the adverse humanitarian consequences of their conflict, they will, in many instances, be unwilling or unable to address them until the post-conflict phase has clearly been reached.

The US also must realize that where the parties are still intent in making war upon each other, the introduction of US or other international forces in a limited noncombatant role is likely to motivate one or both parties to use and manipulate the intervention to further its own objectives. The US can expect the parties to the conflict to work to persuade or compel intervening parties to support their respective causes, if not to enter the conflict on their side. The results of such machinations can range from the obstruction or diversion of humanitarian relief efforts to the unintended involvement of the US in hostilities for which we are unprepared and have no real stake. International efforts to provide relief to the victims of the conflict in the former Yugoslavia have been plagued by the constant whipsawing of UN peacekeepers and of relief workers by the warring parties. Indeed, these parties consistently have refused to respect the international contingent's neutrality.

The Enabler Syndrome

Where intervention does succeed in ameliorating or eliminating the human suffering which it is designed to remedy, outside intervention may have the unintended consequence of facilitating the continuance of the conflict and the subsequent carnage. A combatant's civilian population being fed and cared for by others alleviates a key concern for him and may free up additional resources to devote to the war effort. This paradox recalls the "Twelve-Step" self-help movement's concept of the enabler—the friend or relative of the alcoholic who compassionately cares for the drunk and his affairs so he can function despite his addiction, yet in the process assures the latter's eventual destruction. In this regard, it will be interesting to see how long the destitute clans of Somalia will continue their civil war once the remaining international relief efforts are withdrawn.

To the extent that the US has a real or perceived national interest in the outcome of an underlying conflict, onlookers will question the purity of our humanitarian motives and misunderstand our peaceful intentions. Their examination will be a continuing problem for the world's only remaining superpower as long as memories of various past self-interested American interventions persist. Time will determine if the most recent benign US intervention in Haiti succeeds in supplanting local memories of the earlier 19-year occupation of that country by US Marines, let alone effacing the lingering hemispheric effects of a century of heavyhanded US enforcement of the Roosevelt Corollary to the Monroe Doctrine in the Caribbean and Central America.

The Transformation of War

The most dangerous scenario for outside intervention occurs when human suffering, which the intervention seeks to relieve, becomes a deliberate, intended result of the strategy and tactics of one or both combatants' waging the kind of non-Clausewitzian warfare postulated by Martin van Creveld in his book, *The Transformation of War.*[6] In such cases, the essence of the conflict is bound up with what our own society normally sees as an atrocity. In such wars, civilians may be considered legitimate, even preferred, targets. The large-scale human rights abuses and humanitarian tragedy which outside intervention purports to alleviate are apt to be the deliberate, intended results of the strategies and tactics of a style of warfare alien to our culture. Well-intentioned attempts at stopping the killing by outsiders may be tantamount to disarming a combatant who is therefore likely to direct his wrath at the intervention force. It also may draw us into a nontraditional war in which we not only have no interest, but whose rules of engagement bewilder us and for which we are ill-prepared.

It is therefore crucial that the US first carefully analyze the conflictual context of the human rights problems and abuses that we seek to resolve prior to giving serious consideration to address them. Even if we have absolutely no intention of becoming a party to a conflict, the US needs to include a deliberate strategy for avoiding the kind of "mission creep" which results from our inadvertently straying beyond the often fine line which separates combatant from noncombatant. Otherwise, our good intentions may lead us to calamity.

The recent humanitarian interventions in Bosnia, Somalia, Rwanda, and Haiti illustrate the importance of thoughtful consideration of the underlying conflict. A brief review and analysis of these important recent operations is instructive at this point, as the record of success and failure in the humanitarian crises of the past several years has established some parameters for future interventions. These episodes have also shaped how American and international leadership and world opinion have come to think about humanitarian intervention; they will inevitably color our approach to future crises.

The Balkan Cauldron

Most observers have come to view the ethnoreligious conflict in Bosnia-Herzegovina as an intractable struggle peripheral to US, if not European, national interests. The US and its allies have sought to remove the cause of the humanitarian tragedy unleashed by the civil war through diplomatic initiatives, the interposition of a UN peacekeeping force, and occasional threats and limited applications of force. At the same time, the US has attempted to alleviate the human suffering through a substantial international relief effort.

This conflict is noteworthy for the advent of the term, though certainly not the historical practice, of *ethnic cleansing*, in which Bosnian Serbs, as a matter of policy, have summarily uprooted, relocated, mistreated, and killed Muslim inhabitants in the territory they control or seek to dominate. While the UN peacekeeping force has been successful in shielding some of the victims of this brutal war from the worst abuses and relief efforts have alleviated the suffering to a degree, note that as long as the conflict continues humanitarian problems will remain.

United States and North Atlantic Treaty Organization air assets have mounted a few small tactical strikes to intimidate the Serbs and push them back to the bargaining table. However, the US has studiously avoided outright involvement in the conflict, largely maintaining its neutrality despite widespread outrage at the Serbs' behavior and their frequent depiction as aggressors. The parties to the conflict have campaigned to manipulate both the UN peacekeeping force and the international relief effort. The winning Serbs strive to remove the check on their political goals and the hindrance on their military objectives, which their international presence represents, while the losing Muslims vainly seek to compel our entry into the conflict on their side or at least cause the lifting of the international arms embargo.

Meanwhile, the conflict continues unabated, although the presence of UN peacekeepers, coupled with international relief efforts, seems to have had prolonged sieges and forestalled the Serbs' capture of UN-declared civilian "safe areas" and Muslim pockets of resistance. Although the US has avoided involvement in the conflict, extensive efforts to end it have failed. While the debate on policy and alternativc courses of action continues in the US and Europe, the realization of the clear limits of an outside nation to address humanitarian concerns in Bosnia has grown. The only exception involves the willingness of a nation to take sides and mount an outright military intervention to end the civil war.

Feeding the Somalis

The US intervention in Somalia and its UN follow-on are, as of this writing, reaching their sad conclusion. Compelled largely by vivid televised images of mass starvation, President George Bush decided in late 1992 to commit US military forces to a large-scale humanitarian intervention to provide security for and delivery of relief supplies and services to the afflicted civilian population of a strategically marginal country torn by civil war. Unlike the situation in Bosnia, the lack of any semblance of competing governmental authority, coupled with the extremely poor organization and equipment of the Somali clans, made it likely that the insertion of US and allied forces would be safe and uncontested, which turned out to be the case.

Although relief operations subsequently proceeded smoothly enough, concurrent and subsequent US and UN diplomatic efforts to achieve the political settlement necessary to end the turmoil and remove the root cause of the humanitarian crisis did not materialize. All went well on the ground until the unprovoked ambush of a Pakistani unit by Mohamed Aideed loyalists led the US commanders to undertake a manhunt for Aideed, effectively making US/UN forces parties to the conflict. US Rangers then suffered 18 dead in a courageous but militarily insignificant gun battle with Aideed partisans; one of the victim's body was videotaped being dragged through the streets by cheering Somalis. American public support of the operation quickly changed from lukewarm support to strong opposition. President Clinton increased the US forces and equipment, while announcing a timetable for their departure and eventual replacement by non-US troops under UN command.

Aideed and his clan thus demonstrated that the center of gravity of any UN contingent is likely to be its US core and that the infliction of significant casualties on US forces is likely to lead the American public to call for their withdrawal. The smaller and weaker residual UN force which remained in Somalia after US withdrawal proved less successful at maintaining order and keeping the Somali factions from continuing their civil war, which seems to have been Aideed's aim. Nonetheless, the warring sides were bent on pursuing their internecine battles irrespective of the consequences to their own civilian populations.

With the US-aided extraction of the remaining UN forces, humanitarian assistance has been abandoned, and Somalia seems to be slipping inexorably back into chaos, anarchy, and starvation. While it is clear the intervention did save many lives, success was fleeting, and achieved at a great cost. The enduring lesson of Somalia is that, even in cases where humanitarian intervention appears at first glance to be militarily risk-free, it may not be. Moreover, outside interventions to alleviate the humanitarian consequences of civil strife appear futile in the long term, absent the host nation's commitment to resolve the internal conflict responsible for generating them.

The Rwandan Holocaust

The early 1994 multilateral operation in Rwanda was much smaller in scale and less military in nature than the Somalia episode. A plane carrying the presidents of Rwanda and neighboring Burundi crashed under mysterious circumstances in the Rwandan capital. This incident caused widespread massacres and dislocation of minority Tutsi tribesmen by members of the dead presidents' tribes, the majority Hutus, who viewed the shootdown as a Tutsi assassination plot. This view, in turn, spurred the formerly quiescent Tutsi-dominated Rwanda Patriotic Front (RPF) insurgency into action. Breaking a truce which had held since the 1990 civil war, RPF forces mounted a successful campaign to seize the capital and overthrow the Hutu-dominated successor government, driving away large numbers of Hutu civilians before it went into exile in nearby Zaire. Vivid media images of the starving, homeless multitudes in the refugee camps helped to spur a nonhostile international humanitarian operation to address the humanitarian needs of the legions of refugees. As relief operators directed their efforts at the termination stage of a conflict that was already quiescent, they noted that Rwanda did not present serious security problems. Their objectives were similar in character, if not in scope, to earlier international assistance surges provoked by sudden refugee flows but which did not involve US military participation.

In any refugee scenario, the long-term solution calls for a change in conditions in the refugee source country so that most, if not all, of the refugees will feel safe should they return to their homes. As of early 1995, the situation in Rwanda seems to have stabilized, yet it may remain quite fluid in the long term. Soldiers from the deposed Hutu-led government reportedly have kept Hutu refugees in Zaire from returning to their homes in Rwanda to apply pressure on the Tutsi-dominated, RPF-led, successor government, which they oppose. The long-term future for human rights in Rwanda seems dim, and the prospect of continuing the age-old cycle of violence between Hutu and Tutsi seems likely.

Nation-Building in Haiti

In late 1994, the US-led intervention in Haiti came in direct response to reports of systematic human rights abuses by the military regime which had overthrown the duly elected government of President Jean-Bertrand Aristide. In this case, however, there appears also to have been an intermediate-level US national interest at play in the form of a need to stop the flow of Haitian boat people proceeding across the Caribbean toward the US. Ostensibly fleeing the tyranny of the despotic Raoul Cedras regime, these destitute refugees generated considerable pressure on the US to intervene to stop the human rights abuses and restore Aristide to power, thus removing the impetus for their flight and obviating the need to resettle them in the US or elsewhere. A successful last-minute diplomatic mission led by former President Jimmy Carter persuaded the Cedras regime to let US troops land unopposed, thus permitting direct movement into the post-conflict phase. American forces helped to restore the Aristide government, and public order was reestablished almost bloodlessly by US forces, who were welcomed quite warmly by the Haitian people. The operation has since evolved into a nation-building exercise in preparation for a smaller UN successor contingent, which will include US troops. Time will tell if Haiti, with no historical or cultural tradition of democracy and facing acute economic problems exacerbated by earlier international sanctions meant to force the military regime from power, can stand alone as a peaceful, more prosperous, and stable nation which respects the human rights of its own people.

An Uncertain Balance Sheet

What are the key strategic-level lessons to be drawn from the experience of the recent past? What implications do these lessons hold? First, onlookers have reaffirmed that the US military indeed possesses an unsurpassed ability to provide security for, and execute if requested, large-scale humanitarian operations. However, the magnitude of the resources required to accomplish these tasks has become evident; it is now clear that, in this age of shrinking budgets, this capability to support humanitarian objectives will remain. The tradeoff between the resource base needed to maintain combat readiness and resources expended on military operations other than war has become even more apparent. The current debate over the funding of UN peacekeeping operations illuminates the resource shortfalls and difficult decisions which lie ahead.

Second, the mixed record of success of the operations undertaken so far has underscored the difficulty of achieving really lasting solutions to human rights abuses and humanitarian crises absent the resolution of the underlying conflict. In Bosnia, the bitterness, intractability, and character of the civil war, where human rights violations seem to be an integral aspect of the type of war being fought, has kept outside forces from putting a stop to the abuses flowing from it, let alone end the fighting. In Somalia—where the warring factions did not seize the opportunity to resolve their differences, which the largely successful US/UN intervention provided—a return to an anarchic, violent warlord-style society seems foreordained. The case of Rwanda makes it seem highly unlikely that the long cycle of violence between Hutus and Tutsis has been broken permanently. Even in Haiti, without a doubt the most successful operation to date, it remains to be seen whether a fundamentally changed society can emerge from what has been, after all, a massive, if benign, occupation by an overwhelming military force.

Unilateral or Multilateral

A key question for the failure of humanitarian operations focuses on the extent to which the US intervenes unilaterally or acts with other members of the international community (i.e., other nations, international governmental and nongovernmental organizations, domestic and private voluntary organizations, regional groupings, and alliances). None of the operations discussed above has occurred unilaterally in a strict sense, and it is unlikely that any of them will. As in the recent past, several variations will appear, ranging from truly multilateral efforts mirroring operations in Bosnia to essentially unilateral US initiatives, such as the Haiti operation, which are covered only by an allied "fig leaf." It behooves the US to train and equip increasingly for combined humanitarian operations. The US must be prepared for the prospect, however uncomfortable, of operations which will lack the tighter unity of command which unilateral operations usually achieve. As in war fighting, the US must also be prepared to act alone. One key factor affecting US involvement in multilateral operations will be the near-certain refusal of America's political leadership to place US troops under UN or other non-US command.

A common feature of several recent operations has been the initial use of overwhelming US force to restore order and get the relief supplies flowing, followed by a US withdrawal and its replacement by a smaller, truly multilateral force (possibly including a sizable US contingent) until they have established a desired end. This strategy seems to reflect the American military tradition of meeting any threat with overwhelming force, yet quickly packing up and going home once they feel the "war" has been won. Other nations tend to be comfortable with this arrangement because they realize the US does have a major comparative advantage in the military sphere, and if we offer them a free ride, so much the better. However, the Somali experience and initial nation-building efforts in Haiti have shown that later phases may become the hard part. We may find it difficult to persuade less capable foreign military and civilian establishments to remain, particularly when the umbrella of a strong US military presence is removed. Furthermore, it may be unreasonable of us to expect other nations to put their own troops in harm's way when we are not. In any case, simply "handing [affairs] over to the UN" is not a real answer: the UN, to a large degree in this post-cold-war world, is us, and it will be difficult to escape a leadership role, if we are to participate at all. Absent strong US political, financial, and military support, the UN and other international organizations seem destined to remain an inefficient, and largely ineffective, vehicle for addressing the most difficult phases of humanitarian operations. If substantial strengthening and reform of the UN system is to be undertaken, we will have to take the lead in achieving it.

The Military's Role

Military leaders and civilian defense officials over the past decade have expressed understandable misgivings concerning the growing tendency to use the military for essentially nonmilitary purposes and such tasks as humanitarian operations. Two factors account for this hesitation. First, traditionally the military has been trained and equipped for warfighting, not social work. While the military can easily convert some of its support activities to other roles and missions, it devotes the heart of its force structure to preparing for and engaging in combat. Therefore, the military has a natural reluctance to perform functions for which its units are ill-prepared and at which they may not succeed. Second, even if the military considers a particular nontraditional role or mission as neither logical nor attainable (i.e., provision of airlift to transport relief supplies), it may still believe that the devotion of those assets to essentially nonmilitary purposes will detract from their primary mission, thereby consuming scarce resources and detracting from combat readiness.

In spite of considerable opposition, a clear-cut and probably enduring trend has emerged over the past several years concerning increased use of military assets for nonmilitary roles and missions. That trend will likely continue for a number of reasons. One reason holds that the inaccurate-yet-widespread perception that military assets are free or come at a marginal cost. Another centers around the strong perception of competence and confidence in the military's capabilities. This view remains half a decade after the successful prosecution of the Gulf War, which captured the public's imagination. The military's own long-standing, can-do attitude and admirable tendency to want to assist with any job it is handed, along with its professional, workmanlike response to the humanitarian operations of recent years, also are contributing factors. Finally, in this current era of shrinking budgets and military and civilian downsizing, the military's uniformed and civilian leadership can view the need to perform these new roles in missions as leverage in the bureaucracy's resource wars and as a mean to obtain increasingly scarce resources also needed to accomplish more traditional roles and missions.

In the past, the armed forces have been reluctant to prepare for such nontraditional activities as humanitarian interventions so as not to create a further impetus for the military's employment in such operations. The time has now come to recognize reality and to discard that reluctance. The military should fully and deliberately integrate humanitarian roles and missions into its recruitment, training, equipment, planning, and doctrine. It should consider such steps as increasing manpower within such relevant functional categories as Army civic affairs. The leadership should also reconfigure its Professional Military Education (PME) curricula to include heavy doses of military operations other than war, something the mid-level Air Force PME curriculum is currently doing with the development of a new course in "war termination."

The real challenge will be to retain war-fighting capabilities amidst shrinking budgets and expanding requirements. Taking full advantage of the revolution in military affairs (RMA), which many believe to be under way, may represent means of achieving this difficult resource balancing act. Notwithstanding the pitfalls discussed earlier in this chapter, no effective alternative exists to some use of the military in major humanitarian crises, if we are to respond in anything other than a token, and probably ineffective, way. Neither the civilian sector, government or private, nor the international community has any probability of acquiring (too cost prohibitive) the capability to respond quickly to major humanitarian crises on anything other than an ad hoc, piecemeal basis. While, for the reasons stated earlier, we should enter into humanitarian crises with as much care as we approach actual conflict, the US military increasingly needs to stand ready to do so. "If not us, who?" is an appropriate clarion call.

Conclusion

The current US national security strategy seeks, as have those of previous administrations, to ensure the security of the US through the coordinated application of the military, economic, and political instruments of power. Unlike that of the Bush administration, however, President Bill Clinton's concept of engagement and enlargement offers an offensive rather than a defensive approach, as it seeks to extend the Zone of Peace rather than merely preventing the encroachment of the Zone of Turmoil.[7] While this strategy sought to forestall such future humanitarian crises as we have recently faced in Bosnia, Somalia, Rwanda, and Haiti, the obvious mismatch between means and ends will make its success difficult. We cannot hope, at least in the near term, to address the roots of the conflicts which have caused human right abuses and humanitarian crises. Nor can the US confront an unpleasant choice between situational Band-Aid solutions or doing nothing at all. Resource constraints and compassion fatigue will be limiting factors, but only time and further experience will determine how extensively and capably we answer the world's humanitarian "911 calls."

Notes

1. Max Singer and Aaron Wildavsky, *The Real World Order* (Chatham, N.J.: Chatham House Publishers, Inc., 1993), 6–7.
2. Karl P. Magyar, "Conflict in the Post-Containment Era," in *War and Conflict* (Maxwell AFB, Ala.: Air Command and Staff College, 1994), 51–53.
3. Alvin and Heidi Toffler, *War and Anti-War* (Boston, Mass.: Little, Brown and Co., 1993), 18–19.
4. Robert D. Kaplan, "The Coming Anarchy," *Atlantic Monthly* 273, no. 2 (February 1994): 44–76.
5. Martin van Creveld, *The Transformation of War* (New York: Macmillan, Inc., 1991), 192–223.
6. Ibid.
7. Singer and Wildavsky, 32.

PART III

ECONOMIC ISSUES

7

Anticipating the Twenty-First Century

Economic Sources of Conflicts

Maris McCrabb

Economic issues have now reached a level of parity with traditional defense concerns because of the virtual elimination of a common military security threat (the Soviet Union and Warsaw Pact) and because the traditional friends of the United States (US) are now engaged in a wide-ranging series of conflicts with the US over such issues as trade and resource access. This essay surveys potential areas of economic conflict in the twenty-first century among those traditional allies that largely comprise the developed world, and between the developed and developing world.[1]

For the US in the twenty-first century and the world in general, there will be a lowered economic imperative for war, but while the economic rationale for war between developed and developing nations will be of medium importance—largely confined to increasing concerns over global environmental degradation—economic rationales for war between developing states will remain high. There are several reasons for this. Technology has reduced the natural resource composition of goods through more efficient production processes and the invention of man-made material substitutes that are often more effective and cheaper than natural materials.[2] This technology has eliminated the "territorial imperative" (i.e., physical capital or wealth from the land or the produce of the land) and has enhanced the "people imperative" (i.e., human capital or wealth arising from the creators, distributors, and users of knowledge[3]), thus eliminating a historic economic cause of war. However, this technological advancement largely has been confined to the developed world. Territorial imperatives still loom large in the developing world because developing nations often still perceive territory (and the natural resources therein) as a means of increasing national wealth. Furthermore, while technology has reduced the dependence of the developed world on natural resources largely found in the developing world, it has not eliminated that need in all areas. Oil is the most obvious example of this dependence, but other natural resources, including tungsten and uranium, are just as important, though less visibly so.

To examine these issues, this essay first establishes the context of economic conflicts during the cold war era to demonstrate the centrality of that event and how it had both positive and negative effects on the presence and resolution of conflicts. Concurrent with the cold war, the economies of the developed world became more globalized, especially with the rise of transnational corporations and highly mobile factors of production, especially capital and human resources. This globalization has affected and continues to impact both the developed and the developing world.

Second, this essay details the current and future trends of these conflicts—given the end of the cold war. It also discusses the implications these trends have for global stability, US security policy, and potential US military requirements.

These two sections show that while some concerns will linger over resource and market access issues between advanced economies, the major sources of conflict will arise within the developing world over territory. Between the developed and the developing world, the focus will center on widening income disparity and the pressure that it brings to migration patterns and flows, critical natural resource access, continuing global environmental degradation, and the conflict that is perceived to occur over the quest for development by the poorer states and the quest for cleaner environments by the richer states.

Third, this essay contends that emerging trends emanating from the demise of bilateralism and the rise of regionalism offer both challenges and opportunities that, if used improperly, could increase the chances for conflict to escalate to the point of war, or opportunities, if used wisely, to lessen conflicts.

The Post–World War II Era

Efforts in the closing days of World War II to create an open and a liberal trading system were based on a belief that economic "beggar-thy-neighbor" policies of the 1930s—policies (for example, currency devaluation) that, while improving current domestic economic conditions, worsened international economic conditions that ultimately worsened domestic economic conditions—were substantially responsible for the war.[4] The division of the world into two ideologically opposed camps in the late 1940s both stimulated and stifled these attempts. It stimulated more open economic relations between the "free world" states. Economic conflicts of interests, which in previous years would have spoiled the entire range of relations between these countries, were now purposefully glossed over or resolved precisely to maintain Western cohesion deemed essential in the face of a monolithic foe who, it was believed, would use force to impose a global economic structure antithetical to the capitalistic system.[5]

The ideological division stifled the spread of open markets in dealings with the "nonaligned" world, those countries not overtly identified with either communist states or liberal democracies. Relations between Western and nonaligned countries were denominated in the currency of East-West conflict, and Western governments viewed assertions of a "third way" (neither Soviet-style socialism nor Western-style capitalism) to economic development as a tilt to the Soviet orbit.

The clearest examples where the commonly perceived threat resulted in economic conflicts being resolved in favor of maintaining security modalities include the Marshall Plan, the rebuilding of Japan, the creation of the European Economic Community (EEC), and the series of General Agreement on Tariffs and Trade (GATT) negotiations on lowering tariff levels. The US saw these agreements as a means of strengthening countries domestically when they were threatened with having communist governments. Further, such countries were viewed as a source of military forces to counter growing Soviet military power in Europe and East Asia. Finally, the transformation of large corporate entities from multimarket firms to transnational corporations and the role they played as a conduit of technology diffusion between developed states further accelerated the rise in living standards of the developed world.[6]

These trends resulted in the greatest rise in living standards in history. For example, from the devastation of war, the West German per capita gross domestic product (GDP) rose 7.9 percent annually from 1949 to 1956 and averaged 3.2 percent per year for the period from 1956 to 1985. Rates for the victors exhibited similar growth: the French GDP rose an average 4.1 percent from 1956 to 1985, and the British rate of increase was somewhat lower but still historically high at 2.3 percent per year. The US data stood at 3.1 percent growth over the same period.[7]

Unpredictably and unfortunately for the postwar planners, the ideological division of the cold war also impacted and enhanced conflict between the developed and developing states. Surprisingly, most of those charged with creating the institutions and regimes of the new world order of the late 1940s did so from an overtly liberal perception that viewed increased prosperity in the developed world as the engine of economic growth for the developing world. Unfortunately, the conflict between the developing and developed world rapidly took on an ideational aspect *on both sides* that often clouded the mutual gains available to each from increased economic collaboration.

This cleavage between rich and poor is reflected in the per capita GDP disparity between them. By the end of the 1980s, the gap between those states the World Bank classifies as low-income economies and those as high-income economies was a staggering sixty-fold. The composition and amount of trade between rich and poor states explain this dynamic. In 1970 extractive materials (fuels, minerals, and metals) and primary commodities accounted for 72 percent of the exports from the low-income states as compared to 27 percent for the high-income countries. Of the remaining exports for the third world, nearly one-half were accounted for by such relatively low-value added goods as textiles and clothing.[8] In other words, the poorer states export relatively low-value added goods such as minerals and clothing, while the richer states export higher value goods such as manufactured items.

Two points emerge from this brief review of the postwar economic environment. First, while economic conflicts within the developed world took second place to maintaining Western cohesiveness, they did not go away. Particularly relevant was the growing breech between the US and the EEC over the proper role of government intervention into ostensibly free markets in pursuit of other social objectives such as employment, lifestyle maintenance, and conflicts over perceptions of unfairness in terms of market access, investment rights, and government support via industrial policies.[9]

Second, the conflict between developing and developed states began to change shape as calls for a new economic order ran aground. The first shoal was the failure of developing countries' internal economic policies (encapsulated in the theory of import substitution[10] as a shortcut to modernization). The second was the developing world realization that, except for a very few cases, the developed world was less dependent on—and increasingly becoming even less dependent on—the developing world. At the same time, the developing world was becoming more dependent on the developed world, especially for markets and an almost continual need for capital.

Before examining future economic sources of conflict, it is worthwhile to present the big picture of the world economy in the late twentieth century. In 1991 the world's combined GDP was estimated at $21.6 trillion with 79 percent of that in the 22 high-income states (as defined by the World Bank). This estimation left 105 countries to share the rest. (These are not all the countries of the world. The World Bank lists separately 73 other nations that have sparse economic data or populations less than one million people.)[11] The US share of the total was 26 percent (the next closest country, Japan, held 15.5 percent). Merchandise trade exhibits a similar disparity between developed and developing states. In 1991 world exports totaled $3.3 trillion (15 percent of world GDP) and imports were $3.5 trillion (16 percent of GDP). The high-income states accounted for 79 percent of merchandise imports and exports.[12]

Another simmering issue between developed and developing states is the worsening trend of the ratio of export to import prices. Organization for Economic Cooperation and Development (OECD) indices show, over the period 1990–94, that developing countries' export prices fell 5 percent for food and 10 percent for minerals, ores, and metals (groups which comprise the major exports of developing states) at the same time that OECD manufactures' export prices fell less than 1 percent.[13] This situation—where developing states earn less for their exports but pay more for their imports—accounts for the large increase in external debt in developing states. And the poorest states are hit the hardest. Forty low-income economies saw their total external debt as percent of exports go from 105.5 percent in 1980 to 225.7 percent in 1991. For the middle-income states, the increase was 21 percent over the same period.[14]

One final issue is the vulnerability of both developed and developing states to vagaries in world trade flows. For developed states, this vulnerability can come from either exposure to trade (that is, the percentage of GDP made up of imports and exports) or from reliance on a critical resource or market for their economy. For example, Austria's trade exposure is 71 percent, with 39 percent of its exports and 43 percent of its imports going to or coming from Germany.[15] In other words, every time the German economy sneezes, Austria's catches a cold. Likewise, Japan is highly dependent on imported oil: it constitutes 29 percent of their domestic power consumption,[16] and it takes 17 percent of their merchandise export earnings to pay for their energy imports.[17]

For developing states, vulnerability arises when a country is highly dependent on a single commodity for export earnings. For example, Saudi Arabian oil exports comprise 81.3 percent of all its exports, and Gabon's export of oil accounts for 79.5 percent of its exports.[18] Hence, these countries are vulnerable to adverse changes in world prices for oil. Saudi Arabia found itself in this situation during 1994 when its earnings from exports were insufficient to pay for its imports and when a threatened budget deficit caused it to reduce government spending 20 percent.[19]

Future Sources of Conflict

The historic patterns of conflict between the developed and developing world and within the developed world have been profoundly affected by the end of the cold war. This section examines those changes and assesses the likelihood that one or both might flare into open hostilities.

Despite the projections of Max Singer, Aaron Wildavsky, Francis Fukuyama,[20] and others that armed conflict between the mass-wealth industrialized nations is highly unlikely, three issues pose at least some possibility for conflict between these countries. The essentially unanswerable question left is whether any of these conflicts would be serious enough to result in open hostilities. I think not.

The first area, and one with the lowest probability of hostile conflict, is disagreements over resource access. Two phenomena are occurring that may cause resource access to become an irritant which, along with other conflicts, could generate enough heat to ignite a spark. One phenomenon is user-supplier agreements where firms, through contract, attempt to secure for themselves guaranteed access to raw materials. An example of this is Japanese firms who, through direct foreign investment to build or modernize extraction facilities, secure supplies of ores for smelting plants in Japan and third-party countries.[21]

Another phenomenon is more direct conflict over resources. An example is the sporadic outbreaks of fish wars, where fishermen of one country have been fired upon by boats and naval craft of another country over alleged poaching on national fishing grounds.[22] Such conflicts have already occurred on several occasions.

The second area that has only medium probability of conflict is over market access. The two biggest concerns in this area are the rise of regional trading blocs and the increasing use of nontariff trade barriers. Trading blocs raise fears of a return to the autarkic economic policies of the 1930s such as Germany's *grossraumwirtshaft*[23] and Britain's sterling area that implied discriminatory preferences for members of the bloc over outsiders. Nontariff barriers are means nations can use to circumvent negotiated market access agreements. The European ban on US beef containing growth-inducing hormones and the Japanese banning other US agricultural products for similar health concerns are but two examples of this use of administrative regulations to keep out foreign competition.

The third area provides the catalyst for the previously mentioned two phenomena. The economic slowdown of 1990–94 injected enormous stress into the liberal economic arena that was manifested in various ways: high unemployment in Europe, stagnating wage growth in the US, and drastically reduced growth rates in Japan.[24] All result in demands for government action by the populace. Additionally, all, to one degree or another, call into question the open trading system that has existed since the end of World War II. Perhaps the clearest example of this questioning is the rising protectionist movement in the US, especially over a belief that the large and growing trade surplus with Japan (and China) is the result of "unfair" trading practices.[25]

Three areas of potential conflict between the developed and developing world in the next century focus on widening income gaps, resource issues, and environmental degradation. North-south income disparities likely will be manifested primarily through migration issues. Potential trouble areas range from North Africa to Western Europe, from Eastern Europe to Western Europe, and from Latin America and Asia to the US and Canada. Paul M. Kennedy places the problem squarely on the too rapidly expanding world population—particularly in the poorer areas of the world.[26] Many countries of the world attempted to address this issue at the September 1994 United Nations (UN) Cairo Conference on Population.[27]

Economic development, environmental degradation, and population growth are all tied symbiotically: as per capita wealth increases, population growth falls,[28] and financial resources—and the political pressure—become available to tackle environmental quality concerns. Unfortunately, as the contentiousness of the Cairo Conference demonstrated, population control arguments run up against deeply held cultural and religious beliefs.

Mass media have captured the images of boat people, streams of bedraggled refugees, and others moving from devastated areas—whether caused by political instability, economic deprivation, or natural catastrophes—towards believed safe havens, many of them located in developed states.[29] These migrations, in turn, have generated backlashes bordering on nativism in some states. The rise of neo-Nazism in

Germany and far-right National Front leader Jean-Marie Le Pen in France[30] and calls for repatriation of refugees from the US are all examples of a growing fear in developed states over unrestrained migration of third world people to their shores.

It is unlikely that migration will be the *casus belli* between emigration states and the refugees' target states. It is likely, though, that immigration issues will be a contributing factor to conflicts between states. First, disagreements between losing and gaining states over border access and treatment of the refugees once inside the receiving state will increase tensions and instability between the two as the developed states pressure the developing countries to take measures to stem the flow of people. For example, during 1994, the US pressured Cuba and Haiti to stop their boat people from trying to get to the US. Likewise, the poor nations will attempt to use migration fears to wrest increased aid and technical assistance from the developed world.[31]

Second, migration issues will arise between developing states (e.g., the war in Rwanda resulted in huge numbers of refugees flowing into neighboring Zaire, putting pressure on an already poor state). Calls to the developed states for assistance from nongovernmental relief agencies and the UN, even when answered, generate their own difficulties. In the case of Rwanda, relief workers claimed Western nations, especially the US, after providing crucial aid to fight the cholera epidemic that broke out in the refugee camps, left immediately whenever the issue no longer occupied the front pages of the Western press, leaving unresolved the long-term relief effort and the underlying issues that started the crisis. These situations, then, may degenerate into huge hostilities. Furthermore, it is not unlikely that in times of economic stress within the developed world, pressures will be placed on governments to ignore some humanitarian crises—particularly those that are not perceived as having a direct bearing on the nation (e.g., such as Rwanda's alleged lack of strategic significance to the US) because of the costs involved, thus accelerating festering conflicts.

Despite product and process technological improvements that have reduced the per unit natural resource content of many of the developed world's goods, resource access issues will continue to be a source of conflict between supplier and user states in the twenty-first century. These issues will continue to breed problems in the first case due to—ironically—the decline of such supplier cartels as the Organization of Petroleum Exporting Countries (OPEC) and in the second case due to depletion issues. The declining power of such organizations as OPEC increases instability between suppliers and users in two ways: first, users lose the certainty, however onerous, of a common bargaining agent with some control over quantity and prices; second, such organizations provide a useful forum for producer states to iron out disagreements, without which states often engage in beggar-thy-neighbor policies. The geopolitical closeness of many OPEC members, plus their deep ideological divisions, offers the prospect of overt conflict between these states. The developed world has ample evidence of the disrupting effect of previous conflict between OPEC states (for example, during the Iran-Iraq war) and will likely be willing to use force to secure access.

The third potential major source of conflict is the issue of environmental degradation. In essence, the developed world—belatedly recognizing the fragile ecosystem, its interdependencies, and the adverse effect that industrialization has on the earth—is pressing the developing world to undertake environmental protection as a humanity-wide public good.[32] Specific concerns are raised over air quality in the emerging megacities of the third world, water quality and the common resources of the oceans, and development versus environmental cleanup or preservation.

Conflict over environmental issues was the centerpiece of the UN Conference on Environment and Development held in Rio de Janeiro, Brazil, in June 1992.[33] At the Earth Summit, industrialized states, which by and large have embraced environmental protection as public policy, sought to tie official development aid and technology transfer to increased environmental protection policies and enforcement in the developing world. The poorer states argued that, due to their constrained resources as a result of economic underdevelopment, such policies are counterproductive because they deny developing nations the tools they need to implement the policies. Tied to this argument is the third world's distrust of the World Bank's Global Environment Facility. This organization allocates billions of dollars for global warming, biodiversity, international water quality, and ozone regeneration projects. The bank is viewed as an unrepresentative agency that too often intrudes into domestic policy-making.[34] On the other hand, the developed states see the bank as a means to provide reliable oversight.

If the dire predictions of the science community are true—the divergent goals of the developed and developing countries over this issue—environmental degradation issues may become the central area of conflict between these states in the twenty-first century.[35] While it is highly unlikely that military means would be used directly to force environmental cooperation, nonmilitary pressure against developing states (for example, cutting of commerce or loans or getting transnational corporations to close plants) could lead to more open conflict such as state-sponsored terrorism.

This section has briefly examined some possible future sources of economic conflict within the developed world and between the developed and developing world. Note that most of the probabilities assigned by the author to the likelihood of open hostilities were low. But two points must be raised. First, in no case was the probability judged to be zero. Second, the probabilities assigned were in light of each conflict being the sole conflict. The author made no judgment on the possibility of several of these converging and sparking armed hostilities between two states.

Implications for the United States

Given at least the possibility that the above scenarios—or some derivation thereof—might occur, what are the implications, especially in the security arena broadly defined, for the US? Two phenomena of the twenty-first century—the end of bilateralism and the emergence of regionalism—offer both challenges and opportunities for the US. The challenge arises because diplomatically, militarily, and economically bilateralism is the United States' comparative advantage. In any possible dyad in those areas, the US is clearly the dominant actor.

Regionally, the challenge derives from the US being unquestionably the leading player in the Americas, while it is considerably less strong (and some argue growing weaker) in other regions, especially Europe and Asia, that are predicted to at least match if not surpass the US in economic power in the early years of the next century.[36]

Yet these trends offer opportunities for the US and other nations to reduce the potential for economic conflict which might spark a more active, possibly even violent, situation. Broadening the negotiation regime offers an algebraic increase in linkages where compromise and agreement in one area may spill over into resolution in another, more contentious issue. Likewise, despite the global telecommunications revolution, most states still identify closer with their region than with an amorphous world community concept.

Three trends mark this movement towards regionalism. First, in the military security field, the Partnership for Peace program of the North Atlantic Treaty Organization (NATO) promises to bring the emerging democratic and free market states of central and eastern Europe closer to the states of western Europe. This alignment offers a clear example of both the challenges and opportunities of regionalism. The challenges lie in a delicate balance of two related issues: the speed at which these states are brought into NATO forums and Russia's response to these accessions. If, for example, states were admitted into NATO under ambiguous guidelines and timetables that resulted in certain states gaining full membership ahead of others, this advantage could lead to instability rather than stability. Likewise, if Russia perceives further accessions of former Warsaw Pact states as a threat to its interests, it could feel obligated to revert to czarist or Soviet imperial policies once again.[37] On the other hand, this program offers the opportunity that NATO institutional arrangements could be used as conflict resolution forums to settle long-simmering debates over borders, environmental degradation issues, access, and immigration.

Closely related to this is the issue of widening and deepening of the European Union (EU). In 1995 Austria, Finland, and Sweden completed their accessions into the EU.[38] Such states as Turkey, Malta, Cyprus, Poland, Hungary, and the Czech

Republic hold associate memberships in the EU and wish to become full members. Mirroring the same concerns outlined above for widening NATO, if some of these states do gain full membership while others are left waiting, the possibility for conflict increases. This concern will hold special interest if the original EU member states continue to experience high unemployment and stagnating economies. The lower wage states are seen as a threat to the jobs and living standards of the richer EU countries. Hence, pressures may arise to limit exports from those states and erect other nontariff barriers to limit the competition from the East.

Outside of Europe, other regional economic arrangements provide the same sort of challenges and opportunities that might arise from increased economic ties. Though less an overt security implication, efforts at an expanded North American Free Trade Agreement (NAFTA), a more robust and unified Caribbean Common Market (CARICOM) and Southern Cone Common Market (MERCOSUR), and a more active Asia-Pacific Economic Cooperation (APEC) forum may be sources of increased conflict or means to reduce conflict over economic issues. If these regional arrangements are seen as efforts to manage trade with other nonregional states or if they are perceived as means whereby one (or a few) large economy within the region attempts to maintain dominance over the smaller economies of the region, they may in fact foster instability. On the other hand, if they are used as forums to negotiate and discuss common economic concerns and reduce trade and investment conflicts, they will mitigate tensions.

Note that the US holds memberships in nearly all of these just-mentioned groups. This revelation points to the pivotal role the US will continue to play in ensuring regional and global stability in both the security and the economic arenas.[39] Charles Kindleberger argues in his analysis of the Great Depression that there is not a viable alternative for continued US engagement and leadership in world affairs.[40] This pronouncement is never more true than in the increasing interdependent and interconnected world of the twenty-first century.[41]

Following the Gulf War and the breakup of the Soviet empire, many commentators believed the era of the UN had finally arrived. Yet, especially in the economic area, this assessment has proven to be overly optimistic for at least two reasons. First, the UN traditionally has played only a minor role in world economic affairs. Second, those UN forums that focused specifically on economic issues have been perceived by developed states as a means developing states have used to force a reordering of the world economic order to the detriment of the developed countries.

Indicative of this perspective is the debate among the developed states, especially the G-7, and between developed states (primarily the US) and developing states over two issues the US wants to include on the future trade agenda of the GATT: environmental standards and worker rights.[42] As exemplified by the debate in the US over the ratification of the NAFTA in 1993 and the Uruguay Round in 1994, groups within the US believe the developed states should use trade, especially market access, to induce changes in the internal political behavior of developing states. Because the wealthy states' markets are more critical to the developing states than their market (either as consumers or as suppliers) is to the developed states, restricting trade is a low-cost option to force recalcitrant states to allow workers there to organize, collectively bargain, gain wage increases commensurate with productivity increases, and improve working conditions that are admittedly deplorable by Western standards. Developing countries counter that such restrictions are thinly disguised attempts by the developed countries to keep the developing world from modernizing and improving living standards and that such restrictions only harm the workers the developed countries seek to help.

One final implication must be addressed. Trends in the late twentieth century point to the increased use and viability of embargoes and sanctions to change the behavior of rogue states. During Desert Shield and continuing on to the Balkan wars and Haiti, the US has led multilateral efforts through the UN to wage economic warfare with mixed results.[43] In this regard, the US military establishment may play an increasing role. Advanced technologies and capabilities in the surveillance and reconnaissance areas and rapid—and precise abilities to target violations selectively with a high degree of confidence of success and little collateral damage—may increase the options of political decision makers and hence increase the likelihood that US armed forces may find themselves as the enforcers of sanctions and embargoes. While these have been traditional sea power missions, the global presence and global reach of airpower may change the balance more towards air forces. Airpower also offers the advantages of relatively low visibility vis-à-vis target states.

Conclusion

Table 1 summarizes the predicted sources of economic conflict and assesses the probabilities they will evolve into something approaching armed hostilities between developed states, developed and developing states, and developing states.

Table 1

Summary of Possible Economic Conflict

Between	Conflict Sources	Probabilities of Armed Hostilities
Developed States	Raw Materials*	Very Low
	Market Access	Low
Developed and Developing States	Raw Materials	Low
	Environmental	Medium
	Immigration	Medium
Developing States	Raw Materials	Medium
	Immigration	Medium
	Borders	High

*Includes conflict between two developed states over raw materials from a third party, another developed state, or a developing state.

Note: While border conflict is not precisely an economic conflict and one not argued extensively in this essay, it is included here for two reasons. First, border conflict often arises over resource issues (either ownership or access). Second, since it is rated as a high probability for armed hostilities, it provides a benchmark for the other probabilities.

This essay has advanced two broad trends in economic conflict and implications for the twenty-first century. First, there is a broadening in the meaning of national security in two senses of that phrase. One, for each nation, but more so for developed nations, economics is less exclusively national and more accurately portrayed as global in nature. This trend is also becoming more true for the developing nations who seek access to markets, technologies, and capital in the developed world. Two, there is the merging of economics with defense into the concept of security because for most political decision makers in both the developed and the developing world, living standards, economic development, and quality of life concerns have become the dominant issues. Security is no longer exclusively measured by the size of armies or the number of combat aircraft a nation possesses; it is increasingly measured by the size and growth of per capita GDP and its distribution, wage rates, and quality of life indices.

These changes point to the second broad trend identified by this essay: because economic issues are becoming more important to the relations between states, conflicts that arise over these issues may exacerbate conflicts that arise in the traditional political and military arenas. Hence, while hostilities over purely economic issues will be quite rare, political conflicts may be fanned into violence due to the presence of unresolved economic conflicts; as when deteriorating economic conditions may lead to civil war. Furthermore, the likelihood of this occurring between developed states or between a developed state and a developing state is quite low, but the possibility of it occurring between two developing states is somewhat greater.

The key implication of these two trends for the US armed forces, and the US Air Force in particular, is that they may be called on to support economic warfare missions in the form of sanction and embargo enforcement. The US will likely avoid direct engagement in wars between developing states but rather will attempt to apply economic pressure against one or both of the warring parties to stop the fighting.[44] This observation points to an important strategic military change where the value of heavily equipped ground forces will be relatively low while the value of high technology and sophisticated air and space assets will grow in importance.

Notes

1. There is no agreed upon definition of a developed or a developing state. The World Bank, for example, divides nations on the basis of their per capita gross national product (GNP). Many economists use a $5,000 per capita GNP to separate the two levels of development. That convention will hold in this chapter.

2. For one view of the implications of this, see Lester Thurow, *Head-to-Head; The Coming Economic Battle Among Japan, Europe, and America* (New York: William Morrow & Co., 1992).

3. A cogent analysis of the knowledge revolution implications can be found in Robert B. Reich, *The Work of Nations* (New York: Vintage, 1992).

4. Paul M. Kennedy argues the postwar economic system was not established for purely altruistic reasons. See his *The Rise and Fall of the Great Powers* (New York: Vintage, 1984), especially chapter 7.

5. A series of excellent articles on these issues can be found in Graham Allison and Gregory F. Treverton, eds., *Rethinking Americas Security* (New York: W. W. Norton & Co., 1992).

6. The role these trends played in US security policies can be found in Robert Gilpin, *US Power and the Multinational Corporation: The Political Economy of Foreign Direct Investment* (New York: Basic Books, 1975).

7. See Andrew Graham with Anthony Seldon, *Government and Economies in the Postwar World; Economic Policies and Comparative Performance 1945–85* (London and New York: Routledge, 1990), chapters 3, 4, 5, and 11.

8. See the World Bank, *World Development Report 1993* (New York: Oxford University Press, 1993).

9. The developed states also disagreed over the use of trade to influence the behavior of the Soviet Union. See Michael Mastanduno, *Economic Containment; CoCom and the Politics of East-West Trade* (Ithaca, N.Y. and London: Cornell University Press, 1992).

10. This theory suggests that developing states should close their markets to imports from other states to foster domestic industries that will make those goods.

11. *World Development Report 1993,* 305 (technical notes). Therefore, the GDP total should be used as a conservative estimate. Furthermore, the inequality is not solely confined to between developed and developing states. Within the developing world, large disparities exist. For example, the poorest country listed by the World Bank, Mozambique, has about $80 per capita while the much "richer" Gabon has almost $3,800 in per capita wealth, almost 50 times greater than Mozambique.

12. *World Development Report 1993,* tables 3 and 14.

13. *OECD Economic Outlook* (Paris: OECD, December 1992), table 82.

14. *World Development Report 1993,* table 24.

15. United Nations, *1992 International Trade Statistics Yearbook.*

16. *Business Week*, 22 June 1992, 76. Nuclear power is second, contributing 27 percent of domestic energy consumption, followed by gas (21 percent), hydroelectric (13 percent), and coal (10 percent). Japan recognizes

their vulnerability and has established a 145-day emergency supply of petroleum. *Platts Oilgram News*, 29 October 1992, 6.

17. *World Development Report 1993*, table 5.

18. *1992 International Trade Statistics Yearbook*. The second largest export from Saudi Arabia is chemicals (slightly more than 9 percent); no remaining export category exceeds 1 percent of the total. The vulnerabilities are lessened if the country commands an overwhelming percentage of world trade in that commodity. Unfortunately, Saudi Arabia's world market share is only 5 percent (by value) while Gabon's is only slightly more than 1 percent. Ibid.

19. See "Saudi Arabia, Its Purse Thinner, Learns How to Say 'No' to the US," *New York Times*, 4 November 1994, 1; and "Saudi Arabia Is Facing Debts and Defections That Test US Ties," *Wall Street Journal*, 25 October 1994, 1.

20. See Max Singer and Aaron Wildavsky, *The Real World Order* (Chatham, N.J.: Chatham House Publishers, 1993); and Francis Fukuyama, *The End of History and the Last Man* (New York: Free Press, 1992). However, this democratic peace thesis is the subject of intense scholarly debate. For opposing views see, Christopher Layne, "Kant or Cant; The Myth of the Democratic Peace," *International Security* 19, no. 2 (Fall 1994): 5–49; and David E. Spiro, "The Insignificance of the Liberal Peace," ibid., 50–86.

21. See David B. Yoffie, ed., *Beyond Free Trade: Firms, Governments, and Global Competition* (Boston: Harvard Business School Press, 1993).

22. See David Rohde, "Worldwide Fish Depletion Sparks Gunboat Diplomacy Over Share of the Catch," *Christian Science Monitor*, 24 August 1994, 7.

23. Large economic area. For the economic policies of Nazi Germany and the origins of the Second World War see, Alan S. Milward, *War, Economy and Society, 1939–1945* (Berkeley, Calif.: University of California Press, 1977).

24. See Paul Krugman, "Europe Jobless, America Penniless?" *Foreign Policy* 95 (Summer 1994): 19–34.

25. For opposing views on this issue, see Roger C. Altman, "Why Pressure Japan?" *Foreign Affairs* 73 (May/June 1994): 2–6; and Jagdish Bhagwati, "Samurais No More," *Foreign Affairs* 73 (May/June 1994): 7–12.

26. See Paul M. Kennedy, *Preparing for the Twenty-First Century* (New York: Random House, 1993).

27. For various reports on this conference see, Victor Chen, "Crisis of a Crowded World: Population and Development," *Audubon* (July–August 1994): 50–54; Marguerite Holloway, "Population Summit: Women's Health and Rights Shape Cairo Document," *Scientific American* (June 1994): 14–16; and "UN Proclaims 1996 as Poverty Eradication Year: Progress on Agenda for Development," *UN Chronicle* (March 1994): 78–81.

28. In many developed countries in Europe, such as France and Germany, population rates have stopped growing since 1970. See *World Development Report 1993*, table 26. Another side of this issue is that as development increases, so does environmental degradation. For example,

China—the fastest growing economy in the world—is on pace to become the largest source of acid rain in the world by 2010 and the third largest emitter of greenhouse gases by 2025. See Peter Schoettle, "Key Geostrategic Trends," *Naval War College Review* 48, no. 1 (Winter 1995): 67.

29. For two views on this issue see, Matthew Connelly and Paul M. Kennedy, "Must It Be the Rest Against the West?" *Atlantic Monthly* (December 1994): 61–84; and Virginia Abernathy, "Optimism and Overpopulation," ibid., 84–91.

30. The National Front, at one time thought to be the second largest political force in France (behind the moderate-right alliance), favors strict control on immigration, along with reducing French participation in the EU; removing French peacekeepers from Bosnia; and even opposed French participation in the Gulf War. See "Enough of Le Pen," *The Economist*, 30 January 1993, 48–49.

31. An interesting analysis of migration as a form of strategic nonviolent conflict can be found in Gene Sharp, *The Politics of Nonviolent Action*, pt. 2, *Methods of Nonviolent Action*, pt. 2 (Boston: Porter Sargent, 1973).

32. See Graciela Chichlnisky, "North-South Trade and the Global Environment," *The American Economic Review* 84 (September 1994): 851–74.

33. See Peter M. Haas, Marc A. Levy, and Edward A. Parson, "Appraising the Earth Summit," *Environment* 34 (October 1992): 6–33.

34. Another favorite target of the developing states is the International Monetary Fund (IMF). At the recent fiftieth anniversary of the World Bank gathering in Madrid, Spain, a north-south split emerged over increasing global liquidity. See "The Fight for the Fund," *The Economist*, 8 October 1994, 85–86.

35. That environmental changes are not all bad, see Robert Mendlesohn, William D. Nordhaus, and Daigee Shaw, "The Impact of Global Warming on Agriculture: A Ricardian Analysis," *American Economic Review* 84 (September 1994): 753–71.

36. See "War of the Worlds; A Survey of the Global Economy," *The Economist*, 1 October 1994. This study forecasted that by 2020 seven of the top 15 economies (as measured by total GDP expressed in purchasing power parities) will be in Asia (China will be the largest economy of all), five will be in Europe (the largest economy there, Germany, will only be the sixth largest in the world), and three will be in the Western Hemisphere (the US, number two in the world; Brazil; and Mexico).

37. Russian Federation president Boris Yeltsin echoed these very fears at the Conference for Security and Cooperation in Europe (CSCE) meeting held in Budapest, Hungary, on 5 December 1994.

38. Norwegians voted down, for a second time, membership in the EU.

39. For a more complete argument over this issue, see Robert Gilpin, *The Political Economy of International Relations* (Princeton, N.J.: Princeton University Press, 1987), especially chapter 10.

40. See Charles P. Kindleberger, *The World in Depression, 1929–1939* (Berkeley, Calif.: University of California Press, 1973).

41. For two authors who dispute the US decline thesis, see Henry R. Nau, *The Myth of America's Decline* (New York: Oxford University Press, 1990); and Joseph S. Nye, Jr., *Bound to Lead; The Changing Nature of American Power* (New York: Basic Books, 1990).

42. These countries include the US, Japan, Germany, France, Italy, Great Britain, and Canada.

43. For an analysis on the efficacy of economic warfare means in the 20th century, see Gary Clyde Hufbauer, Jeffrey J. Schott, and Kimberly Ann Elliot, *Economic Sanctions Reconsidered: History and Current Policy*, 2d ed. (Washington, D.C.: Institute for International Economics, 1990). For an analysis that ascribes somewhat greater utility to economic warfare, see David A. Baldwin, *Economic Statecraft* (Princeton, N.J.: Princeton University Press, 1985).

44. See the discussion on where and when the US might engage militarily in *A National Security Strategy of Engagement* (Washington, D.C.: Government Printing Office, 1994), 10.

8

The Third World's Nonviable States

A Major Source of Conflict in the Twenty-First Century

Gary A. Storie

Like the tectonic forces that move continents around on the surface of the earth, the end of the cold war and other recent developments portend massive shifts in the "historic tectonics" of human civilization.[1] One such shift is in the area of global conflict.

Introduction

Following World War II, and to the end of the cold war, the greatest security fear was an all-out war between the two superpowers that would culminate in the use of nuclear weapons. With the end of the cold war, however, global conflicts are almost conclusively occurring in developing countries. During 1993, 42 countries experienced 52 major conflicts and another 37 countries suffered from political violence. Of these 79 countries, 65 are in the developing world.[2] While these conflicts presently do not have the potential to erupt into a nuclear holocaust, they do pose the threat of widespread regional destabilization with fearsome death tolls and massive refugee problems.

Many of the emerging global conflicts are arising from disintegrating nation-states (politically unstable states lacking in socioeconomic progress). Some examples follow.

Somalia

Years of clan-based civil war resulted in the collapse of the central government. By 1992, drought and conflict combined had led to 300,000 deaths. A mission that began as a humanitarian one had turned into a frustrating attempt at nation-building. The cost to the UN has been $3 billion and the lives of 130 peacekeepers, 26 of them American. Currently, the UN is bankrolling the activities of 15,000 UN soldiers in Somalia at a cost of nearly $80 million a month.

Haiti

With a history of political instability and no strategic resources, Haiti is one of the most environmentally degraded countries in the world. It is the poorest country in the Americas; in remote villages, most houses are made of earth and have no windows. To restore democracy and promote human rights, the US deployed 17,500 troops in the fall of 1994, at a huge cost. UN plans called for a 6,000-member force to be deployed to Haiti in 1995, with the US supplying about half. As of January 1995, the mission (to provide security) was plummeting. At that time, the *Christian Science Monitor* reported, "Crime has hit this Caribbean nation full force, past and present members of the military have clashed in violent confrontations, and the basics of running a country—from providing electricity to whisking away garbage—have further decayed."[3]

Rwanda

The genocide that took hundreds of thousands lives in Rwanda in 1994 has passed, but the country still desperately needs help. Real stability within Rwanda remains elusive—indeed impossible—while more than a million Rwandans are still in exile in neighboring African countries. Safe repatriation of the civilians is absolutely necessary to prevent renewed war, but many are afraid to return to their villages because they fear reprisals.

Other countries in various stages of disintegration include Afghanistan, Angola, Iraq, Mozambique, Myanmar, Yugoslavia, Sudan, Zaire, Ethiopia, Nigeria, and Bangladesh. With armed conflicts increasing in disintegrating states, it is no wonder that the UN spent $4 billion on peacekeeping in 1994. As more countries disintegrate, the consequences will have regional and global implications. Indeed, the components of human security are interdependent. When the security of people is endangered anywhere in the world, other nations are likely to become involved. Spin-offs such as famine, disease, pollution, drug trafficking, terrorism, ethnic dispute, and social disintegration will not be confined within national borders. Like it or not, developed countries must not ignore the disintegration of third world countries—or else face the consequences. More in-depth analysis is thus needed to determine the root causes of disintegration.

The underlying reason for disintegration goes beyond ideological, economic, political, or cultural conflicts—it is a question of "viability." Somalia, Rwanda, Liberia, and Mozambique experienced numerous types of clashes, but the ultimate reason they disintegrated was that they were nonviable entities in the international system. As Dr Karl P. Magyar states in the *Washington Times*, "The problem is nonviable, or 'collapsed states'—or put more graphically, the impending 'Somalianization' of a huge part of the Third World." Magyar further states, "As the gulf widens between the two worlds (rich and poor), more states become nonviable and thus potential sources of instability."[4]

The thesis of this chapter is that many third world nonviable states will become major sources of conflict across the globe, presenting serious security implications for the United States and the world. We will review how the concept of nonviability evolved with the proliferation of small states in the 1960s, and how it is applicable to both small and larger states today. We will then examine nonviable states from economic, military, and political perspectives, and how the problem will be manifested and most likely will escalate to affect more and more international actors. Finally, we will examine the prospects for a peaceful resolution to conflicts that emerge from the nonviability problem.

Microstates and the Nonviability Issue

In the field of international relations, the "nonviability concept" began to appear in the literature following the emergence of small states in the 1960s. In only three decades, the spirit of what President John F. Kennedy called "a worldwide declaration of independence" has transformed more than 1.25 billion people occupying nearly 14 million square miles of territory into 109 new nations.[5] The world currently comprises 191 independent states and 58 dependencies. In the decades following World War II, many states, particularly very small states, came into being when they achieved independence from their former colonial rulers. Most of these so-called "microstates"—generally with small land sizes and populations of less than one million people—had, and continue to have, too few financial resources to ever be self-sufficient.[6]

Microstates of this sort first attracted attention with the admissions of the Republic of Maldives (population 143,000) and The Gambia (population 592,000) to the UN in 1965. Many asked, why should such microstates have an equal or even a *legitimate* vote in the United Nations? Of current interest is the Republic of Nauru, which lies in the Pacific Ocean, 2,480 miles northeast of Australia. This island of only 8.2 square miles and 9,400 people has been exploited for its phosphate deposits (its only resource). Mining has left 80 percent of the island uninhabitable and uncultivatable, and the phosphate deposits are due to run out soon. Should this country have a legitimate vote in the UN General Assembly? Indeed, the very fact that small states can today participate in the activities of various international organizations advertises and underlines the basic and persisting conditions of international politics: the formal equality of sovereign states (regardless of size, resources, and responsibilities) and their substantive inequalities.

The nonviability of microstates centers around the concept of *dependency*. Is a state viable if it is "overdependent" on another for jobs, electricity, resources, and protection? For example, Lesotho, a country of 1.8 million people entirely surrounded by South Africa, is economically dependent on its neighbor, which provides all land transportation links with the outside world. Financial aid, over 50 percent of which comes from the Southern Africa Customs Union (SACU), provides 26 percent of Lesotho's Gross National Product (GNP). Furthermore, about 38 percent of Lesotho's male labor force is comprised of migrant workers from South Africa.

Vulnerabilities contribute to the microstates' nonviability. Their particular difficulty emanates from their greater vulnerability to crises and their lower capacity to respond to them. Their size makes them particularly susceptible to both natural and man-made disasters. A coup in a small state will have a far greater chance of success, for example, than in a larger area where rebellious troops might be contained—and one hurricane can destroy the economy of a small state that is dependent on a single crop. Because of their strategic positions, many of these states or territories—in the Caribbean, the Indian Ocean, and the Pacific—can easily become pawns in the game of international power politics. The Falkland Islands in 1982, Grenada in 1983, and Kuwait in 1991 are just three recent examples of small-state crises in peripheral areas that have had much wider repercussions. In his article, "Small is Beautiful but Vulnerable," Shridath Ramphal argues that small states by their very nature are weak and vulnerable: "Sometimes it seems as if small states are like small boats pushed out into a turbulent sea, free in one sense to traverse it; but, without oars or provisions, without compass or sails, free also to perish. Or, perhaps, to be rescued and taken on board a larger vessel."[7]

What Constitutes Nonviability?

Thus far, we have looked at the evolution of nonviability with the proliferation of small states in the 1960s. However, as Magyar points out, the nonviability issue is no longer restricted to small states. "The second dimension of the viability problem concerns the consequences of the proliferation of many such small states as well as large, but noncompetitive, nonviable states in the international system."[8] One example of a large emerging nonviable country is Bangladesh. With a population of 119 million, Bangladesh depends on foreign aid for more than 90 percent of its capital spending. The country is highly dependent on jute, which accounts for over 40 percent of its Gross Domestic Product (GDP). Furthermore, Bangladesh is highly vulnerable to its violent and unpredictable climate (a recent typhoon resulted in 144,000 deaths and wiped out practically an entire year's jute and rice crops).

Assessing a country's nonviability is a highly subjective process. Attempts have been made to establish operational criteria based on quantitative analysis using measurable variables such as population, size, wealth, resources, and military might. But analysts must go beyond quantitative variables to explore qualitative aspects, such as how well the country is managed. What is the country's ability to conduct international relations? Is it competitive? What is its ability to balance its budget? What is the country's ability to bring about political stability, economic development, and social transformation? Is the state able to maintain certain specified levels of public services, international representation, and a capable military establishment? To better understand this concept, we will first look at viability in three separate dimensions—socioeconomic, military, and political. Then the three will be evaluated in aggregate to establish the degree of overall viability.

Socioeconomic Viability

An assessment of socioeconomic viability must measure how well a country is able to "convert its resources into socioeconomic progress for its inhabitants in accordance with the more advanced standards of the international community."[9] Early literature that addressed economic viability focused on size, resources, and population. But, Magyar contends "viability . . . has a qualitative aspect which means that more than only quantifiable criteria [e.g., size and population] must be considered."[10] Singapore is a good example of economic viability that is not proportional to its small size or population. With only 2.9 million people, Singapore occupies the 47th position in world GNP rankings.

Abundance of strategic resources is another physical characteristic that has little correlation with economic viability. Switzerland, for example, a small country of 6.8 million people, is poor in natural resources, having no valuable minerals in commercially exploitable quantities. Yet, Switzerland has a GNP per capita almost 100 times that of resource-rich Nigeria. Japan is another example of a viable country with almost no resources. Whereas population, land size and fertility, and resources (physical characteristics) once were prerequisites for economic might, we now see this isn't necessarily the case today. Other characteristics may better reveal the socioeconomic viability of a state.

Michael Porter, a noted economist, argues that "productivity is the prime determinant in the long run of a nation's standard of living."[11] Probably the most often used statistic to measure a state's productivity is to look at its GNP per capita (the value of a country's final output of goods and services in a year, divided by its population). It reflects the value of a country's economic activity and the income of its residents. However, GNP should not be the only indicator of socioeconomic progress because a country that appears to be wealthy and productive may be managed poorly. If so, general development suffers. Raymond Bonner believes that the mayhem in Rwanda was not simply an eruption of long-simmering ethnic hatred between the Hutus and the Tutsis; it was also due to bad leaders and poor management.[12]

Another economic indicator is economic output per sector, which is the percentage of gross domestic product devoted to agricultural, industrial, and service activities. Generally, countries with more than 30 percent of their GDP derived from agriculture are still in a "first wave"[13] economy; that is, they are producing agricultural goods primarily for the export market and are vitally dependent upon that market (usually the richer countries). It is not surprising that many African and Asian countries fall into the first wave category.

Because national economic progress tends to be measured by GNP data alone, analysts have looked for a better, more comprehensive method that includes not just economic but social development as well. In 1990 the UN introduced a new way to measure human development, combining life expectancy, educational attainment, and income into a composite human development index (HDI).[14] The HDI offers an alternative to GNP for measuring socioeconomic progress. It enables people and their governments to evaluate progress over time and to determine priorities for policy formulation. It also permits instructive comparisons of different countries.

The HDI appears to have a high correlation with a country's socioeconomic viability. According to the *Human Development Report*, countries with an HDI below 0.5 are considered to have a low level of human development, those between 0.5 and 0.8 a medium level, and those above 0.8 a high level.[15] It is reasonable to conclude that countries with an HDI below 0.4 are currently legitimate candidates for socioeconomic nonviable status. Table 2 lists those countries with an HDI below 0.4, most of which are in Africa.

Table 2

HDI Values for Least Development Countries (LDC)

Country	HDI	Country	HDI
Madagascar	0.396	Rwanda	0.274
Laos	0.393	Uganda	0.272
Ghana	0.385	Angola	0.271
India	0.382	Benin	0.261
Côte d'Ivoire	0.382	Malawi	0.260
Haiti	0.370	Mauritania	0.254
Zambia	0.354	Mozambique	0.252
Nigeria	0.348	Central African Republic	0.249
Zaire	0.341	Ethiopia	0.247
Comoro Islands	0.331	Bhutan	0.226
Yemen	0.323	Djibouti	0.226
Senegal	0.322	Guinea-Bissau	0.224
Liberia	0.317	Somalia	0.217
Togo	0.311	Gambia	0.215
Bangladesh	0.309	Mali	0.214
Cambodia	0.307	Chad	0.212
Tanzania	0.306	Niger	0.209
Nepal	0.289	Sierra Leone	0.209
Sudan	0.276	Afghanistan	0.208
Burundi	0.276	Burkina Faso	0.203
Equatorial Guinea	0.276	Guinea	0.191

Source: *Human Development Report* (New York: Oxford University Press, 1994).

Analysts should evaluate a country's HDI by observing it over a period of time. Trend analysis will provide a better picture of a country's viability and whether it is or is not declining. Figure 4 depicts some examples in HDI performance since 1960. The HDIs of Somalia, Nepal, and Sierra Leone increased at a snail's pace while Malaysia's and the world's HDIs grew at a much higher rate. Such comparative data highlights the emergence of nonviable states.

Socioeconomic viability analysis shouldn't be considered complete with only a quick look at the HDI—a much more thorough look is warranted. Breaking the HDI into its components—life expectancy, adult literacy, years of schooling, and GDP per capita—yields further data on the country's degree of socioeconomic viability.[16]

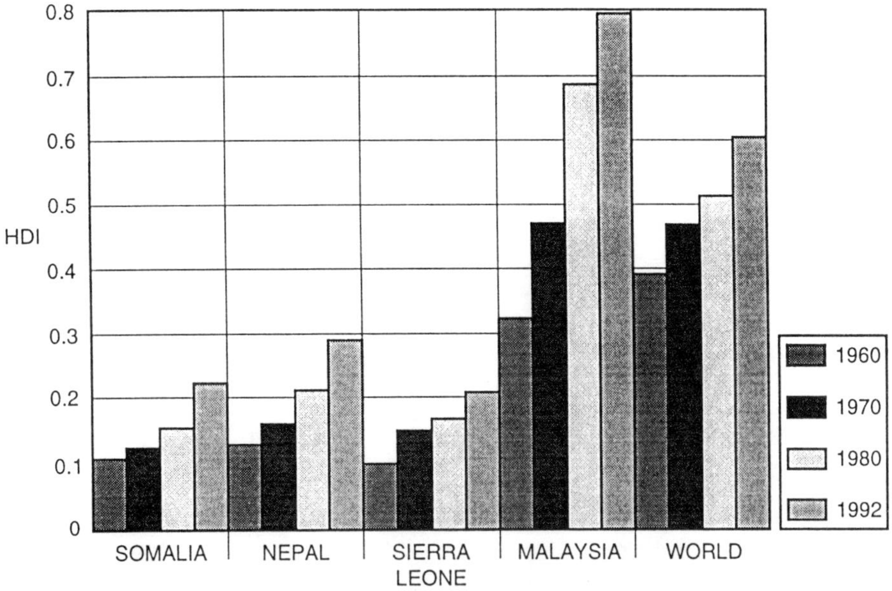

Source: Human Development Report (New York: Oxford University Press, 1994), 105.

Figure 4. HDI Values, 1960–92

Table 3 depicts the wide disparities between Malaysia, considered to be a third world industrializing state, and the nonviable states of Sierra Leone, Nepal, and Somalia, where many people are so poor they are not assured of their basic needs.

Table 3

Human Development Index Components

	Life expectancy at birth (years)	Adult literacy rate (%)	Mean years of schooling	Real GDP per capita (PPP$)
Country/Group	**1992**	**1992**	**1992**	**1991**
Nepal	52.7	27.0	2.1	1,130
Somalia	46.4	27.0	0.3	759
Sierra Leone	42.4	23.7	0.9	1,020
Malaysia	70.4	80.0	5.6	7,400
Industrialized	74.1	97.3	12.2	14,000
Developing	68.0	80.4	4.8	3,420
Least Developed	55.8	47.4	2.0	1,170

Source: *Human Development Report* (New York: Oxford University Press, 1994), 105.

An additional measure called purchasing power parity (PPP) is introduced in table 4. PPP refers to the units of a country's currency that are required to buy the goods in its domestic market that one US dollar would buy in the US market. One can further judge socioeconomic development by looking at what the government spends on internal development programs such as education and health. For example, Malaysia spends 5.6 percent of its GNP on education and has one doctor per 2,708 people. By contrast, Mozambique spends virtually nothing on education and averages one doctor per 39,500 people.[17]

Table 4

Comparison of Economic Aid Received to GNP in 1990

	(A) Economic Aid Received per capita US$	(B) GNP per capita US$	Aid/GNP per capita Ratio (A)/(B)
Bangladesh	17	184	0.092
Nepal	20	168	0.119
Haiti	25	324	0.078
Rwanda	36	279	0.129
Sierra Leone	15	146	0.103
South Asia	6	341	0.018
Sub-Saharan Africa	37	327	0.113
Latin America	11	1,618	0.007

Source: Ruth Leger Sivard, *World Military and Social Expenditures 1993* (Washington, D.C.: World Priorities, 1993), 42–51.

The HDI is a good measure for the internal analysis of a country's socioeconomic development. However, when assessing economic viability, analysts must not ignore external linkages to the world economy. What are the external vulnerabilities that contribute to a country being nonviable or noncompetitive? To address this question, we must analyze two areas—trade and aid.

In the area of trade, analyzing a country's merchandise exports can indicate the degree of competitiveness in the world economy. Merchandise exports are the goods a country produces and sells to other countries. The money a country earns from these exports helps determine how much it can afford to spend on imports and how much it can borrow abroad. Developing countries pay for imports mainly with the money they earn by selling exports to industrial countries.

Manufactured goods can generally be sold at a higher price than primary goods, but they are often more complicated and expensive to produce. Nonviable countries such as Nepal, Mozambique, Rwanda, Somalia, and Haiti each export less than $300 million of merchandise goods annually. Malaysia, with a population about one-tenth that of Bangladesh, exports almost 16 times as much.[18] South Africa, with an economy equivalent to that of Massachusetts, accounted for more merchandise exports ($18,454 million) than 33 of the 35 remaining sub-Saharan countries combined. Since economically nonviable countries are primarily single-commodity producers and exporters (such as the small island of Nauru), they must import primary goods and energy to sustain the population. But if they earn little from exports, what then is the source of their operating funds?

One characteristic of economically nonviable countries is that they don't have surplus capital with which to purchase imported goods such as food and energy. The only way they can survive is to borrow money and depend on aid, as is the case with Bangladesh. In the 1960s and 1970s, many developing countries were able to import more than they exported because they borrowed money from overseas banks, international institutions, and the governments of industrialized countries. To repay the principal and interest on those loans, most of these developing countries had to cut spending on imports in the 1980s, even though they were earning more from their exports. By 1986, developing countries were spending about 20 cents of every dollar earned from exports to pay off old debts. (In 1970, it was 10 cents; developing countries could not borrow as much in the 1980s because interest rates were higher and banks were less willing to make additional loans).[19]

Because borrowing had become more difficult and more expensive, many least developed countries (LDC) became even more dependent on aid. An economically nonviable country must receive external aid to survive. This aid originates from several sources, including international organizations, individual donor countries, and nongovernmental organizations. In analyzing aid dependency, comparing economic aid received per capita to GNP per capita proves to be highly revealing.

Table 4 reveals that extremely poor countries are highly dependent on aid for their survival. We see that particularly in sub-Saharan Africa: for every $100 produced by the economies, approximately $11 is received in aid. Not surprisingly, that region contains many nonviable states.[20]

Up to this point, we have examined several characteristics that exhibit a degree of socioeconomic viability. We have seen that many nonviable countries have in common the following characteristics:

1. Greater than 30 percent of GDP derived from agriculture
2. HDI below 0.4
3. Life expectancy at birth around 40–55 years
4. Adult literacy rate below 30 percent
5. Mean years of schooling usually below three
6. Real GDP per capita generally well below $1,200 (PPP$)
7. Merchandise exports well below $1 billion annually

Socioeconomic characteristics and their accompanying statistics can tell us only part of the story of socioeconomic viability, but they constitute an important and measurable part. They can serve as guidelines, but many aspects of economic and social development cannot be measured by statistics. Examples are the attitudes and feelings of people, their cohesiveness, their industriousness and ability to innovate, their values and ideas, their social and political systems, their history and culture, and the quality of their leadership.

Military Viability

Another important measure of viability is the military dimension. What constitutes military nonviability? A state is militarily viable if it has the capability of "maintaining domestic order and at least the capacity to assert its sovereignty vis-à-vis regional challengers to the point of discouraging an ill-conceived external military threat to the state."[21] If these criteria were applied to the world today, there would be arguably many socioeconomically viable states that could be judged militarily nonviable. A recent example is the country of

Kuwait in 1990. Its flat, almost featureless landscape conceals huge oil and gas reserves, making Kuwait the world's first-ranked oil-rich state. Dependent on oil for over 80 percent of its export earnings, Kuwait ranks 51st in the world in GNP per capita and 64th in HDI. However, it failed to deter an external military threat when its 11,000-strong, partly volunteer army was easily overrun by vastly superior Iraqi forces in August 1990. Kuwait has become militarily more viable since its externally engineered liberation, having signed defense pacts with the US, the UK, France, and Russia. Kuwait is now rearming rapidly with weapons purchased from major Western suppliers.

Another country failing to meet the test of military viability that resulted in conflict was Cuba. Under Jose Miguel Gomez, Cuba prospered economically from 1909 to 1925 due to US investment in tourism, gambling, and sugar. From 1925 to 1956, two military dictators, first Gerardo Machado and then Fulgencio Batista, were unable to suppress guerrilla activities and maintain domestic order. This situation led to Fidel Castro's rise to power in 1959. Castro declared Cuba a Marxist-Leninist state and formed political, economic, and military linkages with the Soviet Union. Cuba had been militarily nonviable before these linkages were established, and its military nonviability was a key contributor to the US-Soviet confrontation that could have resulted in nuclear war. Now, with the end of the cold war, Russia continues to weaken its ties with Cuba—and Cuba is becoming increasingly nonviable economically and militarily. More conflict could be on the horizon for Cuba.

Many of today's conflicts are occurring in third world countries that are militarily nonviable. Chad, Rwanda, Liberia, Angola, and Mozambique, for example, have failed to assert their sovereignties vis-à-vis regionally abetted internal challengers. And many countries' civil wars can be traced to their inability to thwart external interference—and once the wars were underway, anarchy followed. Hundreds of thousands have starved to death; others have been murdered. Still others have left their homes for refugee camps in neighboring countries, thereby destabilizing entire regions.

Political Viability

Political viability is another dimension of the concept. Whereas much of economic and military viability can be measured objectively (many economists have developed computer models or projections to measure economic development), political viability is difficult to quantify in many third world countries. However, the inability to build a viable economy closely parallels a poorly developed political apparatus. Haiti, Rwanda, and Yugoslavia are prime examples of countries in which political instability and poor management have led to their disintegration. But precisely what is it that constitutes political nonviability?

According to widely accepted convention, a state must have these four attributes to be a state: (1) territory, with clear boundaries; (2) a population; (3) a government, not answerable to outside authorities, with control over the territory and the population; and (4) sovereignty, or recognition by other states as a legally equal player in the global environment.[22] The latter two characteristics are closely related to Magyar's description of political viability: "the ability to gain international recognition but also to demonstrate the progressive development of institutions responsive to the reasonable expectations of its citizens for social and economic peace, progress and justice."[23]

There are, of course, many current examples of governments failing to gain international recognition or legitimacy and not being responsive to its citizens. Since the death of Tito in 1980, political instability in the former Yugoslavia has led to greatly mismanaged economic and social reforms. Unable to settle political issues that cut across religious and ethnic lines, the former Yugoslavia fractured into five republics, each vying for autonomy. Political nonviability rendered the Yugoslavian government unable to provide social and economic peace and justice. The result has been civil war, economic collapse, externally imposed sanctions, and ethnic cleansing.

Another example of a politically nonviable country is Zaire, a classic case where the leadership has not been able to translate its substantial advantages into sufficient socioeconomic development. Located in Central Africa, Zaire is one of the continent's largest countries. Its population comprises approximately 40 million people. With its huge mineral, agricultural, and energy resources, Zaire should be rich. Instead, political instability and 25 years of mismanagement have reduced it to one of the world's poorest states. From 1990 to 1993, real GDP declined by an average of 8 percent a year; in 1993, it declined by more than 12 percent. Copper and cobalt output has collapsed since 1990, and diamond smuggling is booming. Zaire has oil reserves, and its hydro potential could supply much of Africa if fully exploited. Instead, lack of maintenance has shut down many existing power turbines and forced power cuts in most urban areas. Despite rich soils and the fact that 80 percent of its people are involved in farming, Zaire is not self-sufficient in food. Political crises and economic collapse have exacerbated Zaire's long-standing problems of corruption and human rights abuses. Politically linked "death squads" are prevalent, as is ethnic violence. President Sese Seko Mobutu, under international as well as internal pressure to resign, has lost the support of his once-closest allies—Belgium, France, the US, and the European Union (EU). Most countries have stopped all except humanitarian aid. Clearly, Zaire's managerial incompetence is to blame for its nonviable status in the international arena.

Politically nonviable countries are characterized by improperly constructed governments that are unable to settle political issues requiring wide domestic legitimacy. A strong argument can be made, particularly in sub-Saharan Africa, that the major causes for disintegration can be traced to incapable governments, a lack of managerial talent, and political corruption. Since the independence era, countless deaths in Africa have been a direct result of governmental ineptitude and mismanagement. Despite having inherited economic and administrative infrastructures from colonial powers, and despite having access to modern technology, information, education, investment capital, and international markets, many countries have declined (e.g., Liberia, Ethiopia, Somalia, and Zaire). These governments are unable to conduct international relations effectively or to be responsive to their citizens. Even some economically and militarily viable countries may be doomed to disintegration because of poorly constructed governments.

Potential Consequences of Nonviable States

We have elaborated the socioeconomic, military, and political dimensions of nonviability separately to help conceptualize this phenomenon. In reality, however, these three dimensions are closely intertwined, and the so-called "collapsed states" (such as Haiti, Rwanda, Burundi, Somalia, Comoro Islands, and Equatorial Guinea) exhibit nonviability in all three dimensions. As mentioned in the introduction, 65 of the 79 countries involved in major conflicts and political violence are in the developing world. Many of them may be judged to experience some or all dimensions of nonviability. These conflicts have taken the lives of four to six million people in the last decade, and have caused millions of others to flee across their borders to avoid repression and death. The major refugee-generating countries of the past decade were clearly nonviable: Afghanistan (4.3 million), former Yugoslavia (1.8 million), and Mozambique (1.7 million).[24]

These conflicts, despite having gained worldwide media attention at times, have had minimal effect on the US and the world. However, we must realize that these collapsed countries have had populations of generally less than 10 million people and have had minimal external linkages to the international system. As we move rapidly towards the twenty-first century, more and more nonviable countries may fail. Many of these countries may have substantially greater population numbers (Zaire, Bangladesh, and Nigeria, for example). And since the global population increases by 93 million each year, the problems facing these politically unstable countries will intensify: "Even states with a recent history of stability such as Algeria are tottering toward disintegration."[25]

The proliferation of nonviable states could have cascading and catastrophic effects on the international system in the twenty-first century. Major challenges to human security, though originating within nonviable countries, will emanate beyond national frontiers. Millions of people will migrate to other countries in search of survival (Haitian refugees are a recent example). The rapid rate of population growth—coupled with a lack of development opportunities—will continue to overcrowd the planet, adding to the enormous pressures that already exist on diminishing nonrenewable resources. Ethnic tensions will spill over national boundaries. International terrorism, crime, and drug trafficking could be major spin-offs. Clearly, it will not be possible for the community of nations to achieve any of its major goals (peace, environmental protection, fertility reduction, social integration) unless it seriously addresses the problem of nonviability.

Conclusion

There are no easy solutions to the nonviability problem. If nonviable countries are to survive and prosper, particularly in sub-Saharan Africa, those governments must make the necessary reforms to become more viable. They must be able to provide internal and external security to their people. They must also be able to build infrastructures that promote socioeconomic development and sustainability. Finally, they must find a way to instill managerial competency, which nonviable states so badly lack. With the help of developed countries, there is still a sliver of hope left for these countries.

Developing countries have tended in the past to argue that almost all their economic problems spring from an inequitable international order. There certainly are many changes needed in global economic affairs—including freer flows of trade, technology, capital and labor—but developing countries now recognize that no amount of external assistance can ever substitute for the fundamental reforms needed in their domestic economies.[26]

Possibly the brightest hope for nonviable states is to become more viable by "sublimating their nationalistic political aspirations and to acknowledge the need for pooling their individual economic resources in the interest of the collective community."[27] Most nonviable states lack all or some of the necessary political, military, and economic ingredients to become competitive in the global economy, effective in international relations, and competent to provide necessary services to the people. Magyar, a proponent of "confederal integration" for Africa, argues:

> By forming greater regional-based economic units, they would benefit by the factor of economies of scale, specialization, maximum use of infrastructure (ports, roads, airports, energy, etc.), trade, joint

> financial institutions, common currency, aid, development plans and strategies, industrial decentralization, attraction of foreign investments, and above all, the greater ability to bargain for the sale of their primary products.[28]

He goes on to say that these regional entities, specifically in Africa, could be managerially viable if designed properly. Magyar believes we can assist by first being prepared to accept possible changes in Africa's present borders. "The process of national disintegration may sweep the continent, and our natural tendency will be to arrest this process. We should rather prepare to accept this development."[29] After the disintegration, Magyar believes we can assist in reintegrating Africa's fragments into four or five viable regional economic units.

Another proponent of the confederation concept is Kenichi Ohmae. In his article, "The Emergence of Regional States," Ohmae states that "the nation state has become an unnatural, even dysfunctional unit for organizing human activity and managing economic endeavor in a borderless world."[30] He believes that in today's borderless world there are natural economic zones, and what matters is that each possesses, in one or another combination, the key ingredients for successful participation in the global economy.

Professor Mike Faber, director of the Institute of Development Studies at the University of Sussex, offers a federation approach as a possible scenario for nonviable states. In theory, he argues "federal structures are able to provide many of the advantages of a larger economic unit, if factors of production, including labor, are allowed to flow freely within the component parts of the federation." In practice, however, he believes that political strains will cause the federal structures to come apart as they did at the end of the colonial era.[31]

The proliferation of nonviable states, and the conflicts resulting from their nonviability in the international system, will present enormous challenges to the US and the world. However, the US must resist the temptation to become engaged in conflicts involving nonviable states, if US involvement cannot be avoided, we must be prepared for these types of conflicts, which means establishing entirely different doctrine, force structures, and training from that which we have grown accustomed to during the cold war. Nonviability will be at the root of many conflicts in the twenty-first century: we must learn to recognize it and deal with it.

Notes

1. Michael T. Klare, "The New Challenges to Global Security," *Current History 92*, no. 573 (April 1993): 155.

2. *Human Development Report* (New York: Oxford University Press, 1994), 47.

3. Kathie Klarreich, "Haitians' Hooray Fades as Troubles Drag On," *Christian Science Monitor*, 13 January 1995, 7.

4. Karl P. Magyar, "Dealing with the Failures of Democracy," *Washington Times*, 16 August 1994.

5. *World Reference Atlas* (London: Dorling Kindersley, 1994), 14.

6. G. R. Berridge, *International Politics: States, Power, and Conflict Since 1945*, 2d ed. (New York: Harvester Wheatshelf, 1992), 20. Both the United Nations and the British Commonwealth define a microstate as "a state with under one million inhabitants," though evidently the real hallmark of a microstate is the absence of anything other than a token defense force.

7. Shridath Ramphal, "Small is Beautiful but Vulnerable," *The Round Table* no. 292 (1984): 368.

8. Karl P. Magyar, "The Emerging Post-Cold-War International Order and Changing Conflict Environment," in Karl P. Magyar, ed., *Challenge and Response: Anticipating US Military Security Concerns* (Maxwell AFB, Ala.: Air University Press, 1994), 10.

9. Ibid.

10. Ibid.

11. Michael E. Porter, *Competitive Advantage of Nations* (New York: Free Press, 1990), 6.

12. Raymond Bonner, "Rwanda Now Faces Painful Ordeal of Rebirth," *New York Times*, 29 December 1994.

13. Alvin and Heidi Toffler, *War and Anti-War* (Boston: Little, Brown and Co., 1993). *First wave* connotes an agrarian society.

14. *Human Development Report*, 91. The HDI sets a minimum and a maximum for each dimension and then shows where each country stands in relation to these scales—expressed as a value between 0 and 1. So, since the minimum adult literacy rate is 0 percent and the maximum is 100 percent, the literacy component of knowledge for a country where the literacy rate is 75 percent would be 0.75. Similarly, the minimum for life expectancy is 25 years and the maximum is 85 years, so the longevity component for a country where life expectancy is 55 years is 0.5. For income the minimum is $200 and the maximum is $40,000 PPP (purchasing power parity: the units of a country's currency required to buy the goods in its domestic market that one US dollar would buy in the US market). Income above the average world income is adjusted using a progressively higher discount rate. The scores for the three dimensions are then averaged in an overall index.

15. Ibid., 92.

16. Ibid. GDP per capita in international dollars is converted at purchasing power parity.

17. *Human Development Report*, 129–30.

18. *The Development Data Book & Teaching Guide*, 2d ed. (Washington, D.C.: The International Bank for Reconstruction and Development/The World Bank, 1988), 12–15. Bangladesh, with a population of 119 million, exported $880 million in merchandise goods in 1986. Malaysia, with a population of 18.8 million, exported $13,874 million in 1986.

19. Ibid., 11.

20. Ruth Leger Sivard, *World Military and Social Expenditures 1993* (Washington, D.C.: World Priorities, 1993), 42–51. Figures are from 1990 or latest year available. Economic aid received includes estimated receipts per capita of official loans and grants made to promote economic development. Military supporting assistance is excluded from these figures insofar as it is possible to do so. There is, however, a gray area of quasi-military transactions which may appear in some national totals.

21. Karl P. Magyar, "Managing Africa: The Strategy of Confederal Integration" (Unpublished paper, University of Durban-Westville, South Africa, 1985), 24.

22. Barry B. Hughes, *Continuity and Change in World Politics*, 2d ed. (Englewood Cliffs, N.J.: Prentice Hall, 1994): 64.

23. Magyar, "Managing Africa," 24.

24. *Human Development Report*, 47.

25. Youssef M. Ibrahim, "Algeria is Edging Toward Breakup," *New York Times*, 4 April 1994.

26. *Human Development Report*, 61.

27. Magyar, "Managing Africa," 29.

28. Ibid., 30.

29. Karl P. Magyar, "Sub-Saharan Africa: Political Marginalization and Strategic Realignment," in *U.S. Foreign Policy in Transition*, eds. James E. Winkates, J. Richard Walsh, and Joseph M. Scolnick, Jr. (Chicago: Nelson-Hall Publishers, 1994), 258.

30. Kenichi Ohmae, "The Emergence of Regional States," *Vital Speeches of the Day* 58, no. 16 (June 1992): 487.

31. Mike Faber, "Island Micro States: Problems of Viability," *The Round Table* no. 292 (1984): 375.

9

When the Water Runs Out

Jan Kinner

By the end of the 1990s, water problems in the Middle East will lead either to an unprecedented degree of cooperation, or a combustible level of conflict.

—Sandra Postel

Oil has been a catalyst for conflict around the globe, from court battles over environmental damage to Alaskan shorelines to the US-led coalition war against Iraq. Yet for all its influence upon humanity in recent years, oil cannot compare with the impact of one of our most vital resources: water. Throughout time, water has been vital to the development and survival of civilizations. The first great civilizations arose in the valleys of the great rivers: the Nile Valley of Egypt, the Indus Valley of Pakistan, the Huang He Valley of China, and the Tigris-Euphrates Valley of ancient Mesopotamia. Fresh water is a prerequisite to human existence, yet its scarcity is a problem of global proportion. Water has been a cause of armed conflict throughout history, and if the world's demographic trends continue, water will become an even greater catalyst for conflict, especially in the Middle East. This essay explains the critical nature of the world's water shortages and reveals how these shortages have led, and will continue to lead, to conflict in the future.

The Global Water Problem

Although more than 70 percent of the earth's surface is covered by water, precious little of it is fresh. The total volume of water covering the globe is immense—about 1.41 billion cubic kilometers (km^3)—but 97 percent of this total volume is salt water, which is difficult to use without removing the salt (an expensive and highly energy-consumptive process). The remaining 3 percent is fresh water, but less than 1 percent of that amount is readily available as surface water (lakes, rivers, and streams) and ground water (aquifers).

The remainder is inaccessible, being in polar ice caps, glaciers, deep aquifers, and the atmosphere.[1] To put fresh water in perspective, consider this: if the world's total water supply were only 100 liters, the usable supply of fresh water would be only 0.003 liter, or one-half teaspoon.[2]

The amount of fresh water available for man's use at any one time is dependent upon the amount of precipitation, the rate of water use, and the quality of the available water. Precipitation is the source of all fresh water as it renews or recharges surface and ground waters (man's primary sources of fresh water). Low levels of precipitation threaten many countries of the world; at least 80 arid and semiarid countries, with about 40 percent of the world's population, have serious periodic droughts.[3] On the African continent, the worst drought of the century continued in 1993. Many of Africa's crops were totally destroyed, raising concerns that, if the drought continues, mass starvation may become as common as the world witnessed in Somalia. Precipitation patterns directly affect the amount of water available in those areas.

The second factor affecting the amount of fresh water available is the rate at which the water is withdrawn from its source for agricultural, industrial, and domestic uses. World water withdrawals have increased more than 35-fold over the past three centuries, the majority of which have supported the world's agricultural base.[4] Approximately 67 percent of the world's water supply is used to support agricultural production. Agriculture uses 82 percent of the available water in Asia, 40 percent in the United States, and 30 percent in Europe. For some countries, the numbers are even more revealing. In Egypt, more than 98 percent of all water used is for crop production while China and India use approximately 90 percent of their water supply to support agriculture.[5] As the world's population continues to increase, the demand for water to support food production will increase as well, thus putting a further strain on fresh water sources.

Water is also used extensively by industry. Almost one-quarter of the world's fresh water supply is used to support manufacturing processes, electricity production, and mining operations. Manufacturing, like agriculture, uses large quantities of water to produce an end item. For example, between 7,000 and 34,000 liters of water are needed to produce 1,000 liters of gasoline while 8,000–10,000 liters are needed to produce a single ton of steel.[6] The amount of water used for industrial applications varies according to each nation's level of technological development. In Canada, industry accounts for 84 percent of all water used; in India, it takes a mere 1 percent.[7] Water is also used extensively for cooling in nuclear power plants that produce electricity as well as in the extraction of ores and minerals in mining operations. Industrial development therefore impacts the amount of water available for other uses, including agricultural and domestic.

The remaining 8 percent of the world's fresh water supply is used for domestic purposes. The quantity of water used daily varies with population, standard of living, education, customs, and climate. It's no surprise that industrialized nations use significantly more water per person than agrarian nations. Thus, the way water is used directly affects the amount of water available; conversely, the amount of water available directly impacts a country's future economic development.

The third factor affecting the amount of fresh water available is water pollution. Agriculture is the leading source for water pollutants such as sediments, pesticides, and nutrients, as farmers increase crop yields through the use of fertilizers and pesticides that run off into streams or percolate into ground water.[8] The diversion of water for irrigation to support agriculture can also dramatically affect water quality. The Aral Sea, which straddles the borders of Kazakhstan and Uzbekistan in west-central Asia, is a case in point. In 1960, the Aral was the fourth largest inland body of water in the world. However, because of extensive withdrawals for irrigation over the past 30 years, the sea has lost 40 percent of its area and 67 percent of its volume. In addition, its salinity is now four times that of oceans.[9] Industry is also responsible for polluting surface and ground waters. Pollutants are discharged into surface and ground water sources as by-products of manufacturing processes or from the leaching of pollutants buried in solid-waste dumps. A 1980 study by the Worldwatch Institute revealed that about 70 percent of all heavy metals in Germany's Ruhr River came from industrial sources.[10] In Malaysia, many of the major rivers were officially declared dead in 1979, the result of industrial pollution.[11] And according to the Worldwatch Institute, "Industrial discharges, combined with untreated sewage and agricultural runoff, have contaminated most rivers, lakes, and seashores in Eastern Europe and the Soviet Union."[12] Inadequately treated sewage from domestic sources also introduces large quantities of pollutants into surface waters. In developing nations, more than 95 percent of urban sewage is discharged into surface waters without treatment. An example is Bangkok, Thailand, which relies on four rivers and a series of canals to dispose of an estimated 10,000 metric tons of raw sewage and municipal waste every day—without being treated.[13] A survey by the World Health Organization found that only 35 percent of the populations of all the developing nations had access to relatively safe drinking water and only 32 percent had proper sanitation.[14] Given these factors, the issue of water quality has considerable bearing on water supply. A source of fresh water may be readily available and able to provide reliable amounts of water, but when much of it is polluted, it has the same impact as if it were not available.

The amount of fresh water ultimately available for man's use is dependent upon the amount of precipitation, the rate of water use, and the extent of water pollution. Arid and semiarid countries, with growing populations and hoping to develop agricultural or industrial bases, will often find themselves lacking critically needed water. Industrialized and developing nations, on the other hand, often have to contend with pollution, which severely restricts the amount of water available for agricultural and domestic uses. The amount of fresh water is limited, and man's use of this resource constrains it further.

Water Scarcity

Water shortages occur where the demand for water exceeds the available water supply. Water use is increasing at dramatic rates, the result of population growth and industrial/agricultural development. According to the *Global 2000* study, increases of at least 200–300 percent in world water withdrawals are expected over the 1975–2000 period.[15] At the global level, the *average* annual use (for all uses) is currently 650m^3 (650 cubic meters) per person per day, with annual average per capita water use varying widely by region: 1,700m^3 in North and Central America, 725m^3 in Europe, 525m^3 in Asia, 475m^3 in South America, and 245m^3 in Africa.[16] The amount available per capita depends in part upon a country's population. An increasing population, in other words, acts as a "thumb screw" on the amount of water available for other uses. Malin Falkenmark, a noted Swedish hydrologist, estimated that the needs of the temperate zone industrialized regions can be met by between 150m^3 and 900m^3 per person per year. Irrigated semiarid regions, by contrast, need about five times as much—between 700m^3 and 3,500m^3 per person per year. And semiarid industrialized regions, such as the lower Colorado basin of the United States, need even more—2,700m^3 to 7,000m^3 per person per year.[17]

Falkenmark also defined what she called "water competition intervals." Countries having 10,000m^3 of water *available* per person per year (for all uses) or more have what she called "limited water problems" (quality and dry-season problems); those with 1,670m^3–10,000m^3 of water have "water stress" (general problems); those with 1,000m^3–1,670m^3 suffer from "chronic water scarcity"; and those with fewer than 500m^3 of water per person per year are beyond what Falkenmark calls the "water barrier."[18] When a country passes the "water barrier," the need for water exceeds the current supply. In other words, any economic development that would increase the standard of living of the population becomes almost impossible to accomplish.

Falkenmark estimated that 10 African countries, with a combined population of 1.1 billion, will be water stressed by the year 2025, with another 15 countries beyond the "water barrier."[19] Robin Clarke, another hydrologist, expanded on Falkenmark's work. In his global study, he excluded waters entering the country and all nonrenewable water sources (e.g., deep water aquifers, which can take thousands of years to renew) because such water was not controllable by the host country. For example, a country upstream could dam a river, stopping or slowing its flow. Or an upstream country could utilize a larger share of a river's flow for irrigation. Additionally, an adjacent country could overdraft an aquifer, causing the water table to drop on the other side of the border.

Clarke's work paints a bleak picture for many parts of the world. Israel's total internal water supply, according to Clarke, can only provide 370m^3 of water per person annually. This is 130m^3 below Falkenmark's "water barrier" and 280m^3 below the world's average. Egypt's total internal water supply can provide only 40m^3 of water per person annually, well below Falkenmark's "water barrier" and 610m^3 below the world's average. When Egypt's exogenous sources (e.g., Nile River) are included, Egypt extracts and uses 97 percent of its total water supply to meet its agricultural, industrial, and domestic needs. If the Nile's waters were dammed or significantly reduced by upstream countries like Sudan or Ethiopia, Egypt's agricultural base, which uses the greatest share of Egypt's total water supply, would collapse. Would Egypt, or other nations dependent upon water originating outside their countries, allow such a scenario to occur? Or would the Egyptian government take some action to persuade the upstream countries to change their behavior? It is apparent that water shortages can lead to conflict among nations.

Water as a Source of Conflict

Water has been called the "fugitive" resource because it moves. As such, water has been the source of numerous conflicts throughout history. Where a river has been used as a boundary between nations, the shifting of the water has caused conflict over lines of political demarcation. Examples of boundary disputes include India and Bangladesh over the Ganges River, Mexico and the United States over the Rio Grande, and Czechoslovakia and Hungary over the Danube. The latest conflict involving a border defined by water involved the Shatt al Arab, which separates Iraq from Iran. In September 1980, Saddam Hussein claimed Iraqi sovereignty over the entire Shatt al Arab and initiated the Iran-Iraq War. Hostilities have not overcome the problems caused by the elusiveness of water, however.

Where water flows across political boundaries, as it does in 246 out of the 253 river basins in the world, conflict often results when significant changes occur in either quality or quantity.[20] Natural upstream erosion in one nation may endanger downstream ports, channels, and reservoirs in another nation. Irrigation projects upstream may deprive a downstream nation of adequate supplies of water for established domestic, industrial, and agricultural uses. Pollution from upstream users may cause downstream nations to install expensive purification works to prevent danger to health and industry, and to allow for future development. An example of this occurred in 1988 when the Polish government asked Czechoslovakia to pay damages for contamination of the Polish stretch of the Odra River caused by a heavy fuel leak in November 1986.[21] Other countries currently embroiled in conflict over the pollution of multinational river basins include Czechoslovakia and Germany over industrial pollution in the Elbe; Hungary and Romania over industrial pollution in the Szamos; Bolivia and Chile over salinization of the Lauca; Egypt, Ethiopia, and Sudan over siltation of the Nile; and Mexico and the United States over agrochemical pollution of both the Rio Grande and the Colorado.[22]

Downstream nations, dependent upon the flow of water, often find themselves in a weak position to negotiate formal agreements whereas nations controlling those water resources can wield formidable power. This precarious worldwide situation is intensifying as limited resources come under increasing pressure from growing populations, particularly in arid and semiarid downstream countries that are already short of water. The situation is exacerbated when the upstream country is facing its own water shortages. When upstream water resources have become increasingly scarce, nations have not hesitated to take action to ensure their own supply, even at the expense of downstream nations. In regard to the growing demand on fresh water supplies, Dr Mostafa Tolba, executive director of the United Nation's environment program, said, "National and global security are at stake . . . shortages of fresh water worsen economic and political differences among nations and contribute to increasingly unstable perceptions of national security."[23] Nowhere is this more vivid than in the Middle East, where disputes over water are shaping the political landscapes and economic futures of its countries.

Middle East Water Problems

The Middle East water problem has become a crisis because of world demographic trends and a scarcity of water. Falkenmark says the crisis is so acute that "in the near future, water, not oil, will be the most sought after resource of the Middle East."[24] The Middle East is a microcosm of the world, and the root causes of conflict over Middle East water are only extreme examples of the problems facing the rest of the world: water scarcity caused by low levels of precipitation, the multinational nature of water supplies, water quality problems, and expanding populations that require and demand more water.

Population growth rates throughout the Middle East are currently among the highest in the world. In 1983, the World Bank reported that the population of the Middle East was expected to grow from 217.4 million people to 337 million by the year 2000.[25] These numbers prompted Israeli prime minister Shimon Peres to write:

> Rapid growth in population within the Region is not matched with a concomitant growth in food production, so poverty is worsening. Available water shrinks each year, and the quality of that water is compromised from overuse that results in salinization and desertification. All these factors have an adverse affect on public health and lower the standard of living. Thus, we get sucked into a vicious cycle; the worse the poverty, the more the population grows, the worse the water shortage becomes, the worse the poverty gets, the more the population grows.[26]

Demographic data analysis reveals that the populations of water-hungry Iraq, Syria, Jordan, and Saudi Arabia are growing between 3 and 4 percent per year. This growth rate will result in a doubling of their populations in less than 20 years. Turkey's, Lebanon's, and Kuwait's population growth rates are around 2 percent per year while Israel's rate is approximately 1.5 percent. (Israel's growth rate does not include an expected 1 to 2 million immigrants from the former Soviet Union.)[27] Using the lowest available estimates, per capita consumption rates could increase by 20 percent, putting almost all Middle East countries beyond Falkenmark's "water barrier." Detailed demographic data also shows that 67 percent of all Arabic-speaking people rely upon transboundary water from non-Arabic-speaking areas, and that approximately 24 percent of all Arab people live in areas with no year-round surface streams.[28] Thus, the problem of scarcity versus increasing need is compounded by the international nature of existing supplies within the Middle East. The major river basins—Tigris, Euphrates, Jordan, Orontes, and Nile—do not respect national boundaries. And a sixth basin, the Litani, though entirely within Lebanon, is a focus of interest in other nations. Over 50 percent of the Middle East's population is dependent upon waters originating from these six river basins.[29]

In addition to being in short supply, much of the Middle East's fresh water is now polluted. This pollution is a result of the "increasing discharge of untreated or inadequately treated domestic wastes, emissions from agroprocessing plants and unregulated or misinformed agrochemical use, and hazardous and toxic industrial wastes into water bodies serving as a source of supply for other users," says a representative from the Food and Agricultural Organization of the United Nations.[30] Also, overdrafting in many of the aquifers (in support of agriculture) has resulted in saline intrusions from the seas, which renders the water nonpotable. These and other problems in water quality have increased, thus magnifying the water crisis which, in the past, has been punctuated by armed conflict between Middle East nations—and water supply remains a source of increasing tension today.

Potential Conflicts

Today, the Jordan River basin presents the Middle East's most intractable water management problem. From its headwaters in Syria and Lebanon, the Jordan River flows south into the Sea of Galilee and then to the Dead Sea between the West Bank and Jordan. Users of this 360-kilometer basin include Israel (including the occupied West Bank), Jordan, Syria, and Lebanon. Its principal tributary, the Yarmuk River, forms the border between Syria and Jordan and, further downstream, between Israel and Jordan. While the Jordan River basin is shared by four riparian nations that have a deep and long-standing enmity towards one another, most of the problems have emerged between Israel and Jordan. Both nations depend upon the Jordan River for fresh water and for replenishment of their aquifers. Thomas Naff and Ruth Matson, noted Middle East correspondents, contend that an increase in water-related Arab-Israeli hostility was one of the major factors that led to the 1967 war.[31] John K. Cooley, also a noted Middle East correspondent, asserts that Israel went to war "partly because the Arabs had unsuccessfully tried to divert into Arab rivers Jordan River headwaters that fed Israel."[32]

The aftermath of the 1967 war had a direct impact on the management of the Jordan River basin. Israel's occupation of the Golan Heights prevented the Arab nations from diverting the headwaters of the Jordan, and Israeli occupation of the West Bank secured the Yarqon-Taninim aquifer, the source of between 20 and 40 percent of Israel's sustainable water supply. Israel has severely restricted the amount of water West Bank Arabs can pump from this aquifer, even as it continues to overdraft the aquifer for its own use. The measures taken to restrict pumping on the West Bank have been described by Israel as defensive in nature to protect its coastal wells and the integrity of the water system as a whole.

The Israelis argue that unchecked Palestinian water development and pollution in the hills west of the watershed line will endanger both the quality of the water and the quantity of the water sources on which the heavily populated coastal plain of Israel relies. But these restrictions on water access have angered the West Bank Palestinian population. The agreement between Israel and the Palestine Liberation Organization (PLO) may require that Israel return some of the territory it has occupied since the 1967 Arab-Israeli war. Since many of Israel's prime water sources are located in the disputed areas, this would mean relinquishing control over much of its fresh water supply. A study by the Jaffee Center for Strategic Studies at Tel Aviv University concluded that Israel cannot afford to give up captured water sources unless its future supplies are guaranteed. Joseph Alpher, director of the center, wrote: "Water is essential. It doesn't mean you can't withdraw, but you can't withdraw without making certain that Israel's supply is secure and that there is guaranteed access to the water resources."[33] With no water guarantees currently forthcoming, water rights in this area will remain a source of tension between the PLO and Israel.

Another portion of Israel's water supply comes from the water catchment area for the Sea of Galilee. Located in the Golan Heights, this formerly Syrian area was captured by the Israelis in the 1967 war and annexed in 1981. The Sea of Galilee, fed by the Jordan River, is Israel's largest surface water reservoir. It provides water for a pipeline and a canal, which transport it from the north towards the Gaza Strip. However, overpumping the Sea of Galilee has created salinity problems in the reservoir. To counter a potential water crisis, Israel has developed plans to build a canal that would pump water from the Mediterranean to the Dead Sea, and to construct reservoirs above the Jordan Valley. These plans have led to a conflict with Jordan, which fears that pumping water into the Dead Sea will waterlog areas of irrigated agriculture in the East Ghor Canal region.

Control of the Golan Heights has given Israel access to the Yarmuk River, one of the last major undeveloped tributaries in the basin. Entering the Jordan River from the east, the Yarmuk is of great importance not only to Syria, its source, but also to Israel and Jordan. Jordan has already overreached its renewable supply, and water rationing is in effect there. This situation is expected to worsen as Jordan's population doubles in size over the next 20 years. And Jordan depends on irrigated agriculture for much of its income as its underground aquifers, which have been substantial sources of water, are depleting rapidly. Jordan views increased use of the Yarmuk as vital to its interests, and wants to build, with Syria, a dam on the Yarmuk. But Israel has managed to block actual construction, at least temporarily, claiming that the dam would reduce flows into the Jordan River.

Israel's third source of water is the coastal aquifer, which borders the Mediterranean. Years of overdrafting have caused extensive saline intrusion in parts of this aquifer. Additionally, approximately 25 percent of the aquifer is polluted. In fact, water officials in Israel predict that a fifth of all wells may need to be closed over the next few years—an action which will increase Israel's dependence on the West Bank's Yarqon-Taninim aquifer.[34] And Cooley wrote—in 1984—that "present aquifers can scarcely meet the country's current needs or greater levels of consumption much beyond 1990. Another major water source will be needed."[35] Israel's need for water has become known as the "hydraulic imperative," which has been interpreted as the need for Israel to acquire—by military means if necessary—a larger water supply to ensure the continued growth of Israel's economy and population.[36] Likely losers in such a gambit include Syria, Jordan, and Lebanon.

Another river basin which has been a source of conflict in the Middle East is the Tigris-Euphrates. From headwaters located in Turkey, the Tigris and Euphrates rivers flow through Syria into Iraq, where they join to form the Shatt al Arab. Although Turkey, Syria, and Iraq have engaged in intermittent discussions over the waters of these rivers for decades, they have been unable to agree on a permanent tripartite treaty. In fact, the construction of dams in the early 1970s by Turkey and Syria precipitated a major Syria-Iraq crisis that brought the two nations to the brink of war. Iraq, downstream to both Turkey and Syria, claimed that Syria had reduced the Euphrates flow by 75 percent, endangering the livelihood of Iraqi farmers who use the waters of the Euphrates to irrigate their farmland.[37] Syria and Iraq exchanged threats, Turkey indicated a readiness to take any action necessary to restore the flow of the Euphrates, and Syria claimed it was passing on to Iraq most of the water received from Turkey.[38] The situation was resolved only when Syria released substantially larger amounts of water to Iraq—a result of mediation efforts by the Saudis.

This situation almost repeated itself when Turkey's massive Ataturk Dam started operating in 1990, depriving Syria of badly needed water. Instead of attacking Turkey directly, however, Syria and Iraq have supported Kurdish guerrilla activities in eastern Turkey as a means of pressuring the Turkish government into releasing more water.[39] Turkey, in response, has continually threatened to cut the flow of the Euphrates in an attempt to force Syria to curtail its support for Kurdish activities in the southeast Anatolia region.[40]

The Ataturk Dam is only one of a series of 22 dams, 25 irrigation systems, and 19 hydropower stations that Turkey is constructing as part of a massive economic development project called the Grand Anatolia Project (GAP). When completed, the GAP will boost Turkey's hydropower capacity to 7,500 megawatts and double its irrigated area. Syria and Iraq fear the GAP will reduce the Euphrates flow into Syria by 35 percent in normal years—substantially more in dry ones—while polluting the river with irrigation drainage.[41] Iraq, the last downstream country, would also see a reduction, and the Iraqi government has continually expressed concerns about Syria's plans to tap more and more of the Euphrates.

Syria's population, which will double in the next 18 years, will dramatically impact the cities of Damascus, Homs, and Aleppo, each of which is already suffering severe water shortages. Syria depends upon the Euphrates for a large part of its energy, and the city of Aleppo depends upon Euphrates water for both domestic and agricultural uses. As the Ataturk Dam starts to fill, water levels below the dam are expected to remain low for five to eight years while existing tensions between Turkey, Syria, and Iraq are expected to increase.

Tensions are also running high in the Nile River basin. The Nile, the world's longest river, provides water for nine countries. About 85 percent of the Nile's flow is generated by precipitation in Ethiopia. It flows as the Blue Nile into Sudan before it enters Egypt. The remaining 15 percent comes from the White Nile system, which has headwaters in Tanzania and which joins the Blue Nile near Khartoum. The last country in line and the one most dependent upon the waters of the Nile is Egypt, which is already beyond the "water barrier."

Egypt's water problem is especially serious. The Aswan High Dam, built in the 1950s, was intended to guarantee a constant source of water even in times of drought. However, the water levels behind the Aswan Dam are rapidly declining due in part to evaporation and seepage caused primarily by the extended drought that affected the entire northeastern region of Africa. Thus, the amount of water available to irrigate cropland is diminishing as Egypt's population is rapidly increasing. By the end of the current decade, estimates indicate that Egypt's population will increase from 52 million to 70 million. To get more water, the Egyptian government is focusing more of its attention on its southern upstream neighbors—Sudan in particular.

If additional water allocations cannot be gained through diplomatic means, a war could erupt between Egypt and Sudan. In 1958, there was a military confrontation when Egypt unsuccessfully attempted to reclaim disputed border territory from Sudan. The confrontation occurred because of differences over water allocations. An agreement was eventually reached in which Egypt was entitled to 55.5 billion cubic meters (bcm) of water from the Nile each year while Sudan was allocated 18.5 bcm. Ten years later, and after completion of the Aswan High Dam in Egypt, the situation almost repeated itself when the Egyptians claimed that their larger population entitled them to a larger allocation of water than Sudan. The Sudanese rejected this, claiming they had first rights to the river's water because of their upper riparian status. Negotiations followed because "the positions of both parties were hardened by domestic nationalist politics."[42] No agreement has been reached, and tensions remain high between the two countries.

In 1990, Egypt's total water supply from all sources was 63.5 bcm. Unfortunately, even "best case" trends show Egypt's demand rising to 69.4 bcm by the year 2000—about 9 percent more water than is available now.[43] The situation could worsen substantially if Ethiopia begins to dam the Nile's headwaters—a move that is under consideration. In 1990, Egypt was reported to have temporarily blocked an African Development Bank loan to Ethiopia in response. Egypt feared that the project would reduce downstream supplies. As Egypt's water security becomes increasingly jeopardized by new projects along the Nile, tensions will continue to build. The current secretary general of the United Nations, Boutros Boutros-Ghali, while serving as Egypt's foreign minister, made the realities of the water situation in this region crystal clear: "The only thing which could make Egypt ever go to war again would be an attempt by Ethiopia or another power to divert the Nile."[44]

While the Middle East is an obvious hotspot, there are other places in the world where water has been a source of conflict in the past or will be a source of conflict in the future. In 1947, the Indus River was used as a line of demarcation between

India and Pakistan. A year later, the Indian province of East Punjab attempted to claim sovereign rights over the water within its territory by stopping the flow into two large canals that were the source of irrigation for some Pakistani land. East Punjab's decision was the catalyst that provoked a water dispute between the two countries that almost resulted in war. The crisis was resolved 13 years later through ongoing diplomatic efforts when the two parties signed the Indus Waters Treaty, which established a joint commission and provided equitable water allocations to both countries.

Other conflicts have arisen in the Mekong River basin and in the Ganges River basin. In 1992, Thailand angered the downstream countries of Cambodia, Laos, and Vietnam when it announced plans to divert water from the Mekong River near Nong Khai/Vientiane to irrigate Thailand's arid northeast region. The Vietnamese government fears that this project will divert enough water from the river to disrupt its flow into the Mekong Delta in southern Vietnam. A reduction in flow would likely result in increased saltwater intrusion—a situation that already threatens the delta's fertile rice fields. Diplomatic efforts to date have failed to provide a solution that is acceptable to all parties involved.

The Ganges River basin conflict is between India and Bangladesh. Bangladesh officials contend that some of India's upstream activities (e.g., deforestation and the dumping of raw sewage into the Ganges River) threaten the fertile delta region where a preponderance of Bangladesh's rice crop is grown.

As populations in the Middle East and elsewhere continue to grow, water resources will be stretched to their limits. The result can only be increased conflict over this scarce resource. It is clear that riparians are willing to sound the call to arms when their source of water is threatened. Any resulting conflict will revolve around efforts to gain control of vital water-related assets.

United States Interests

Rising populations and increased levels of industrialization in the Middle East are placing enormous burdens on the limited water supplies there. As regional tensions increase, so will conflicts. Whether such conflicts can be resolved through diplomatic means remains to be seen. The closest thing to a negotiated settlement on water rights was the Johnston Plan for the Jordan River in the 1950s. Working with functional experts, Eric Johnston, chairman of the US International Advisory Board of Technical Cooperation, was able to get the riparians (Jordan, Israel, Syria, and Lebanon), traditional political adversaries, to agree on water allocations for their countries. Unfortunately, the plan was never ratified due to the parties' inability to overcome the political and ethnic barriers that divided the region. Despite this, reports indicate that Jordan and Israel are today still voluntarily abiding by the quotas set by the Johnston Plan. It is this type of "functional diplomacy" which the United States should adopt, especially as national military security concerns diminish and environmental and resource security issues move to higher importance on our foreign policy agenda. Such functional diplomacy appears to be our best bet to quell the brewing conflicts in the region.

Applied properly, functional diplomacy can lead to mutually beneficial functional projects, which help in circumventing conflicts. Projects of this nature create a social and economic interdependence between the rivals, making armed conflict contrary to their own interests. In practice, functional diplomacy creates teams of functional experts from specific problem areas and supplements them with specialists from ancillary areas. The methodology involves bringing together teams from each of the rival sides. Multilateral negotiations led by technical experts produce workable concepts for resolving regional problems. The final products of negotiations are well-defined projects designed for political approval. The US's role as a world leader, and its expertise in hydrological engineering, make it ideally qualified to serve as a trusted neutral party in the Middle East or elsewhere. The US can offer expertise and guidance in both planning solutions and implementing the agreed-upon solution. This method weaves an increasing degree of interdependency between traditional rivals that mirrors the global characteristics of the 1990s and which functions as a foundation for overcoming traditional political hurdles. In short, functional diplomacy offers active engagement targeted at the root causes of conflict.

Summary

The availability of fresh water is limited, and man's use of this vital resource constrains it further. As populations continue to grow, there will be increasing competition between nations for a larger share of the available water for agricultural, industrial, and domestic uses. The demands for larger shares of the available water will inevitably lead to conflicts. Nowhere is this more true than in the Middle East, which has one of the highest population growth rates in the world. There, the need for additional sources of water has reached crisis proportions—and ethnic and religious tensions already exist. Whether this will explode into armed conflict depends upon the willingness of the nations to seek cooperative regional solutions. The United States' role could be one of facilitator under the moniker of "functional diplomacy." The one certainty is that water is a necessity of life; without it, civilizations die.

Notes

1. *World Resources: A Report by the World Resources Institute and the International Institute for Environment and Development, 1990–1991* (New York: Oxford University Press, 1990), 23.
2. Michael Parfait, "Sharing the Wealth of Water," in "Water: The Promise, and Turmoil of North America's Fresh Water," in *National Geographic* 184, no. 5A (November 1993): 24.
3. World Resources Institute, *The 1992 Environmental Almanac* (Boston: Houghton Mifflin, 1992), 104–6.
4. *World Resources: A Report by the World Resources Institute and the International Institute for Environment and Development, 1992–1993* (New York: Oxford University Press, 1992), 160.
5. Robin Clarke, *Water: The International Crisis* (London: Earthscan Publications, 1991), 28.
6. Julio A. Barberis, *The International Groundwater Resources Law* (Rome: Food and Agricultural Organization of the United Nations, 1986).
7. Ibid.
8. *World Resources, 1992–1993*, 168.
9. *World Resources, 1990–1991*, 171.
10. *World Resources, 1992–1993*, 168.
11. Clarke, 25.
12. Hilary F. French, "Restoring the East European and Soviet Environments," in *State of the World 1991*, ed. Linda Starke (New York: W. W. Norton & Co., 1991), 97.
13. *World Resources, 1992–1993*, 167–68.

14. Clarke, 6.

15. Gerald O. Barney, *Global 2000: The Report to the President* (Washington, D.C.: Seven Locks Press, 1988), 26.

16. *World Resources, 1992–1993,* 161.

17. Malin Falkenmark, "The Massive Water Scarcity Now Threatening Africa—Why Isn't it Being Addressed?" *Ambio* 18, no. 2 (1989): 31.

18. Ibid., 115.

19. Ibid., 113.

20. *Systematic Index of International Water Resources Treaties, Declarations, Acts and Cases by Basin* (Rome: Food and Agricultural Organization of the UN, 1978), 385.

21. French, 97.

22. Robert Mandel, "Sources of International River Basin Disputes," *Conflict Quarterly* 12, no. 4 (Fall 1992): 52.

23. Mostafa Tolba, *Environment and Conflict* (London: Earthscan Publications, 1984), quoted in Clarke, 92.

24. Malin Falkenmark, "Middle East Hydropolitics: Water Scarcity and Conflicts in the Middle East," *Ambio* 18, no. 6 (1989): 350.

25. US Army Corps of Engineers, *Water in the Sand: A Survey of Middle East Water Issues* (Washington, D.C.: Government Printing Office, 1991), 4.

26. Shimon Peres, *The New Middle East* (New York: Random House, 1993), 24.

27. US Central Intelligence Agency, *Atlas of the Middle East* (Washington, D.C.: Government Printing Office, 1993), 55–63.

28. John Kolars, "The Course of Water in the Arab Middle East," *American Arab Affairs* 33 (Summer 1990): 58.

29. *Systematic Index of International Water Resources Treaties, Declarations, Acts and Cases by Basin*, 385.

30. Barberis, 42.

31. Thomas Naff and Ruth C. Matson, *Water in the Middle East* (Boulder, Colo.: Westview Press, 1984), 44.

32. John K. Cooley, "The War Over Water," *Foreign Policy* 54 (Spring 1984): 3.

33. Joseph Alpher, quoted in Nicholas B. Tatro, "Mideast Thirsts for Solution to Water Shortage," *Montgomery Advertiser*, 12 December 1993, 6F.

34. Sandra Postel, "The Politics of Water," *World Watch* 6, no. 4 (July–August 1993): 25.

35. Cooley, 26.

36. David Wishart, "An Economic Approach to Understanding Jordan Valley Water Disputes," *Middle East Review* 21 (Summer 1989): 45–53.

37. Ewan Anderson, "Water Conflict in the Middle East—A New Initiative," *Jane's Intelligence Review* 4, no. 5 (May 1992): 227.

38. Naff and Matson, 94.

39. Nicholas B. Tatro, "Mideast Thirsts for Solution to Water Shortage," *Montgomery Advertiser*, 12 December 1993, 6F.

40. Angus Hindley, "Battle Lines Drawn for Euphrates," *Middle East Economic Digest* 34, no. 1 (19 January 1990): 5.
41. US Army Corps of Engineers, 5.
42. Naff and Matson, 146.
43. Postel, 29.
44. Cooley, 6.

10

Transnational Air, Water, and Land Degradation Problems

Michael J. Savana, Jr.

> *You are interested, I know, in the prevention of war, not in our theories. . . . Yet I would like to dwell a little . . . on this destructive instinct. . . . We are led to conclude that this instinct functions in every living being, striving to work its ruin and to reduce life to its primal state of inert matter.*
>
> —Sigmund Freud
> Letter to Albert Einstein

Great minds, scholars, and lay people have tried—and they continue to try—to understand why people fight, and they have debated the specific causes of war. Beyond any normal propensity humans might have for conflict, the prospects for war in some form, emerging over apparently diminishing quality and quantity of natural resources, suffer from a dearth of popular literature. But among those who do study this problem, a bitter conflict between optimists and transformationists has emerged. *The Resourceful Earth* by Julian Simon and Herman Kahn offers an optimistic view.

> Global problems due to physical conditions . . . are always possible, but are likely to be less pressing in the future than in the past. Environmental, resource, and population stresses are diminishing, and with the passage of time will have less influence than now on the quality of human life on the planet. . . . Because of increases in knowledge, the Earth's carrying capacity has been increasing through the decades and centuries and millennia to such an extent that the term *carrying capacity* has by now no useful meaning.[1]

By contrast, ample evidence suggests that global patterns of environmental change are affecting renewable and nonrenewable resources so that conflicts at varying levels are likely to arise either directly or indirectly from those changes. The *Global 2000 Report to the President* in 1980 argued, for example:

> Environmental, resource, and population stresses are intensifying and will increasingly determine the quality of human life on the planet. . . .

> At the same time, the Earth's carrying capacity . . . is eroding. The trends reflected in the *Global 2000* suggest strongly a progressive degradation and impoverishment of the Earth's natural resource base.[2]

Without question humans will fight over diminishing natural resources. Substantial precedent already exists for such occurrences. The archaeological record has described disputes over water resources when, 5,000 years ago, the Tigris River and Euphrates River Valley was used both as a reason for conflict and as a weapon. In one example, the two city-states of Umma and Lagash fought a 100-year war over fertile soils. The contestants either destroyed or diverted the water irrigation systems to effect intended results. Current tensions in the same region center around the attempts of Turkey to harness the Euphrates to produce electric power and irrigation.[3] Further evidence might easily be gleaned throughout history.

This chapter explores the prospect for future conflicts resulting from increasing competition for diminishing air, land, and water resources. For the US military planner, this question might become a critical one. Although US forces might not engage directly in conflicts over resources, they will most likely contend with nations who are so engaged. Viewed previously by many as an ephemeral problem, the United States has for more than a decade signalled warnings of the potential problems related to resource and environmental issues. In 1980 the *Global Report to the President*, stated that "serious stresses involving population, resources, and the environment are clearly visible ahead. Despite greater material output, the world's people will be poorer in many ways than they are today."[4] Regardless of the view one might take, one must understand the state of the *global problematique*, the interconnected matrix of resource and population problems which might be the cause of conflict.[5]

Scarcity and the Resource Paradigm

This chapter also examines the interrelationships and critical issues revolving around what one might consider a trilogy of cause and effect comprised of population pressure, resource depletion and degradation, and scarcity. Each of these linkages are causal of and affected by each other. This trilogy represents a parasequential, deadly spiral with each component directly impacting upon the others.[6] Increasing population densities in a region can have a detrimental cascading effect and result in greater resource damage and depletion that make these assets more quantitatively and qualitatively scarce.[7] The resulting scarcity can mean maldistribution, increased competition, social unrest, population migration, and conflict, with the cycle beginning again in another region. This observation holds true because air, land, and water resources and their social effects do not respect the cartographic boundaries human activity imposed upon the landscape and because each place where people live is endowed with finite resources. Regardless of the sequence of the interplay between the three factors, the result is always greater scarcity and increased competition, a sure source of conflict.[8]

Numerous models depict the interrelationships between people and resources. Three such models can demonstrate how relative abundance influences populations so that adjustments must be made either in the resources themselves or in the density of the population for the region. In Von Liebig's model, for example, water, food, space, heat, energy, and nonrenewable resources (coal and minerals) represent a "resource space." The resource space is the relative "areal" element necessary to sustain that population at its present level. When one or a combination of the resources falls below a minimum level, someone either must replenish or substitute the resource, or the population must change either its consumption rate or size. From this model a fundamental "law of minimum" holds that the resource necessary for survival that is *in shortest supply* limits the size of a population.[9] This law simply means that a population might have ample space into which it can expand, but a lack of available resources usually inhibits population growth and can even precipitate migration to other regions.

William B. Wood's "Provisional Forced Migration Model" offers a broader scope of the law of minimum. It captures ethnic/religious/tribal aspects, political instability, resource availability, and other elements.[10] This model portrays the push-and-pull interplay between elements which cause groups to migrate and illustrates the negative impact upon the regions into which the migration takes place. This model is particularly important because people who have historically fled resource impoverished areas have usually sought less-inhabited regions in which to set up new communities. Finding such areas today presents special challenges and therefore offers increased chances for clashes.

Variations on a model developed by Thomas F. Homer-Dixon, Jeffrey H. Boutwell, and George W. Rathjens also describe the cause and effect of scarcity. In their model, a "scarcity of renewable resources" inextricably links "political and economic factors" and "social conflict." It depicts three origins of scarcity that result from the manner in which the two major social elements interact. The critical aspect of this theory describes first how, in some cases, population growth alone will set in motion social stresses, leading to conflict. Second, it describes how increasing population usually results in scarcity as in the division of a flow of water. Population pressures also can cause a shift in the concentration of resources into the hands of a privileged few. In combination, the depletion, deterioration, and maldistribution of air, land, and water resources are accurately described as causal processes leading to violence.[11]

Earlier in this essay, we introduced an optimistic view of the earth's ability to sustain the demands for resource use. However, more recent analyses show that the rate of deterioration of air, land, and water assets in some regions is accelerating, and that "sustainable development"—the ability for the earth to support economic and social systems' attempts to increase the quality of life—is in a precarious state.[12]

As the world approaches the twenty-first century, war planners often conceal or dilute their motives for a war or armed conflict with other more apparent motives. In some cases groups in contention might not understand the role played by environmental and resource issues in their conflict. The more obvious motive might appear to be economic and social disputes when in fact the underlying causes have a direct link to hunger, deprivation, and scarcity caused by soil depletion or desertification.[13] A report analyzing conflicts after World War II, which itself was a war over resources,[14] has revealed that between 1989–1992 there occurred 82 conflicts, of which 35 were listed as wars resulting in 1,000 deaths or more in a single year.[15] Classic interstate conflicts occurred in only four cases: Iraq-Kuwait, India-Pakistan, Mauritania-Senegal, and USA-Panama. When analyzed relative to their levels of activity or combat, the greatest number of conflicts occurred in developing nations in Asia and Africa, with the Middle East, Central and South America, and Europe following, respectively. This study conducted by the Department of Peace and Conflict Research at Upsala College categorized the motives of these conflicts into only two broad areas—government and territory. Because this study failed to analyze the issue of territory further, it is difficult to conclude that resources played a role in those conflicts. Nonetheless, the issue of resource scarcity is real, pandemic, and frequently one of several contributing motives for conflict.

An important aspect of the resource issue focuses on understanding whether anger over the state of their resource base has provoked some people to engage in some form of hostilities. In a global survey conducted in 24 nations representing a broad range of geographical regions and economies, the Health of the Planet (HOP) survey represented the single largest such survey ever conducted.[16] Surprisingly, observers view the deterioration of resources and the environment in general as serious throughout the full spectrum of respondents in developing and in lesser developed countries. Consequently, it is difficult to show a linkage in all cases, between wars in which resources were the principle motive for conflict, and the level of concern of the combatants over the state of their respective environments. It is clear, however, that within such regions as Asia and Africa, where the preponderance of conflicts persisted, developed and developing countries have acknowledged the poor condition of their environments with about equal concern.

The Third World Context

From a geographical perspective, we recognize that much of the conflict over air, land, and water will take place in large part or at least emerge from the developing or third world nations. Three recurring patterns in these regions support this view: population growth, deteriorating environmental conditions, and economic ties to resources.

Populations and Demands for Water

The third world currently represents the greatest source of population growth. Estimators predict that the global village will contain between eight and 10 billion people sometime between the years 2020 and 2050.[17] Despite poor living conditions and high mortality rates, annual population growth rates in the third world have more than doubled from less than 1 percent at the first half of this century to over 2 percent since 1950.[18] Currently, 80 to 90 percent of the globe's population growth has occurred in the third world, with the greatest concentration in their urban areas, at a growth rate of 3.8 percent or doubling every 18 years.[19] In the context of strained natural resources, it is alarming that although it took thousands of years to produce the first billion humans around the year 1800, it took only the last 13 years to gain the fifth one billion inhabitants.

Nowhere has population growth had as great an effect on water as it did in the Middle East.[20] In this region, ideological, religious, and geographic disputes go hand in hand with water-related conflicts.[21] For example, 97 percent of Egypt's water comes from the Nile River, with 95 percent of the Nile's runoff coming from outside Egypt. Because of Egypt's alarmingly high population growth, that country struggles to sustain a population rapidly approaching 60 million—gaining an additional million every nine months. So great has been the potential for conflict over the Nile's water that Egypt and Sudan, from whose northern border the Nile enters Egypt, signed a treaty in 1959 to help reduce the risk of conflict. Note, however, that none of the other seven nations of the Nile basin signed that treaty.

Water continues to serve as a major focus of peace talks in the Middle East. In 1994 Jordan won rights over land and water in a Jordan-Israel peace treaty. Second, only to the control of weapons in the area, the successful negotiation of shared or leased farmlands, fresh water, and joint construction of dams and desalinization facilities was achieved. However, no treaty has resolved the control and management of groundwater aquifers of the Jordan, Euphrates, and Nile river basins that serve vast territories. The path to peaceful resolution of conflicts concerning water resources is fraught with danger. Turkey, for example, still declares that it has no greater obligation to give away water than Saudi Arabia has to give away its oil. The future paints a pallid picture of water consumption. Global water use doubled between 1940 and 1980 and could double again by 2000. Because 80 countries with 40 percent of the world's population already suffer serious water shortage-related problems, competition for water for industry and domestic consumption will continue to grow.[22]

Deteriorating Environmental Conditions

The third world also represents the worst state of resource consumption, environmental deterioration, and inadequate governmental controls. Even Russia has been guilty of committing government-sponsored "ecocide." Well after the collapse of communism, veils of pollutants still obscured vast areas. Russian fishing boats operating from the port of Kuril'sk into the Sea of Okhotsk bribed local governments to gain access to illegal waters, thus further depleting food resources; and accidental industrial discharges accounted for 2,000 cases of almost irreparable damage to air, land, and water resources. Decades of negligence in the former Soviet Union have resulted in contaminated soil and impure drinking water to the extent that 75 percent of the water currently is unfit for human consumption.[23] The Aral Sea disaster, where the diversion of the Anu Darya and Syr Darya rivers reduced the volume of the sea by 60 percent, has affected vast regions. This reduction has directly resulted in hotter summers and colder winters, with desertification leading to large-scale migration and social unrest.

Additionally, the rate of tropical deforestation which directly impacts soil and water quality has rapidly accelerated in just the past 10 years in Central and South America, India, Indonesia, Southeast Asia, Asia, and Africa. Despite their delicately balanced ecosystems and invaluable sources of revenue, tropical forests still face large-scale destruction, as populations seek to gain additional farming lands. Tensions between Rwandan and Zairian forces, for example, escalated to guerrilla war in January 1995 over "anarchical acts of deforestation, banditry, and pollution," according to reports from Kinshasa. Similarly, as a result of large-scale mechanized farming, a new dimension has been added to an old conflict in the Sudan, where conflicts have arisen between various classes of farmers who clash over cultivable or fresh grazing land. Poor Sudanese governmental controls have resulted in schemes for land distribution or controls that go unmonitored, resulting in unequal distribution of highly valued agricultural assets.[24] Similarly, in the Philippines, land distribution problems contribute directly to guerrilla warfare. Poor land reforms by local and national governments resulted in massive devastation of forests in a few decades, thereby producing floods, reduction of fresh water, soil erosion, and diminished agricultural productivity. These reforms directly strained political, economic, and social systems and contributed to social unrest.[25]

Amidst the great interest over the US and United Nations involvement in Somalia, a major underlying cause of internal conflict originated in the 100-year-long migration of Somali clans from nomadic grazing regions that had become overpopulated and the soils depleted. A struggle to control the nation's best remaining farmland could be at the heart of conflict in that region according to the *Christian Science Monitor*. One hundred degrees to the east, rebel forces operating in the highlands of Bougainville in the Solomon Islands are engaged in a war with Australia, in which a struggle for independence conceals anger over pollution of rivers, poisoning of fish, acid rain, and dead water fowl. Simultaneously, conflict festers in the region among four different groups following the shutdown of a highly profitable, Australian-owned copper mine by the Bougainville Revolutionary Army (BRA) as a direct result of the adverse impact of years of Australian mining operations on the environment. These cases represent clear examples in which air, land, and water assets represent economic assets domestically and globally.

Economic Factors

In the context of current conflicts in the regions of greatest diminishing resources, the future planner should count on committing forces for a third and instrumental reason. This planner views natural resources, specifically land and the things it produces, as economic assets and sources of power.[26] Many of those resources represent substantial portions of trade between the United States and the third world in the forms of ores, minerals, textiles, and agricultural products. Peter J. Schraeder states cogently, "The Third World is an increasingly important focal point for US trade and investment."[27] He points out that the US Department of Commerce revealed that in 1988 imports from the third world amounted to $164.2 billion (37.2 percent) out of a total US imports of $441.3 billion. Concurrently, US exports to the third world during that same year amounted to $114.5 billion (35 percent of total US exports of $320 billion). Considering also that US private investment in the third world exceeded $78 billion (yielding almost 32 percent of all US profit from overseas private investments), observers can assume that US interests are present at least in part in third world regions, which present the greatest potential for conflict over natural resources.

Recently, overfishing has been recognized to pose serious dangers to national economies. Although not included in the catalogue of developing nations, Britain and Argentina have disputes over fishing rights in the South Pacific. Such other nations as Japan, South Korea, Canada, Poland, Iceland, Spain, and the United States could see fishery-related disputes increase as they harvest fish beyond the level of sustainable yields of this resource that is both a source of sustenance and financial gain.[28] Some of these countries already have been involved in hostilities over fishing practices.

It might not be obvious, but the atmosphere as a resource is an economic entity. Although skeptics might claim that global warming is far from a proven fact, substantial economic costs imposed on many nations already impact the atmosphere. The wealthy nations, with less than one-eighth of the world's population, produce roughly one-half of such emissions as carbon dioxide, sulfur dioxide, and chlorofluorocarbons. Because climate models predict future deterioration of the general state of the atmosphere and the ozone layer, resulting in global warming and climate change, policymakers must accept these developments as a "clear and present danger"[29] and take drastic measures to prevent future damage. The potential for conflict lies in the substantial economic implications of the corrective actions. Pressure has been applied on nations to reduce gasoline and energy use and also industrial fossil fuel emissions. Although most policies to reduce these kinds of emissions are domestic, they have important international implications. Increases in fuel taxes, increased electricity costs, "pollution taxes," and research and development costs to search for alternative energy and innovative industrial production will bring with them enormous economic strains. Within the context of the third world, many developing countries insist that they literally cannot afford "green consciousness."[30]

The environment and its resources comprise only one of several variables from which political, economic, and social conflicts might arise.[31] A number of alarming global military trends leaning towards a "deadly convergence" also exist,[32] which, when overlain with the third world, portend US military involvement in areas where the environment already is one aspect of the conflict. First, the conventional arms trade has greatly expanded in the third world, resulting in the import of record numbers of weapons into the hands of those already predisposed to conflict over resources. Sudan offers an example. Second, almost nondeterrable proliferation of nuclear weapons technology in the third world challenges attempts to achieve regional stability. From these factors, the means exist for countries to at least attempt to achieve resource security in the near term where previously the opportunity did not exist. This security is important because there is an increased likelihood of the use of military force by third world nations to ensure access to diminishing resources, especially in the face of increasing environmental, population, and economic pressures.[33] In short, an adage for the next century might be a revelation from Patricia M. Mische: "Ecological security is a prerequisite for peace; and peace is a prerequisite for ecological security."

To summarize, we may envision the potential for conflict over resources at varying levels. Rapidly escalating population growth will make air, land, and water resources more scarce by either degrading or depleting them. The scarcity of life-sustaining resources has already resulted in a phenomenon of large-scale forced migrations or "environmental refugees."[34] This real problem is represented by noting that between 1984 and 1985, for example, 10 million Africans fled their homes.

Although there is a long history of natural nomadic movement throughout Africa, much of this modern transmigration emanates directly from deteriorating resources. For example, in the case in Somalia, members of the Gosha clan have been literally dispossessed of their arable land. Although wars have always compelled people to leave their homes, analysts can make the case that people compelled to abandon their homes to seek new resources, could, in turn, cause war themselves.

Humankind has imposed upon the face of the earth lines of political demarcation that don't necessarily coincide with the needs of the people who live within these regions. Migration across recognized borders exert social pressures that result in new conflict and exacerbate the cycle of the resource trilogy.[35]

Conclusion—Patterns for Cooperation

Preliminary records show that the world is experiencing the early phases of an epoch fostering negotiation and cooperation over environmental and resource issues. It is almost impossible to predict how global resource changes will intensify specific social conflicts or even spawn new forms of conflict unimaginable today.[36] Unless met head-on, the problems discussed in this chapter most likely will instigate significant changes in ideologies and national interests, and increase the probability for conflict both within and across national borders. For the near term, however, if recent trends continue, the majority of conflicts arising over diminishing air, land, and water resources will take place mostly within developing nations and will predominate in the form of intrastate clashes caused by people migrating in great numbers.

Regardless of the growing scarcity of resources in certain regions, an international dimension to air, land, and water usage demands accountability for the state of those resources on the part of nations who strive to become and remain players in global markets. For example, the United Nations Conference on Environment and Development (UNCED) and the agreements signed in Rio de Janeiro, Brazil, in 1992, created at least one new international institution. The result, Earth Summit 92, helped to clarify critical issues regarding the deterioration of resources globally, helped to institutionalize a systematic assessment of the *global problematique*, and built the groundwork for resource and conflict management and cooperation. Specifically, the agreements addressed atmospheric, land, and water resources and established economic aid and assistance mechanisms to supplement developing nations to resolve the myriad of environmental problems within and adjacent to their borders.

The bottom line describes the need for exhaustive research to assess the impact of resource regulations and offers alternatives to regulation and national monitoring to understand which strategies work in which situations.[37] International legislative and regulatory coalitions will be critical to and essential for national actors to manage resource damage that transcend national borders and reduce conflicts over future resources. Finally, in most cases, no single legislative approach will be effective unless governments and politicians grasp the critical linkages between air, land, and water resources and social, economic, and political concerns. Resource damage occurs regionally; however, coalitions must develop diplomatic means that reflect the reality of the economic, political, military, and societal costs of the impact of growing populations on the earth's finite resources. They must enforce these means transnationally.

Notes

1. Julian Simon and Herman Kahn, *The Resourceful Earth: A Response to Global 2000* (Oxfordshire, N.Y.: B. Blackwell, 1984).
2. *Global 2000 Report to the President* (Washington, D.C.: Government Printing Office, 1980), 1.
3. George D. Moffett III, "Downstream Fears Feed Tensions," *Christian Science Monitor*, 13 March 1990, 4.
4. Dennis Pirages, *Global Technopolitics: The International Politics of Technology and Resources* (Pacific Grove, Calif.: Brooks Company Publishers, 1988), 39.
5. Ibid., 29.
6. Gro Harlem Brundtland, *Our Common Future, The World Commission on Environment and Development* (New York, N.Y.: Oxford University Press, 1987), 291.
7. Patricia M. Mische, "Peace and Ecological Security," *Peace Review* 6, no. 3 (1994): 275-84 .
8. Brundtland, 291.

9. Dennis Pirages, *The New Context for International Relations, Global Ecopolitics* (Duxbury Press Series in International Studies, 1978), 15.

10. William B. Wood, "Forced Migration: Local Conflicts and International Dilemmas," *Annals of the Association of American Geographers* 84 (4 December 1994): 613.

11. Thomas F. Homer-Dixon, Jeffrey H. Boutwell, and George W. Rathjens, "Environmental Change and Violent Conflict," *Scientific American* (February 1993): 38.

12. Wood, 54.

13. Mische, 276.

14. Ibid., 275.

15. Ibid.

16. Riley E. Dunlap, George H. Gallup, Jr., and Alec M. Gallup, "Of Global Concern," *Environment* (November 1993): 8.

17. Michael S. Teitelbaum, "The Population Threat," *Foreign Affairs* (Winter 1992–93): 64.

18. Ibid.

19. Brad Knickerbocker, "World Bank Turns From Saving Trees to Saving Cities," *Christian Science Monitor*, 27 September 1994, 13.

20. Gleick, 6.

21. Ibid.

22. Brundtland, 292.

23. Vladimir Kotov and Elena Nikitina, "Russia in Transition, Obstacles to Environmental Protection," *Environment* 35, no. 10 (December 1993): 11.

24. Mohamed Suliman, "Civil War in the Sudan: From Ethnic to Ecological Conflict," *The Ecologist* 23, no. 3 (May/June 1993): 104.

25. Mische, 277.

26. Gleick, 7.

27. Peter J. Schraeder, "'It's the Third World Stupid!' Why the Third World Should Be the Priority of the Clinton Administration," *Third World Quarterly* 14, no. 2 (1993): 216.

28. Brundtland, 294.

29. "The Role of the United States in a Changing World, Choices for the 21st Century" (Providence, R.I.: Center for Foreign Policy Development at Brown University, n.d.), 100.

30. Ibid., 103.

31. Homer-Dixon, Boutwell, and Rathjens, 38.

32. Schraeder, 217.

33. Mische, 281.

34. Brundtland, 291.

35. Homer-Dixon, Boutwell, and Rathjens, 40.

36. Paul C. Stern, Oran R. Young, and Daniel Druckmand, "Global Environmental Change, Understanding the Human Dimension," *Report on the Commission on the Behavioral and Social Sciences and Education* (National Academy Press, 1992), 247.

37. Ibid., 150.

PART IV

MILITARY-STRATEGIC ISSUES

11

Nuclear Conflict and Nonproliferation Issues in the Twenty-First Century

Robert H. Hendricks

Current United States national security strategy states that "a critical priority for the United States is to stem the proliferation of nuclear weapons and other weapons of mass destruction."[1] Nonproliferation and the prevention of nuclear conflict will continue as a major security issue into the next decade. This essay examines the strengths and weaknesses of the nonproliferation effort, the current and projected world nuclear environment, possible conflict scenarios and their impact on regional and global security, United States interests and efforts for conflict prevention, and finally, the US military and nonproliferation in the twenty-first century.

Background

Since the invention and subsequent employment of atomic weapons in 1945, United States national security strategy developed a strong focus on preventing further use of atomic/nuclear weapons. This strategy involved two primary components: deterrence and nonproliferation. Deterrence sought to prevent the use of nuclear weapons through the maintenance of a nuclear strike force capable of surviving an attack and carrying out an unacceptable nuclear reprisal upon the enemy. The most likely "enemy" was the Union of Soviet Socialist Republics (USSR). Nonproliferation, on the other hand, attempted to deny nuclear weapons and technology to non-nuclear states, thereby excluding other nations from becoming potential nuclear-armed enemies.

The Soviet response to US nuclear strategy was remarkably similar. Perceiving US nuclear forces as a threat, the Soviet Union developed its own deterrent nuclear force while also actively enforcing nonproliferation. Paradoxically, the two nations competed in a nuclear arms race while attempting to stem the production of nuclear weapons in the rest of the world. While the success of deterrence as the sole factor in preventing nuclear war is arguable, the fact remains that nuclear weapons have not been used in battle since World War II. Nonproliferation efforts cannot claim an equal degree of success.

The Nonproliferation Treaty

Experts describe attempts to stop the proliferation of nuclear weapons simultaneously in terms of both success and failure. The hallmark of the nonproliferation effort is the Non-Proliferation Treaty (NPT), concluded in 1968. It remains in force today with over 160 countries agreeing to its objectives and obligations. According to the US Arms Control and Disarmament Agency (ACDA), the NPT is "one of the great success stories of arms control . . . it has prevented the spread of nuclear weapons, promoted technical cooperation in the peaceful uses of nuclear energy, and served as an essential basis for the reduction of nuclear weapons."[2] The treaty recognizes five nations as nuclear weapons states (NWS): the US, USSR, People's Republic of China (PRC), Great Britain, and France.[3] Since that time, despite dire predictions to the contrary, only one additional nation, India, has overtly joined the nuclear powers with the testing of a nuclear device in May 1974.[4] In "promoting technical cooperation in the peaceful uses of nuclear energy," the NPT has been extremely successful. Today, nearly 500 civil nuclear power plants are in operation or are near completion in 32 countries.[5] Finally, the number of nuclear warheads worldwide has declined since 1986.[6] These facts provide the basis for arguing the success of the NPT and the overall nonproliferation effort.[7] Unfortunately, they do not tell the whole story.

While India is the only former nonnuclear weapons state (NNWS) to explode a nuclear device, experts believe numerous nations throughout the world possess nuclear arsenals or can produce weapons within short time periods. Pakistan and Israel may actually have nuclear weapons.[8] With the dissolution of the Soviet Union, three nations—Belarus, Kazakhstan, and Ukraine—joined Russia as de facto nuclear weapons states.[9]

On 24 March 1993 South African president F. W. de Klerk announced that his country had secretly developed a small nuclear arsenal (seven weapons) between 1974 and 1989 and subsequently had destroyed it by late 1991.[10] Experts also believe that Brazil, Argentina, Iran, and—despite concerted world efforts—Iraq and North Korea have almost achieved nuclear weapons production capability. Additionally, they view Syria, Algeria, and Libya as "aspiring members" of the nuclear "club."[11] Currently, the technology exists for highly developed industrial states to develop nuclear weapons within a very short time, creating a new category of "virtual" nuclear powers.[12] This category includes Japan, Germany, Italy, Switzerland, Canada, South Korea, and Taiwan—all of which observers suspect of conducting nuclear weapons research during the cold war; even Sweden has kept "the nuclear option open."[13] Despite the considerable effort expended to prevent the spread of nuclear weapons, proliferation is rapidly becoming a reality.

The history of the nonproliferation effort demonstrates that nations (or elements within nations) with nuclear weapons technology will share their secrets and equipment under the right circumstances or for the right price. They lack the will and/or capability to restrict access to nuclear weapons technologies and expertise. Additionally, because nations no longer require nuclear tests to ensure the reliability of a nuclear weapon, countries can now develop these weapons while denying their existence, copying the so-called Israeli model. Finally, the nonproliferation regime's inspection agency, the International Atomic Energy Agency (IAEA), does not have appropriate funding or personnel to maintain a high degree of effectiveness. The favorable report following inspection of Iraqi nuclear facilities prior to the Gulf War illustrates this point. Once revealed, the total extent of Iraq's nuclear weapons development program shocked the world.[14]

As noted already, the NPT regime has not achieved the ideal of restricting nuclear weapons to the original five NWS. However, failure to attain that goal should not detract from what the regime has accomplished. The NPT and the nonproliferation regime, which it generated, restricted proliferation well below expected levels, thus reducing the likelihood of nuclear conflict or accidental nuclear detonation. Additionally, it established and spread a global majority opinion against the development and proliferation of nuclear weapons. This negative attitude towards nuclear weapons acquisition, some feel, encouraged South Korea, Taiwan, Brazil, Argentina, and others to abandon their weapons programs.[15] However, the fact of nuclear proliferation remains. Nuclear proliferation, combined with the dissolution of the Soviet Union and the sudden shift to a multipolar world, necessitated a US nuclear proliferation policy revision. To see where adjustments should be made, we must first look at the world nuclear situation and the results of proliferation.

A Case for Stability

In addition to the original five NWS, observers believe that six states—Belarus, Ukraine, Kazakhstan, Israel, India, and Pakistan—either possess nuclear arsenals or possess them beyond the developmental stages and thus represent "unofficial" NWS. A strong case can be made that in each instance the likelihood of actual use of these weapons is extremely low, and that, indeed, each nation's arsenal represents a "stabilizing" case for proliferation.[16] In Ukraine, Kazakhstan, and Belarus, retaining their nuclear arsenals eases fears of Russian imperial aspirations. In a similar manner, Israel's nuclear arsenal (possibly acquired after the June 1967 war) has deterred Arab aggression for more than 20 years, was a factor in ending the 1973 Yom Kippur War, and set the stage for the Camp David and follow-on Middle East Peace accords.[17] Even in India and Pakistan, where long-standing disputes constantly threaten to explode, the existence, or implied existence, of nuclear weapons provides a brake to the escalation of regional disputes toward major war.[18] In these cases, recognition of the catastrophic results of nuclear conflict, both to the attacked and the attacker, provides a stabilizing influence in a region of potential war. Therefore, when determining US proliferation policy revisions, policymakers should recognize instances in which nuclear proliferation proves to be a stabilizing factor.

The "Rogues"

This section discusses the latest group of aspiring nuclear weapons states. These nations—North Korea, Iran, Iraq, and Libya—are either developing nuclear weapons or are attempting to acquire them. Two of them—North Korea and Iran—if not currently in possession of weapons, are certainly close.[19] Much of the Western world perceives these nations as "rogue states" or "irrational actors," who plan to use nuclear weapons for retribution or terror. A brief look from their perspective proves enlightening. North Korea, for example, has been on the edge of war with South Korea and its powerful ally, the United States, for 40 years. North Korea maintains a huge army at the expense of its economic development in response to the perceived threat from the south. Threatened by US nuclear weapons, it relied on its Chinese and Soviet allies for nuclear support. Now the Soviet Union no longer exists, and the Chinese are trading with the South Koreans. North Korean leadership—confronted with an external threat from its southern enemy, an internal threat due to increasing economic hardship, and the knowledge of what relaxing communist standards meant for Soviet and Warsaw Pact leadership—may be addressing the problem in the only manner it sees as "rational."[20]

Similarly, nuclear desires by Iran and Iraq can be seen in light of their regional aspirations for power, the security issues posed by their eight-year war with each other, and the more recent disaster Iraq experienced with US conventional warfighting capability. We can even rationalize Muammar Qaddafi's desires for nuclear weapons in terms of his aspirations for regional leadership and as a deterrent to US or Israeli attacks. Such countries as Libya and Iran, as the next nuclear weapons states, are moving toward nuclear armament for the same primary reasons their predecessors developed the bomb: security and power in a nuclear-armed world.

These states are making the nuclear decision fully aware of the political and economic costs involved. To classify such a decision as irrational, or a particular state as a rogue, is nonproductive and a demonstration of ethnocentrism. The United States' policy on nonproliferation must evolve to deal with the reality of additional nuclear weapons states. In the words of

William C. Martel and William T. Pendley, "Each nation is the best judge of its security interests and the power necessary to protect those interests. . . . Neither the United States nor any other state is in a position to condemn another state's decision to possess nuclear weapons."[21] The nuclear decision is not in and of itself irrational, nor is the addition of a nuclear state automatically destabilizing. It is instead reality, and it will be in the next century.

Nonstate Actors

The possibility that a state which professes support for terrorism might give a nuclear weapon to a nonstate actor such as a drug or terrorist organization does, however, represent a potential for destabilization. Three concerns are associated with that potential.[22] First, once turned over to a nonstate actor, tracking a nuclear device and identifying who controls it present an extremely difficult problem. Second, nonstate actors are not governed by the constraints of physical territory, borders or "accouterments of sovereign statehood."[23] Hence, fears of retaliation have less impact on their actions. Third, in their total dedication to a cause, some of these groups will use whatever means is at their disposal and may choose nuclear weapons as the ultimate weapons of terror. Nonproliferation policy should, therefore, target nonstate organizations primarily. That there are no cases to date where states turned over dangerous technologies to a terrorist organization has mitigated somewhat the fear of proliferation to nonstate actors.[24] The states recognize the leverage such weapons would give a nonstate actor, leverage which it could easily apply against the technology provider.

The US works diligently to keep nuclear weapons from states which support terrorist groups. If allowed to possess nuclear capability, such states as Algeria, Iran, and Libya might then disperse nuclear weapons to nonstate actors. However, the US should realize, in light of the examples of India, Pakistan, Israel, and South Africa, that there is little we or our allies can do to prevent a determined nation from entering the ranks of the nuclear-armed states. Three facts support this statement. First, nuclear technology has existed for more than

50 years. The information on building nuclear weapons is widely available; especially available are large numbers of trained personnel. Second, nations determined to develop nuclear weapons readily circumvent IAEA controls established by the NPT to control fissile materials. Third, the collapse of the Soviet Union has introduced the prospect of readily available fissile materials, nuclear scientists and technicians, and the possibility of selling nuclear weapons to the highest bidder.[25] These facts should provide the impetus for reshaping US policy in the direction of managing "the inevitable process of proliferation toward the creation of stability."[26]

The Future Threat

A new proliferation policy must anticipate possible nuclear conflict scenarios in the coming century. Four regions present potential for such scenarios within the next decade. They include the Russian Federation and surrounding nations of the Commonwealth of Independent States (CIS), South Asia, the Middle East, and the Korean peninsula.

The uncertain status of the Russian Federation, in possession of the world's largest nuclear arsenal, poses a major potential for future conflict. Recent fighting in Chechnya symbolizes ethnic tension throughout the country which some observers forecast as the precursor to all-out civil war. One report highlighted over 200 ethnoterritorial conflicts in the former Soviet Union from 1990 to 1993.[27] The potential for large-scale civil war in a country with over 9,000 strategic and 20,000 tactical nuclear weapons holds cause for world concern.[28] A second scenario within the same region involves the organized criminal element in Russia and the questionable accountability and control of the former Soviet tactical nuclear weapons inventory. FBI Director Louis Freeh called the possibility of a nuclear arms sale by members of the Russian mafia to a terrorist group "the greatest long-term threat to the security of the United States."[29] Third, ethnic tensions combined with a lagging economy could bring to power a political extremist like Vladimir Zhirinovsky, who speaks of restoring Russia's imperial frontiers of 1900 through war if necessary.[30] In his campaign speeches he has threatened nuclear retaliation against the US, Britain, and France; to attack Germany, Japan, and Pakistan with nuclear or other forces; and to blow nuclear radiation into Lithuania.[31] Unfortunately, the conditions which are making men like Zhirinovsky popular are not confined to Russia.

Religious and ethnic unrest also account for political turmoil in South Asia. According to Robert L. Gallucci, assistant secretary of state for political and military affairs, "If a nuclear weapon is to be detonated in anger in the next five years . . . the most likely place would be South Asia."[32] Since Pakistan's independence in 1947, the two countries have fought three wars. The latest was fought in April 1990 to contest the northern Indian province of Kashmir. Created from India to form an Islamic homeland, Pakistan suffers from a severe case of insecurity over the likelihood of an Indian attempt to reunite the subcontinent.[33] According to one author, expressing anti-Indian sentiment is one of the few issues that holds Pakistan together.[34] India, on the other hand, faces potential nuclear threats from both Pakistan and China. A "humiliating" defeat at the hands of China in 1962 fueled India's interest in developing nuclear weapons. An invasion of Pakistan by India, which may occur despite the leadership's attempts to contain the conflict,[35] could escalate to a nuclear exchange should Pakistan feel overwhelmed.[36] Alternatively, India, fearing China's intervention on Pakistan's behalf, might feel obligated to use nuclear weapons to offset Chinese conventional superiority, to which China most likely would respond in kind. This is India's worst case scenario, which, combined with internal ethnic divisions that led to the assassination of Prime Minister Indira Gandhi by her Sikh bodyguards, give credence to Gallucci's concern about this region's stability.

A third region which could erupt in a conflict involving nuclear weapons is the Middle East. The Gulf War demonstrated US and international resolve to secure their perceived vital interests in the area. Armed with nuclear weapons, would Saddam Hussein feel emboldened to reattempt annexation of Kuwait or determine to use a nuclear weapon as an ultimate solution to his difficulties with the Kurds? Should border disputes reignite a war between Iraq and Iran? and Would one or both nations resort to nuclear missiles given the option? War could break out in the region over control of critical natural resources, specifically oil and, less publicized but even more valuable in this arid region, water. Finally, ideological issues dividing Islamic fundamentalist and moderate pro-Western Arab states could bring civil or regional war and the likelihood of international involvement.

A number of events also could precipitate nuclear conflict on the Korean peninsula. A conceivable scenario involves North Korean leadership, in a last-gasp effort to maintain power, initiating an all-out war against the south. If the United States still maintained troops there, such an attack would demand a US response. Whether the US became immediately involved, the conflict certainly would demand the attention of such regional powers as China, Russia, and Japan. In advance of such an event, over the next decade South Korea and Japan may respond to North Korea's nuclear weapons development with their own programs and may have the means to retaliate in kind to a North Korean attack. A decision by either Russia or China to side with North Korea could ignite a global nuclear war.

A Nonproliferation Policy for the Twenty-First Century

The scenarios described above involve the currently known or currently suspected nuclear powers and could occur tomorrow as easily as they might 10 years from now. One essential factor is the certainty of exponential improvements in technology and informational access making nuclear weapons and technology far simpler to acquire.[37] Therefore, sometime in the next century, possibly within the next 10 years, most major international conflicts will include the possibility of nuclear escalation. US policymakers must face this dichotomy in shaping nonproliferation policy for the future—nuclear weapons will have a stabilizing influence on world and regional conflict, yet they present a horrendous potential in any conflict which may take place. In light of this dichotomy, the following actions should modernize our nuclear proliferation policy.

First, we should not abandon the current NPT regime. Despite the weaknesses it presents, the current regime continues to offer an ideal goal. The United States should continue to pursue the goals of the NPT and aid in strengthening the nonproliferation effort. The US also should vote and campaign for the indefinite extension of the NPT, or at least seek an additional 25-year extension.[38] This extension—combined with mutual (or in Britain's case by default, since it conducts its tests in the US) agreement by the NWS to an agreement on the Comprehensive Test Ban Treaty in 1996—would demonstrate a step toward NWS compliance with treaty provisions calling for disarmament.[39] Additionally, the United States should make a pledge of no first use of nuclear weapons similar to the pledges made by China and Israel.[40] This declaration could be made unilaterally or put forward for vote as a UN resolution banning first use of nuclear weapons. Additional UN action should include the development of a course of action to be taken in response to any nation violating the first use of nuclear weapons. The UN should hold personally and criminally liable civilian and military leaders who permit or direct the first use of a nuclear weapon. It should hold states financially liable for reparations.

Second, while putting greater emphasis on the NPT, the new policy should de-emphasize the importance of nuclear weapons as a measure of prestige/bargaining chip by recognizing the sovereign right of any nation to choose to construct or possess nuclear weapons. The new policy should monitor closely efforts at nuclear weapons development or acquisition and report those efforts to UN members. The findings should prompt neither condemnation and military threats nor an overindulgent economic effort to "buy" the state back to NNWS status with economic incentives. Additionally, the new policy should consider admitting some NNWS, particularly those extensively involved in peace support efforts, to the UN Security Council.

Third, bilateral efforts to reduce the nuclear inventories of the US and Russia should continue according to Strategic Arms Reduction Treaty (START) agreements. The agreements should make every effort to aid Kazakhstan and Ukraine with the destruction of their weapons and safe storage of nuclear material. They should offer technical and financial assistance for the safe storage and dismantling of Russian weapons as well. At the same time, US officials should ensure verification of Russian compliance with treaty arrangements.

Fourth, actions being taken to counter the criminal/terrorist threat are on track and should receive the full support of NPT members. These actions require full international cooperation between the police and intelligence agencies of all states producing fissile material. The establishment of a Moscow office of the Federal Bureau of Investigation appropriately demonstrates US commitment.[41] Additionally, research and development efforts directed at developing space-based sensors to detect nuclear materials represent a first step towards a foolproof monitoring system.[42]

The US Military and Nonproliferation

First and foremost, the United States must maintain a credible deterrent force. This conclusion does not mean we cannot reduce the numbers in our nuclear arsenal. The START II reductions still will leave 3,000–3,500 warheads in the US inventory, more than sufficient to inflict unacceptable damage on any nuclear aggressor. Maintenance of the strategic triad with a highly reliable, flexible, and survivable mix of weapons will ensure the future credibility of the US's nuclear force. However, our deterrent posture may not prevent a regional conflict from "going nuclear" in the next century.

The fact of nuclear proliferation will make the possibility of nuclear conflict an important consideration in any battle plan a commander develops in the future. Planners must develop contingencies which minimize the effects of a nuclear attack. If possible, their staging of forces should take place out of range of enemy delivery systems. Massing of forces will have to be avoided in favor of small, highly mobile units unless some agency develops extremely effective air and missile defenses. In the long term, Japan, the United States, and other nations should combine resources in producing a tactical antiballistic missile system to protect troops deployed in harm's way.

Recently, a "new" mission is being touted for the armed forces—nuclear counterproliferation—the use of military force to deny nuclear weapons to a potential proliferator.[43] The Israeli attack on Iraq's Osiraq reactor in 1981 is the classic example of counterproliferation. Over the years, military planners have considered this option in several different circumstances. During the latest confrontation between the US and North Korea, former secretary of defense James Schlesinger stated in a forum on American defense policy that the North Korean nuclear facilities represented an "ideal set of targets" for airpower.[44] In the wake of the Gulf War, US Air Force airpower advocates quickly wave the banner praising the twin idols of stealth and precision guided munitions (PGM).[45] The Navy also staked a claim to the counterproliferation mission, pointing out their special capabilities in the nuclear arena.[46]

The warrior does not doubt American conventional military capability to project power almost anywhere in the world and destroy a target. The US has the most capable military force in the world today. Unfortunately, any attempt to destroy a modern-day nuclear weapons facility is likely to turn into a very complex affair, involving a number of decisions. The first consideration must be the desired outcome versus risk. An attack on a sovereign nation's territory constitutes an act of war. Are we prepared to wage war to stop the development of a nuclear weapon? The next consideration addresses the possibility of failure. Are we prepared for the consequences of a miss, a lost aircraft or ship (possibly to a "lucky" shot, maintenance malfunction, or bad weather), the possibility of collateral damage, loss of life or captured military members, and the attendant embarrassment in the eyes of the world? Finally, one of the lessons of the Gulf War was that Saddam Hussein learned from the Osiraq attack. He dispersed, disguised, and hardened his nuclear weapons facilities. Inspectors continue to discover segments of the Iraqi nuclear program, nearly four years after the war.[47] Other nations intent on developing nuclear weapons almost certainly will take similar protective measures. By choosing counterproliferation, can we accomplish our goals? These questions do not state flatly that there is never an instance where military counterproliferation is appropriate. However, we must address these issues before we take this large step.

Conclusion

Ten years from now, we will still recognize the world of 1995. Technology will continue to amaze, and information will overwhelm. Given the current trends, there will be fewer nuclear weapons in the world, but more nations will own them. We should do everything we can to reduce the risk of nuclear war, but we also must step carefully to ensure that our efforts don't produce exactly what we seek to prevent. It still will be a very complex world with no simple answers.

Notes

1. The White House, *A National Security Strategy of Engagement and Enlargement* (Washington, D.C.: Government Printing Office, July 1994), 11.

2. United States Arms Control and Disarmament Agency, *NPT: The Non-Proliferation Treaty* (Washington, D.C.: Government Printing Office, 1994), 1.

3. Ibid.

4. The most famous prediction is probably President John F. Kennedy's warning in 1962 that "fifteen or twenty or twenty-five nations may have these [nuclear] weapons by the middle of the 1970s." See Bradley S. Davis, "Arms Control and Proliferation," in Karl P. Magyar et al., eds., *Challenge and Response: Anticipating US Military Security Concerns* (Maxwell AFB, Ala.: Air University Press, 1994), 97.

5. Ibid.

6. Michael Renner, "Nuclear Arsenals Shrinking," *Vital Signs*, 1994, 114.

7. Including regional nonproliferation treaties, nuclear-free zones, efforts to monitor and control dual-use nuclear weapons and delivery technologies (e.g., the Treaties of Tlatelolco and Rarotanga); Group of Seven; Coordinating Committee for Multilateral Export Controls (COCOM); IAEA Lists, Parts I and II; Export of Arms Regulation (EAR); Missile Technology Control Regime (MTCR); Strategic Arms Limitation Treaties (SALT I and II); and the Strategic Arms Reduction Treaties (START I and II).

8. Kosta Tsipis and Philip Morrison, "Arming for Peace," *Bulletin of the Atomic Scientists*, March/April 1994, 38.

9. In the May 1992 Lisbon Protocol all three agreed to join the NPT as NNWS and return their nuclear arsenals to Russia, but compliance has been sporadic. As of September 1994, Ukraine had nine SS-24 and 90 SS-19 ICBMs, and 19 Blackjack and 23 Bear bombers; Kazakhstan, 60 SS-18 ICBMs; and Belarus, 36 SS-25 ICBMs. See "Nuclear Weapons Deactivations Continue in FSU," *Arms Control Today*, November 1994, 33.

10. Bernhard Rabert, "South Africa's Nuclear Weapons—A Defused Time Bomb?" *Aussen Politik*, March 1993, 232.

11. Davis, 89.

12. Marc Dean Millot, "Facing New Nuclear Adversaries," *Washington Quarterly*, Summer 1994, 56.

13. Steve Coll, "Neutral Sweden Quietly Keeps Nuclear Option Open," *Washington Post*, 25 November 1994, 1.

14. Franklin R. Wolf, *Of Carrots and Sticks, or Airpower as a Nonproliferation Tool* (Maxwell AFB, Ala.: Air University Press, July 1994), 16–19.

15. Larry Presler, "Keep the Nuclear Genie Corked," *Wall Street Journal*, 11 May 1994, 15.

16. William C. Martel and William T. Pendley, *Nuclear Coexistence, Rethinking U.S. Policy to Promote Stability in an Era of Proliferation* (Maxwell AFB, Ala.: Air War College, April 1994), 35–38.

17. Martin van Creveld, *Nuclear Proliferation and the Future of Conflict* (New York: Free Press, 1993), 99–107.

18. Martel and Pendley, 36.

19. Van Creveld, 115.

20. Andrew Mack, "A Nuclear North Korea, The Choices are Narrowing," *World Policy Journal*, Summer 1994, 27–28.

21. Martel and Pendley, 134, 136.

22. Ibid., 110–11.

23. Ibid., 111.

24. Ibid.

25. Ibid., 139.

26. Ibid., 147.

27. Bogdan Szajkowski, "Will Russia Disintegrate into Bantustans?" in *World Politics 94/95*, Helen E. Purkitt, ed. (Guilford, Conn.: Dushkin Publishing Group, Inc., 1994), 69.

28. The 1994 figures come from Robert S. Norris and William M. Arkin, "Estimated U.S. and Soviet/Russian Nuclear Stockpiles, 1945–94, Nuclear Notebook," *Bulletin of the Atomic Scientists*, November/December 1994, 59.

29. "Loose Nukes," *Baltimore Sun*, 31 May 1994, 8.

30. Jacob W. Kipp, "The Zhirinovsky Threat," *Foreign Affairs* 73, no. 3 (May–June 1994): 94–107.

31. James W. Morrison, "Vladimir Zhirinovsky, An Assessment of a Russian Ultra-Nationalist," McNair Paper 30 (Washington, D.C.: Institute for National Strategic Studies, National Defense University, April 1994), 34.

32. Robert L. Gallucci, "Non-Proliferation and National Security," *Arms Control Today*, April 1994, 14.

33. Van Creveld, 88.

34. Ibid.

35. Ibid., 86.

36. Mitchell Reiss, "The United States and Pakistan's Nuclear Programme," *Royal United Services Institute Journal*, Summer 1991, 47.

37. James J. Tritten, ed., *Non-Traditional Forms of Intelligence* (Monterey, Calif.: Naval Post Graduate School, August 1993), 2.

38. The NPT Review and Extension Conference will be held at the UN from 17 April to 12 May. See William Epstein, "Give More to Get More," *Bulletin of the Atomic Scientists*, November/December 1994, 15.

39. Ibid., 16. Britain conducts its tests at the Nevada test site.

40. Van Creveld, 69, 102. Advocated by Paul C. Warnke, "Strategic Nuclear Policy and Non-Proliferation," *Arms Control Today*, May 1994, 5.

41. Gill Gertz, "FBI to Open Moscow Office with Eye on Nuke Trafficking," *Washington Times*, 26 May 1994, 3.

42. Wilson P. Dizard III, "Pentagon Presses for R&D in Counterproliferation," *Military and Aerospace Electronics*, 28 November 1994, 1.

43. Dr Gregory Vardall developed a comprehensive definition of counterproliferation: "Counterproliferation is the sum of all measures designed to prevent the spread of weapons of mass destruction (WMD)." It encompasses traditional "nonproliferation," but, unlike the latter, it is "broader and includes proactive elements including military actions such as preemption." Unpublished paper, "Export Control and Nonproliferation," 15 August 1991, 2.

44. James Schlesinger, "American Defense Policy: Crisis & Confusion from Korea to Cuba," address at the Eighth Annual Report of the Secretaries of Defense Conference, Montgomery, Ala., 16 September 1994.

45. Wolf's paper makes a strong case for airpower in a counterproliferation role.

46. Ambassador Linton Brooks, "The New Nuclear Threat," US Naval Institute *Proceedings*, May 1994, 45–49.

47. Diana Edensword and Gary Milhollin, "Iraq's Bomb—an Update," *New York Times*, 26 April 1993, 17.

12

The Other Weapons of Mass Destruction

Chemical and Biological

Bradley S. Davis

The end of the Cold War does not mean the end of political, ideological, diplomatic, economic, technological, or even military rivalry among nations. It does not mean the end of the struggle for power and influence. It very probably does mean increased instability, unpredictability, and violence in international affairs.

—Samuel Huntington

The post-cold-war world of the early 1990s has seen dramatic and historic changes in the political status quo and the concurrent military threat. No longer must the rest of the world fearfully stand by, hoping against hope that the two superpowers do not incinerate themselves and everyone else in a nuclear holocaust. That particularly nasty specter has subsided. Unfortunately, a new—and potentially far more sinister—threat exists for mankind. Chemical weapons (CW) and biological weapons (BW) have emerged from the obscurity of the tunnel-visioned attention the world has lavished on nuclear weapons since World War II. Although the history of CW/BW reaches much farther back than nuclear weapons, the world has finally recognized that CW/BW are also weapons of mass destruction (WMD). Once let loose on an unsuspecting mankind, they are uncontrollable, indiscriminately affecting soldier and civilian alike. The danger that a sovereign nation, especially one in the third world, or a terrorist organization will manufacture or steal lethal CW/BW poses a potentially more significant threat to global security now and in the near future than does the possibility of these same actors acquiring a nuclear weapon. The House Armed Services Committee in February 1993 recognized that while the CW/BW threat had diminished with the passing of the cold war, it had actually increased the potential diversity and the frequency with which such weapons might be used.[1]

Problem Defined

In the twenty-first century, the major threats to global and American security interests will arise from the perceived imbalances of power and political instability among the world's community of nations. Countries with too much power may be tempted to engage in aggressive acts that threaten the world's wavering political, economic, and military balances. Regional imbalances of power can provoke weaker, insecure states to begin a military buildup, potentially including chemical and biological weapons, to protect themselves. In this precarious, competitive environment, states and nonstate actors with a national identity that want to survive must acquire power and use it as they deem necessary to protect themselves. Terrorists wishing to boldly push their unique agenda into the world arena to establish their legitimacy, or to simply take revenge upon an uncaring global society, will revert to weapons which they might easily acquire and employ. Chemical and biological weapons ideally fit that description. They are, however, not terror weapons to be found only in the future. "The threat is real, and it is upon us today. It is not in the future, it is here now," stated former Secretary of Defense Les Aspin to the National Academy of Sciences in December 1993.

The Chemical Weapons Convention (CWC) defines *chemical weapons* as toxic chemicals and their precursors, munitions and devices specifically designed to cause death or otherwise harm through its chemical action on life processes. Toxic chemicals include any chemicals which can kill, temporarily incapacitate, or permanently harm humans or animals. Precursor means any chemical reactant which takes part by whatever method at any stage in the production process of a toxic chemical.[2] Chemical weapons are quite distinct from biological warfare agents (such as bacteria, viruses, and rickettsia). The United Nations defines these agents as living organisms—whatever their nature—or infective material derivatives which cause disease or death in man, animals, or plants. The destructive nature of these derivatives emanates from their ability to multiply in the person, animal, or plant attacked.[3]

Authorities classify chemical agents by their physiological effects as either incapacitating or lethal. Incapacitating agents temporarily impair a person from functioning effectively. These agents are further subdivided into *physical agents* that cause irritation and abnormal bodily behavior, or *psychochemical agents* that cause mental disorientation. Lethal agents vary considerably by effects. *Lung agents* irritate the eyes, throat, and lungs, eventually leading to death from the lack of oxygen. *Blood gases* act faster and attack the blood's circulation of oxygen. *Vesicants,* like mustard gases, damage bodily tissues through burns, blisters, and temporary blindness. In large doses, they can be deadly by causing respiratory complications.

In contrast to chemical agents, biological agents can be divided into *peptides,* genetically mutated amino acids used to affect mental processes, or *toxins,* which are chemical substances produced by living organisms. The most deadly forms though, are the genetically altered bacteria or viruses which can defeat immunity. Biological warfare agents are more potent on a weight-for-weight basis than their chemical agent counterparts.[4] Both chemical and biological weapons, however, can inflict considerable disruptive and indiscriminate damage on civilians and military forces.

Both sovereign states and terrorist organizations see many advantages to the acquisition and ownership of these types of weapons. First, compared to the huge multimillion dollar expense to develop and field nuclear weapons, CW/BW are far more inexpensive to develop, manufacture, store, and deliver—the reason they are often referred to as the "poor man's nuclear weapon." For example, one can manufacture a Type-A botulinal toxin, which is more deadly than some nerve gases, for approximately $400 per kilogram. In fact, a blue-ribbon panel of chemical and biological experts testified in 1969 before a United Nations panel that "for large scale operations against a civilian population, the cost for casualties over a square kilometer using conventional weapons would be $2,000, using nuclear weapons the cost narrows to $800, chemical weapons are slightly lower at $600, but the cost for using biological weapons plummets to a mere $1."[5]

The second reason these weapons are attractive is the short time and relative ease required for their manufacture. Many of the normal agents or precursors used in chemical weapons are legally manufactured around the world for legitimate commercial reasons, as are the associated machinery, equipment, physical plants, and facilities. Manufacturers use these chemicals in a variety of products, which are the mainstay of the world's global economy. To simply ban their use would gravely perturbate or even destroy this fragile economic system, removing those products from legitimate use upon which the world depends. Even in a clandestine environment, both CW or BW can be manufactured by individuals with only moderate technical knowledge and a minimum of tools and workspace. They can quite readily find formulas for manufacturing nerve agents, mustard gas, and other deadly toxins in various scientific and governmental publications. The United States Department of Defense in 1971 declassified the formula for VX, one of the most potent nerve agents. The ease in gathering information concerning these weapons is clearly evident in a publication entitled, "C-Agents: Properties and Protection," produced by the Swedish Armed Forces Research Institute. This handy guide, a must for all those amateur terrorists contemplating the use of these weapons, describes in detail the process of launching a gas attack and includes the formulas needed for calculating wind speed and lethal concentrations.[6]

Compared to the massive numbers of conventional weapons required to hit a target effectively, producers need only a small amount of a chemical or an even smaller amount of a biological agent to offer a credible threat. For example, it has been estimated that only 50 kilograms of anthrax spores in an aerosol form is necessary to cause several thousand deaths if released in a large urban area.[7] In addition, producers can use CW/BW to strike virtually any target, especially civilian population centers. Incredible as it may seem, during mock CW/BW attacks, the shelter under the White House and the command centers in the Pentagon, which have air and water filtration systems, have flunked.[8] Table 5 provides a comparative estimate of the effects

Table 5

Impact of Attacks on Population Centers

Criteria for Estimate	Type of Weapon: Nuclear (1 megaton)	Chemical (15 tons nerve agent)	Biological (10 tons)
Area affected	≈ 300 km^2	≈ 60 km^2	≈ 100,000 km^2
Time delay of effect	Seconds	Minutes	Days
Structural destruction	Over area of ≈ 100 km^2	None	None
Time before normal use after attack	3–6 Months	Limited during contamination period	After end of incubation period or subsidence of epidemic
Maximum effect on man	90 percent deaths	50 percent deaths	50 percent morbidity, 25 percent deaths without medical help

≈ = nearly equal to

Source: Neil C. Livingstone and Joseph D. Douglas, Jr., *CBW: The Poor Man's Atomic Bomb* (Washington, D.C.: Corporation Press, Inc., 1984), 57.

that attacks have upon unprotected population centers using nuclear, chemical, or biological weapons.

Historical Perspective

Although we tend to regard CW/BW only in a modern contextual framework, the origins of this type of warfare are lost in the dark recesses of history. Leonardo da Vinci described in detail shells which could be fired over naval targets, filled with sulfur and arsenic dust. This is not the first recorded use of CW though. In the fifth century B.C., the Spartans used fumes from a combination of burning wood soaked in pitch and sulfur when they attacked the fortified Athenian city of Plataea.[9] The Germans in 1762 besieged the fortress of Schweidnitz in Austria with cannon shells emitting asphyxiating fumes.[10]

However, World War I saw the beginning of chemical warfare in earnest. The British, Germans, and French all began using tear gases almost as soon as the misery of trench warfare broke out on the western front in 1914. The first large-scale gas attack of the war—hence the occasion is historically associated as the beginning of modern chemical warfare—was delivered by the Germans just north of Ypres, Belgium, on the evening of 22 April 1915. From over 5,700 compressed air cylinders manhandled to the front lines, the Germans released chlorine gas, a greenish yellow cloud. The attack instigated the almost immediate collapse of two French divisions in the area, and as the Germans warily advanced into the abandoned Allied territory, they were horrified to witness the dead lying on their backs, fists clenched in the air, and the whole battlefield bleached to a yellow color. The attack devastated the Allies who suffered over 5,000 deaths.[11] The other major combatants, not to be outdone by the Germans, ultimately combined to employ by war's end over 125,000 tons of toxic chemicals, including chlorine, phosgene, and mustard gas. In all, 100,000 people died, and 1.3 million others were casualties of chemical agents used during "The Big One."[12]

Like chemical warfare, the use of biological agents dates back over two millennia. As early as 600 B.C., the Greek statesman, Solon, threw the roots of a plant that caused diarrhea into the river his enemies used for drinking water. An early incidence of natural biological warfare occurred in 67 B.C. when the army of Roman general Pompey was lured into a valley where the honeycomb was known to be tainted with a natural debilitating toxin. The foraging Roman soldiers soon became ill and suffered defeat by the local forces.[13] In 1346 plague-weakened Mongol forces attacked the Genoese-controlled city of Caffa in the Crimea. The Mongols catapulted victims of the plague over the battlements, and a citywide epidemic followed soon after. The strickened Genoese capitulated and retreated to Italy, taking the plague back to Europe with them. Within three years the Black Death had claimed over 30 million victims. The Russians followed the same tactics against the Swedes at Reval in 1710 by throwing plague victims over the city walls.[14] Contamination of wells and drinking water by similar means commonly occurred throughout the ages. In his

Memoirs, Union Gen William Tecumseh Sherman records that Confederate forces, upon their retreat from Vicksburg, drove farm animals into ponds and shot them, so that their 'stinking carcasses' would foul the water for the Union forces.[15] Not only did such actions have a demoralizing impact, but the consumption of the contaminated water probably accounted for many undocumented epidemics of gastrointestinal disease. Sherman's lack of any condemnatory remark, though, implies this was an accepted tactic on both sides.

Although the Japanese were the only country during World War II to have verifiably used chemical agents (on the Chinese), both the Allied and Axis powers stockpiled large quantities of chemical agents and instituted large BW agent research and development programs. One of the greatest mysteries of the war is why the warring nations did not use chemical agents more extensively. Most experts of the time surmised Hitler's overwhelming aversion to chemical gas, having been a victim during World War I, or President Franklin D. Roosevelt's early declaration of the US' no-first-use policy made the difference. But later historians believe it was simply a fear held by all belligerents of how far each side would go to retaliate which caused their inertia. The one notable, and infamous, example was poison gas, the German-preferred method of murdering thousands of Jews and other victims in their concentration camps.

"The limitations applied to the so-called inhuman and atrocious means of war are nothing but international demagogic hypocrisies. . . . Just because of its terrible efficacy, poison gas will be largely used in the war of the future."[16] Giulio Douhet, an early airpower visionary, soon saw his prophecy become fact, and the clear military restraint demonstrated during the war by all but one country was not to be followed in the postwar period. The following list reflects an increasing willingness and capability among a growing number of nations to employ these weapons.

- Yemen (1963–67): Egypt used mustard bombs against Yemenese tribesmen.[17]
- Laos (1975–83): The Vietnamese used Soviet-supplied chemical and toxin weapons, killing 700–1,000 rebellious Hmong tribesmen.[18]

- Cambodia (1978–83): The Vietnamese used chemical agents on Cambodian resistance forces.[19]
- Afghanistan (1979–83): Soviets employed a variety of chemical weapons against the Mujahedin guerrillas. In one case, death was so sudden for three guerrillas their hands still gripped their weapons.[20]

One of the most notorious and publicized uses of chemical weapons happened during the Iraq-Iran war. United Nations' investigation teams positively confirmed the use of sulfur mustard, nerve (tabun), and blood (cyanide) agents during the years 1984–86. The casualty potential of these agents was graphically demonstrated on the village of Halabja, where unprotected Kurdish civilians were singled out for an Iraqi airborne gas attack. This one assault injured some 100,000 people and may have killed several thousand.[21] Though the attack was confirmed and acknowledged by the Iraqis, there was no widespread global protest, only reinforcing the legitimacy of CW.

A sad commentary to the above list of countries found to have used CW includes one more—the United States. During the Vietnam conflict (1965–72) the US used a variety of defoliants or herbicides to clear the jungle that the guerrillas used for concealment. One of the most effective of the applied chemicals was Agent Orange. Without getting into the debate on the military's prior knowledge of the medical effects this chemical had on humans, and recognizing that the use of a herbicidal chemical was legal under international law, it is still painfully clear this compound has caused untold human suffering for both the Americans and the Vietnamese. Additionally, US military forces extensively used the tear gas, CS, to drive the Vietcong out of their underground tunnels.[22] The offensive or first-use employment of these weapons by the United States in the 1960s and 1970s, and then by the Soviet Union in the 1980s, established a critical precedent in the eyes of the world, especially those of the third world. These examples granted a legitimacy to these weapons and to their ownership and use by the very same superpowers who vehemently asked for their banishment, making it one of the main reasons many countries have developed and, in some cases, employed these agents in regional conflicts.

The proliferation of chemical and biological weapons cannot be described solely as the possession of these weapons by an ever-increasing body of nations around the world or even the legal or illegitimate means to produce them. Instead, proliferation resulted from a gradual erosion of the technical, legal, moral, and political constraints which have in the past placed the hand of caution on many nations from producing or using them.[23] Another contributing factor is the widespread global proliferation of industrial, chemical, and biomedical facilities, and the diffusion of the technological knowledge and reciprocal capability to manufacture chemical and biological agents that are useful in both the civilian and military arenas. Despite the requisite technical capability and knowledge level of a prospective CW/BW developer and user having dramatically declined over the years, most countries today could not have established their programs and facilities without some form of outside assistance. Judge William Webster, former director of the Central Intelligence Agency, has recounted that in the cases of the most notorious nations—Iran, Syria, and Libya—the help of foreign companies had been critical in beginning their programs. These foreign industrial suppliers had provided the technical and operational expertise. Outside corporations built these production locations and provided the requisite chemicals, necessary equipment and tooling, trained the host country's personnel, and even provided the parts for the munitions. Judge Webster concluded that over time these countries would develop their in-country expertise in the production of chemicals and the requirements for filling, storing, and handling these munitions.[24]

A Global Problem

Nations acquire CW and BW to advance their own interests. The Soviet Union and US both exercised considerable influence over the security policies of many nations until the end of the cold war. The bipolar nature of this confrontational era allowed the two superpowers to control, but not completely, the spread of WMD by answering the security concerns of many potential proliferators. The emergence of the world's new multipolar international system has agitated security concerns in some regions, causing some nations to consider or reconsider chemical and biological weapons options. Like those who possess nuclear weapons, CW/BW can serve as a deterrent, offering that "equalizing edge" against more powerful neighbors or regional antagonists. Several of the more radical Arab states feel they have ample and legitimate justification for acquiring these weapons, rationalizing the necessity to offset their perceptions of the Israeli nuclear threat. Any country involved in a conflict can threaten CW/BW use to keep the fighting localized, inhibit outsiders who may intervene or, keep the fighting from spreading to other geographic areas. These countries ultimately resort to CW/BW when they perceive themselves in a losing situation and rely on them in one last, desperate gasp. In spite of the defensive characteristics of CW/BW, if any actor possesses an offensive capability, whether used or not, this automatically confers upon the nation a large advantage since any adversary must now provide expensive protective countermeasures, which are at best cumbersome and definitely limit their combat effectiveness. The threat to use these weapons could cause such a public outcry and force the threatened country to succumb to the wishes of the bullying country without firing a shot.

As seen in table 6, the extent of the proliferation of CW and BW technology and/or weapons is extensive and growing. The stark reality of this table is that some of these countries are undoubtedly in possession of an arsenal of CW or BW. The recent post-Persian Gulf War disclosure of Iraq's secret, but very extensive CW/BW program by UN inspection teams, has jolted the world to this reality.

The world in righteous indignation often decries the repulsive nature of these WMD when compared to normal conventional weapons. By contrast, the public's view usually associates nuclear, chemical, and biological weapons with far more suffering, devastation, and cruelty. While this is true, it is only in scale. Throughout history conventional weapons have killed or injured far more people, animals, and plant life than the combined effects of all WMD. However, when we see, or even imagine, the horrendous effects of just one chemical, biological, or nuclear weapon, we find no comparison to conventional weapons. Western civilizations tend to view war and conflict in moralistic terms, and our cultural attitudes and expectations usually guide the decision and potential employment of CW/BW. Why then are we so surprised when confronted with an enemy who does not share these common values of right and wrong that we revere in the West? When a belligerent embraces a victory-at-all-cost philosophy, we must accept the possibility that a country or nonstate actor will use these terror weapons when they consider the situation advantageous or for that matter hopeless. This scenario is especially true when led by individuals, like Saddam Hussein, who view the survival of their personal power and prestige through the survival of the state as synonymous objectives. These individuals may view the use of CW/BW in a much more liberal manner than developed, democratic states, especially the United States.

Table 6

CW/BW Club Membership in Developing Nations

COUNTRIES	CHEMICAL WEAPONS	BIOLOGICAL WEAPONS
Middle Eastern and North African		
Ethiopia	Probable	
Libya	Probable	Probable
Egypt	Probable	Possible
Iran	Probable	Probable
Iraq	Confirmed	Confirmed
Israel	Probable	Possible
Saudi Arabia	Possible	
Somalia	Possible	
Syria	Probable	Probable
Asia		
China	Probable	Probable
India	Probable	
Indonesia	Possible	
Laos	Possible	
North Korea	Probable	Probable
South Korea	Probable	
Myanmar	Probable	
Pakistan	Probable	
Taiwan	Probable	Probable
Thailand	Possible	
Vietnam	Probable	
Others		
Angola	Possible	
South Africa	Possible	
Argentina	Possible	
Cuba	Possible	Possible

Source: House Armed Services Committee, *Countering the Chemical and Biological Threat in the Post-Soviet World*, Report of the Special Inquiry into the Chemical and Biological Threat, 102d Cong., 2d sess., 23 February 1993, 12–13.

The global chemical trade has flourished in part due to the dual-use properties of many of the chemicals, equipment, and technologies involved. A myriad of the most basic chemical compounds are mass produced and traded around the world for completely legitimate civilian purposes. However, these compounds are also the basic ingredients for chemical weapons or the precursors in their manufacture. This reason also accounts for the close relationship between toxic agents and chemical products used for many peaceful, commercial purposes that allows a producer to manufacture chemical weapons in plants that they can convert swiftly from commercial use to weapons production. These facilities have little or no outward differences with which to hint at their sinister internal capability. Experts have noted that with the twist of a few knobs or the simple change in catalyst, producers can convert a facility from producing pesticides to weapons in as little as 24 hours.[25]

The concerns of dual-use capabilities are even more acute when discussing biological warfare because the technology and materials used in the legitimate commercial industry are in essence the same for producing a vaccine or a weapon. A fermentation process in a seed culture can produce anthrax bacteria within 96 hours. Cutting-edge technology in genetic bioengineering is now available that could lead to BW with agents impervious to diagnostic testing, able to defeat a body's immunity, are drug-resistant, and may even be targeted at populations of certain ethnicity.[26]

One additional threat, the use of ballistic missiles, when coupled with either CW or BW, instills fear in the hearts of political leaders around the globe. No country today can defend against these missiles, including the US. The cost of one ballistic missile (about $1–8 million in contrast to the $20–60 million range of military aircraft) when added to inadequate defensive capabilities explains the reasons third world nations have numerous ballistic missiles. It comes as no surprise then to learn that these same countries also possess CW and BW. Comparably, these missiles are vastly inferior to those of the US. They are primitive and inaccurate, but when mated with a CW or BW warhead, they become a credible threat. Saddam Hussein nearly proved that point during the Gulf War, firing many Scud intermediate-range missiles into Israel and Saudi Arabia. Fortunately, he did not use any of Iraq's purported vast stores of chemical warheads, but the threat was there, and it was real.

The Unknown Factor—Terrorism

Today, and in the foreseeable future, the United States stands alone as the world's only superpower, a situation not seen since the height of the Roman Empire, almost two thousand years before. Like then, it seems ludicrous today that a state with a grievance would directly initiate a conventional war. It would cause a massive drain economically, and probably be counterproductive, as Iraq discovered in 1991 after their invasion of Kuwait. The ease with which manufacturers can obtain and produce chemical and biological agents, coupled with the dramatic and devastating effects which users can promise by only incidental use of such weapons, also makes them ideal for terrorists or guerrilla organizations. Barring capture and use of a nuclear device by terrorists, no other weapon system can promise the havoc nor the guaranteed worldwide media attention. The use or threatened use of chemical or biological weapons represents one method by which terrorists could seek to maximize their shock impact, gain widespread publicity for their cause, and demoralize their chosen target by instilling fear and trepidation. The potentially ghastly effects of toxic weapons, the small quantities required to produce significant results against an unprotected community, and the vulnerability of many political, military, and civilian targets add to their attractiveness as terrorist weapons. Extremist groups could use them as revenge weapons or as a means of leverage against a more powerful foe. The biggest advantage terrorists have in using these weapons is they have no sovereign territory upon which targeted countries could attempt to bring political, economic, or military pressure to bear. Terrorists can threaten a particular country, but where can that country in turn apply political pressure against the terrorists, or, if required, retaliate? Terrorists understand they are shadows and cannot be directly touched.

In a Special National Intelligence Estimate the CIA asserted that "one successful incident involving such [lethal] agents would significantly lower the threshold of restraint on their application by other terrorists."[27] Unfortunately, this prediction is in fact a reality, since terrorists already have been found with these weapons, and have clearly demonstrated the will to use them. The Federal Bureau of Investigation has discovered chemical and biological agents in the possession of several revolutionary groups, including cyanide by the Revolutionary Action Movement and the Covenant Sword in the Arm of the Lord; cultures of typhoid bacteria in the hands of the Order of the Rising Sun, a fascist group planning to contaminate Midwestern water supplies; and a nerve agent on an assassin who was planning to kill the US president in Washington, D.C., in 1974.[28] Israeli citrus fruit exports received serious damage when radical Palestinians injected Jaffa oranges with cyanide. Huk guerrillas used the same terror tactic in the Philippines when they poisoned pineapples due for export. In both situations, the rapid response of observant authorities averted these potential catastrophes. Scotland Yard foiled an extortion plot against the government of Cyprus, which had been threatened with explosions around the entire island by canisters containing dioxin. Finally, Parisian police, upon raiding the safe house of the German Red Army Faction terrorist group in 1989, found a growing culture of clostridium botulinum, used in the manufacture of botulinum toxin.[29]

Despite these instances of successful actions by the authorities, these examples highlight the range of problems that any terrorist organization can pose to authorities by using or threatening to use chemical or biological weapons. Also, apparently, fiscal constraints or technological complexity has not hampered this mode of terrorism. Terrorists neither need the support of large-scale production facilities nor the provision of highly reliable delivery systems. The terrorists' aims, capacities, and circumstances would determine the choice of using a chemical or biological weapon. The anticipated large number of casualties which would result from the use of only a small dose of a biological agent would tempt the more radical groups. Using these agents, the terrorists could either cause mass casualties and untold widespread panic by selectively targeting certain urban areas or initially demonstrating their resolve and the credibility of their threat by releasing the agent in aerosol form within the ventilation systems of one or more buildings. The stability, relative controllability, and the ease of production and dispersal of CW would be conducive to a more cautious terrorist group, especially one physically close to the intended victim or some neutral territory. Although biological weapons could produce much larger numbers of injured or dead, chemical weapons would still cause the desired effects the terrorists wish to instill, as well as considerable panic and fear in the targeted population.

Prospects for a Peaceful Solution

Recognizing a need to curtail the insanity of these weapons occurred in the world not just in the last few years, but during the first quarter of this century. The excesses and use by all combatants in World War I spurred the United States, outside the auspices of the League of Nations, to insist on a new international agreement to control these weapons. The outcome of this push was the 1925 Geneva Protocol, which prohibits chemical and biological warfare by international law. While it was conceived as a means to eliminate the conduct of such warfare, unfortunately the protocol did not prohibit the signatories the right to possess these weapons. This agreement simply promised that its members would not resort to their use. The flagrant employment of chemical weapons by Italy in the Italo-Abyssinian War (1935–36) only highlighted the ineffectiveness of the accord. It had no verification regime nor compliance enforcement procedures for violators. It was riddled with problems, but it was a start.

A great deal of debate and discussion occurred throughout the world during the 1950s and 1960s about eliminating chemical and biological weapons. Chemical weapons proved politically difficult for the world to grapple with, so the debate and discussion focused on biological weapons. In a unilateral action, President Richard Nixon in 1969 renounced the US offensive biological weapons program: "Mankind already carries in its own hand too many of the seeds of its own destruction. The US shall renounce the use of biological agents and weapons, and all other methods of biological warfare."[30] One year later he announced the dismantlement of preparations for their use, and between May 1971 and May 1972, all existing antipersonnel BW stockpiles were destroyed. This decision on the part of the president greatly facilitated the 1972 Biological Weapons Convention.

This follow-on agreement to the 1925 Geneva Protocol was co-signed by 103 nations. The Convention on the Prohibition of the Development, Production, and Stockpiling of Bacteriological (Biological) and Toxin Weapons and on their Destruction was commonly referred to as the Biological Weapons Convention. This precedent-setting treaty was the first multilateral arms control agreement crafted to eventually eliminate a complete category of weaponry. The co-signers agreed,

> never to develop, produce, stockpile, or otherwise acquire or retain microbial or other biological agents or toxins, whatever their origin or method of production, of types and in quantities that have no justification for prophylactic, protective or other peaceful purposes; and weapons, equipment or means of delivery designed to use such agents or toxins for hostile purposes or in armed conflict.[31]

The agreement took effect in March 1975 and helped to lessen global concerns over the development and use of BW, but it still had some serious flaws. BW continues even today, unconstrained by a stringent and intrusive monitoring regime equivalent to that found in the safeguards systems for nuclear materials enforced by the International Atomic Energy Agency or by the Chemical Weapons Convention. The agreement lacked strict verification procedures to ensure adherents abided by the provisions of the convention, and it assumed the United Nations would ensure compliance to its tenets by the current 140 signatories.[32] This assumption has not been the case. Since 1992 the United States and several other NATO members have strongly urged the establishment of just such a verification/compliance accord. Many other countries advanced immediate counterarguments, claiming that by their very nature, BW bans are unverifiable. The US, though, still argued for a separate, legally binding protocol detailing the needed procedures at a special conference in Geneva. The deficiency of no verification regime was the exact problem encountered by the Geneva Protocol, and it wasn't until the treaty on chemical weapons was completed that we met President Ronald Reagan's conviction, "Trust, but verify."

Before that chemical treaty became reality, the Australia Group was established in 1984. An informal organization, it was open to any nation seeking to stem CW proliferation through voluntary export controls on certain chemicals and equipment. Currently, the organization has 20 members: the 12 members of the European Community, and Australia, Austria, Canada, Japan, New Zealand, Norway, Switzerland, and the US. Each nation has established controls on the export of certain chemicals deemed useful in the production of CW. Some governments have established formal procedures to prohibit or restrict exports, while others rely on voluntary notification from companies that receive export orders for chemicals on the export control list. The informal nature of the group and the varying abilities of nations to track and control their exports has hampered its effectiveness. Whereas the group today comprises primarily the Western industrialized nations; nevertheless, companies in these same nations have been the source of the materials and technical assistance that have engendered CW proliferation.

The first truly global disarmament treaty finally addressed chemical weapons when, in Paris, on 13 January 1993 member nations opened the Chemical Weapons Convention for signatures. To date 157 nations have signed. US officials received a pleasant surprise during the signing ceremony when four Arab states—Algeria, Mauritania, Morocco, and Tunisia—signed despite the boycott of the Paris ceremony by the 22-member Arab League. Four other Arab states—Kuwait, Qatar, Saudi Arabia, and the United Arab Emirates—signed within the next two months.[33] The treaty is a product of 24 years of negotiation, and it bans

> the development, production, use, transfer, retention or stockpiling of chemical weapons, precludes assisting, encouraging or inducing any state to engage in activity prohibited by the treaty, and requires the destruction of production facilities and chemical weapons within a period of ten years (allowing an extension of five years for any country claiming technical difficulties or extenuating circumstances).[34]

Negotiations on this agreement began during President Lyndon B. Johnson's administration, but it wasn't until after the Persian

Gulf War in 1991 that the discussions got serious. The final document numbered 192 pages and will become law in two years or 180 days after 65 countries ratify it—whichever is later. As of late 1994, only nine had done so.[35] The treaty creates the long-sought-after verification system, under the auspices of the Organization for the Prevention of Chemical Weapons, and a new monitoring and enforcement agency represented by all signers. It tasks them with implementing the complex agreement. This treaty includes no-right-of-refusal challenge inspections, potentially encompassing thousands of chemical plants around the world. The agreement additionally mandates the destruction of CW stockpiles by all signatories no later than 10 years after the treaty enters into force. Under those destruction provisions, it will be the responsibility of each country to pay for destroying its own chemical weapons stocks; a cost expected to exceed $10 billion for Russia (with over 40,000 tons of agents and weapons) and $7 billion for the US (with over 60,000 tons of agents and weapons).[36]

This convention is an extremely detailed and carefully crafted treaty which embodies verification rules far more stringent than those found in any other multilateral disarmament agreement. To cover all contingencies, the treaty language also covers those activities which are not prohibited: industrial, agricultural, research, medical, pharmaceutical, or other peaceful purposes; and protective purposes related to chemical defense. The treaty also prohibits riot control agents as a method of warfare, but it does permit law enforcement to include these agents for domestic riot control (some observers consider the law enforcement allowance as a loophole in the treaty). The treaty protects confidential information gathered during inspections to verify the activities at civilian and military locations. The verification requirements or restrictions of legitimate chemical-related knowledge and material among member states should not hamper the economic and technological development of the affected states. For most of the signatories, this treaty is the first foray into the complexities of an agreement with such extensive reporting requirements and the intrusive verification provisions that will impinge upon military and industrial activities alike. The effectiveness of this convention, though, depends upon their rigor of accomplishing the verification and compliance measures, the number of countries involved, and their determination to strictly enforce its provisions. The limits imposed by this treaty in relation to the Geneva Protocol have become more complete and intrusive, and so to have the consequences of violation and the value of verification increased. The issue of verification has historically suffered through a torturous maze in the negotiating process, for it has been the most difficult and complex requirement to resolve.

Even an effective verification regime can still permit serious consequences, as countries continually push the envelope of the agreement's legal boundaries. One of the most serious of these outcomes may be termed *breakout strategy*. Nations do not have to follow the identical path of the superpowers by manufacturing and stockpiling large caches of chemical weapons. They could, as an alternative, accumulate enough precursors (quite legal under the provisions of the CWC), maintain the dual-use production facilities in their country, and clandestinely manufacture the unfilled munitions and delivery systems. They would then have the requisite pieces to fit together at a moment's notice for a rapid breakout of their chemical weapons should they feel the need to do so. This breakout would have a corollary effect on the signatories to the treaty, lulling them into a euphoria that the convention was effectively controlling these weapons and reducing the fear of other nations spending large quantities of resources on chemical defensive preparations.

This breakout strategy could have even more devastating effects when considering biological weapons. As mentioned previously, the amount of agent required would be less, the dual-use facilities would correspondingly be smaller and more easily concealed in the labyrinth of the commercial field of medical research. In addition, any attacks by these weapons would be difficult to identify, far more so in areas where similar diseases were endemic. A nation's biological warfare defensive program could easily conceal much of the basic research for an offensive breakout, all openly supported by dissemination trials, delivery systems tests, and exercising containment facilities under the guise of defense. These facilities could manufacture in short order the necessary biological agents using state-of-the-art production techniques. Militarily significant quantities of biological weapons can be produced from a seed stock quickly, as in a month or so.[37]

Conclusion

In a speech before the United Nations in 1993 President Bill Clinton stated, "The end of the Cold War did not bring us to the millennium of peace. Indeed, it simply removed the lid from many cauldrons of ethnic, religious and territorial animosity. . . . As weapons of mass destruction fall into more hands, even small conflicts can threaten to take on murderous proportions."[38] The past policies adopted by the global community, and specifically the United States, to confront the use of CW/BW by any nation, especially third world, or by terrorists, will not work today. To totally curb the use of these weapons, nations must agree upon a plan which eliminates the incentives to acquire and employ them. Those countries or nonstate actors who possess CW/BW do so because they believe these weapons have inherent strategic utility. If someone can convince the other nations that the cost of acquisition and employment is too great, and the anticipated benefits too small, then they might have no incentive to have and use them.

Observers have noted glimmerings of hope and progress in the control of these weapons. The membership of the Australia group has recently become larger and stronger with the addition of Finland and Sweden. The list of internationally controlled CW/BW-related materials has increased under US prodding, jumping from 11 to 50 weapons precursors. Controls also have been introduced on chemical and biological weapons-related, dual-use equipment, and entire chemical plants. Regional achievements are also in evidence. Argentina, Brazil, and Chile agreed on a CW/BW-free zone in 1991. East European export controls have greatly expanded; in fact, the Czech republic, Slovakia, Hungary, Poland, and Romania are meeting the Australia Group's standards. Israel, China, and India have adopted some limited export controls as well. The net result of the persistent efforts has been to choke off most of the traditional sources of supply for chemical and biological weapons programs. They cannot hope to eliminate completely the proliferation of these weapons.

Although the Chemical and Biological Weapons Conventions have proved correct and adequate up to a point, member nations must continue to create a complete, verifiable, and enforceable global ban on the development, production, stockpiling, and transfer of these weapons of mass destruction. Simply maintaining a credible chemical and biological retaliatory capability and defensive posture does not offer a panacea to an active global effort to achieve final elimination of CW/BW. In the end, though, verification will never provide complete assurance of this ban, as long as the actors believe strongly in their utility. The world must ultimately develop incentives that provide states positive reinforcement to abandon their proliferation interests. Regional security arrangements may help to build confidence and reduce tensions, addressing the underlying security concerns that fuel the arms races. The goal embraces the total renunciation of these weapons by all nations of the world, and development of all nations' economic, political, and technical status for them to become competitive in their region without resorting to unconventional weapons. The goal is a worthy one. But it is attainable only if we all want it.

Notes

1. Edward M. Spiers, *Chemical and Biological Weapons: A Study in Proliferation* (New York: St. Martin's Press, 1994), 156.
2. *Convention on the Prohibition of the Development, Production, Stockpiling, and Use of Chemical Weapons and on Their Destruction* (Washington, D.C.: Government Printing Office, January 1993).
3. UN General Assembly, *Report of the Secretary General on Chemical and Bacteriological (Biological) Weapons and the Effects of their Possible Use*, A/7575 (New York: United Nations, 1 July 1969), 6, 13.
4. G. S. Pearson, "Prospects for Chemical and Biological Arms Control: The Web of Deterrence," *Washington Quarterly* 16, no. 2 (Spring 1993): 145–62.
5. Neil C. Livingstone and Joseph D. Douglas, Jr., *CBW: The Poor Man's Atomic Bomb* (Washington, D.C.: Corporation Press, Inc., 1984), 7.
6. Ibid.
7. Ibid.
8. Ibid.

9. Christopher Centner, "The Arab View of Chemical Weapons and Its Implications for International Chemical Weapons Treaty Compliance," Defense Intelligence College Seminar Research Paper (Defense Intelligence College, undated), 3.

10. John P. Sinnott, "It was Algerian and Canadian soldiers at Ypres who suffered history's first major poison gas attack," *Military History*, April 1994, 12. The Germans first used an irritant on 27 October 1914 at Neuve Chappelle. The Germans fired 3,000 rounds of 105-mm projectiles filled with sneezing powder at Indian troops and French cavalry. The shells contained shrapnel embedded with the powder, and they were designed to grind and disperse the powder in the explosion. The barrage, however, was so ineffective, the British and French failed to realize that chemical munitions had been used until the fact was uncovered in a postwar investigation.

11. Maj Allen Kirkman, Jr., "CBW—Are We Prepared to Combat the Chemical/Biological Threat," Naval War College Research Paper, Naval War College, 8 February 1994, 5. Interestingly enough, the first casualties were among the Germans who lost three soldiers to gas from the cylinders ruptured by Allied shelling.

12. Richard McCarthy, *The Ultimate Folly* (New York: Alfred Knopf, Inc., 1969), 5.

13. Robert S. Root-Bernstein, "Infectious Terrorism," *The Atlantis*, July 1991, 44.

14. Col Ernest T. Takafuji, MD, MPH, US Army, "Biological Weapons and Modern Warfare," Industrial College of the Armed Forces (ICAF) Executive Research Project S72 (Fort McNair, Washington, D.C.: National Defense University, 1991), 4.

15. J. H. Rothschild, *Tomorrow's Weapons—Chemical and Biological* (New York: McGraw-Hill Book Co., 1964), 18.

16. Giulio Douhet, *The Command of the Air* (Washington, D.C.: Office of Air Force History, 1983), 181.

17. Defense Intelligence Agency, *Soviet Chemical Weapons Threat*, 1985, 21.

18. Charles Bay, "An Update on the Other Gas Crisis," *Parameters*, December 1979, 27–35.

19. *NBC Defense and Technology International* 1, no. 4 (September 1986): 6.

20. Joseph Douglas, "Chemical Weapons: An Imbalance of Terror," *Strategic Review*, Summer 1982, 43, 47.

21. Ibid.; and Spiers, 16.

22. Institute for Defense Analyses, *Summary Report: Chemical Warfare in the Third World War* (Bethesda, Md., IDA, 1987), 2–3. Riot control agents, like CS, were not considered true chemical weapons during this period, but because of America's use in Vietnam, these agents can no longer be used as methods of warfare. See also note 31.

23. Brad Roberts, ed., *Chemical Warfare Policy: Beyond the Binary Production Decision*, Significant Issues Series 9 (Washington, D.C.: Center for Strategic and International Studies, 1987), 36.

24. Senate, *Committee on Governmental Affairs and its Permanent Subcommittee on Investigations*, 101st Cong., 1st sess., 10 February 1989, 11–13.

25. Jill Smolowe, "The Search for a Poison Antidote," *Time*, 6 January 1989, 22.

26. Edward Spiers, *Chemical Warfare* (Urbana, Ill.: University of Illinois Press, 1986), 97–100.

27. Ibid.; and Spiers, *Chemical and Biological Weapons*, 172.

28. Senate, *Hearings before the Subcommittee on Technology and the Law of the Committee on the Judiciary United States Senate*, 100th Cong., 2d sess., 19 May 1988, 15 September 1988, 131.

29. Ibid.

30. National Security Decision Memorandum No. 35, 25 November 1969.

31. Jane M. Orient, "Chemical and Biological Warfare: Should Defenses Be Researched and Deployed?" *Journal of the American Medical Association* 262, no. 8 (August 1989): 644–48. The Biological Weapons Convention, signed by 74 nations on 10 April 1972, was the first disarmament agreement since World War II to involve the actual destruction of weapons. The convention does not apply to such chemical agents as the defoliants and antipersonnel gases used by the US in Vietnam. These were subsequently included in the 1993 Chemical Weapons Convention.

32. Edward J. Lacey, "Tackling the Biological Weapons Threat: The Next Proliferation Challenge," *Washington Quarterly*, Autumn 1994, 53.

33. "News Briefs—Chemical Treaty Gains New Signatories," *Arms Control Today*, March 1993, 27.

34. Ibid.; and Spiers, *Chemical and Biological Weapons*, 130.

35. Rick Maze, "Chemical Weapons Treaty is Mired in Doubts," *Air Force Times*, 24 October 1994, 36.

36. Lee Feinstein, "Chemical Weapons Convention Signed by 130 Countries in Paris," *Arms Control Today*, January/February 1993, 20.

37. Douglas Feith, "Biological Weapons and the Limits of Arms Control," *The National Interest*, no. 6 (Winter 1986/87): 80–84.

38. Graham S. Pearson, "Forging an Effective Biological Weapons Regime," *Arms Control Today*, June 1994, 14.

13

Conventional Armaments

Mapping Warfare in the Twenty-First Century

Mark Browne

In 1995, conventional armaments abound in every corner of the world. The rapid acceleration of conventional weapons acquisition—by governments and by nongovernmental organizations—poses significant challenges to the United States and its allies as the next century approaches. Predicting the nature of these challenges, including the warfare these weapons will generate, requires a careful examination. We must understand the range of these conventional threats if we are to formulate a strategy for coping with them. The most significant challenge to global security in the conventional arena comes from the proliferation of major weapon systems (e.g., F-15 fighters, "smart weapons," tanks) and from the largely uncontrolled commerce in small arms (e.g., automatic rifles, hand grenades, shoulder-operated antiaircraft weapons). The developed nations, led by the United States, are the foremost arms sources, although the primary threat of conflict due to conventional weapons proliferation is in the third world.

This essay will identify the problem by defining and describing conventional weapons and by quantifying world arms transfers of these weapons. The next section will analyze examples of armed conflict, discuss the world's expanding industrial base, and examine the potential for future conflict. The last part will look at the prospects for peaceful solutions, including discussions on nonlethal technology, current diplomatic efforts, and export controls.

Identifying the Problem

Conventional arms are globally plentiful, and are the weapons of choice in most ethnic, substate, and intrastate conflicts. The evidence indicates that conventional arms proliferation itself is destabilizing the globe and is a significant contributor to worldwide armed conflict. Conventional weapons have been described in various ways, but most studies characterize them as "major" weapon systems. Richard Grimmett offers examples of "major" conventional arms:

> Tanks and self-propelled guns, artillery, armored personnel carriers and armored cars, major and minor surface combatants, submarines, guided missile patrol boats, supersonic and subsonic combat aircraft, other military aircraft, helicopters, surface-to-air missiles, surface-to-surface missiles, and anti-shipping missiles.[1]

The world's leading suppliers of major conventional weapons in 1993 are displayed in figure 5. The values of those weapons transfers are indicated vertically at the left.

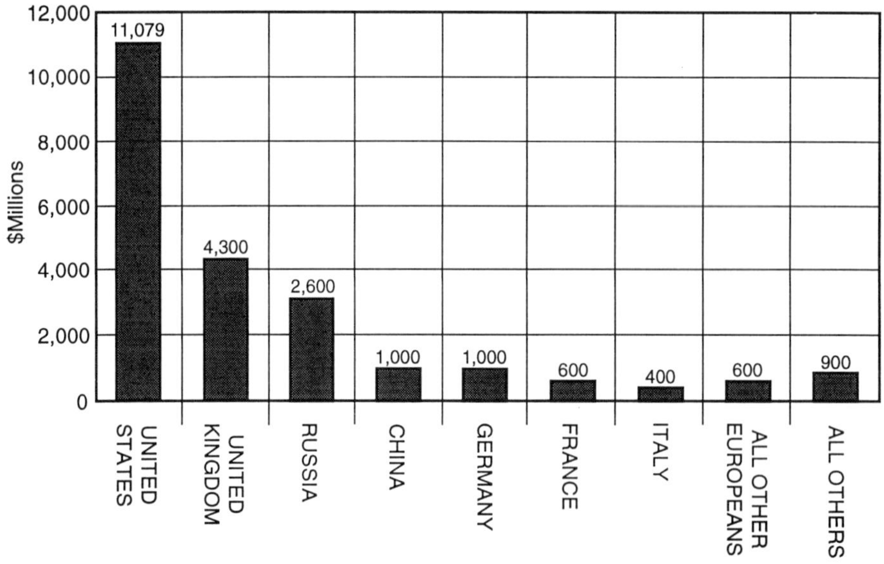

Source: Richard F. Grimmett, *Conventional Arms Transfers to the Third World, 1986–1993* (Washington, D.C.: Congressional Research Service, 1994), 86.

Figure 5. Suppliers of Major Conventional Arms in 1993

As may be seen, the United States ranks first in the world in supplying conventional arms—an interesting paradox as the US participates in worldwide arms control efforts.[2] US weapons from the cold war era are currently being used in conflicts such as those in Afghanistan and Somalia.[3] Russia's share has steadily declined—to third place, behind second-ranked United Kingdom (UK).

The world's leading purchasers of major conventional weapons, and the value of those weapons, are listed in figure 6.

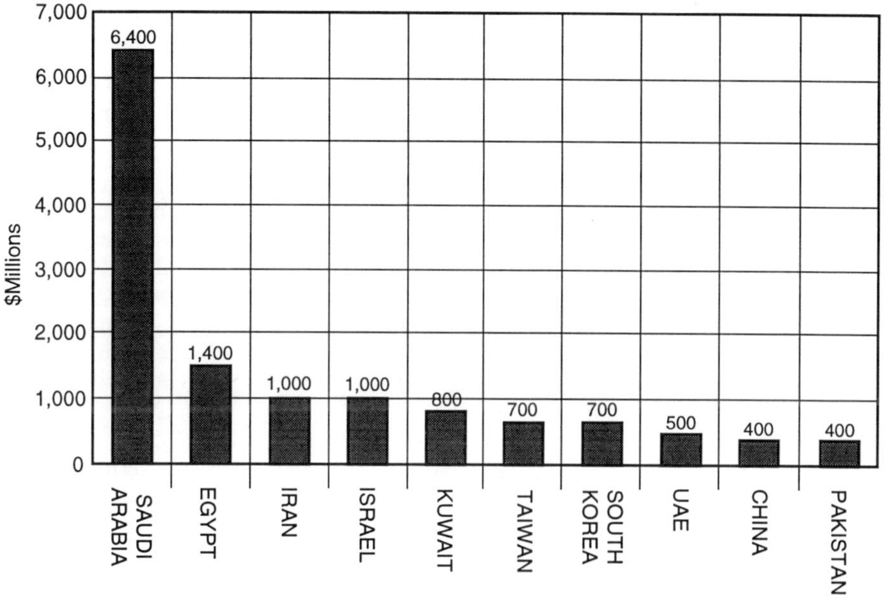

Source: Richard F. Grimmett, *Conventional Arms Transfers to the Third World, 1986–1993* (Washington, D.C.: Congressional Research Service, 1994), 70.

Figure 6. Major Conventional Arms Deliveries in the Third World in 1993

Figures 5 and 6 provide an indication of recent trends in arms sales.[4] They do not, however, illustrate the relative sophistication of these arms; nor do they give any indication of weapon quality.

> The fact that the United States, for example, has not delivered the largest number of weapons in a category to a region does not necessarily mean that the weaponry it has transferred cannot compensate, to an important degree, for larger quantities of less capable weapons systems delivered by Russia, the major West Europeans or other suppliers.[5]

Also, there is no single worldwide database for the accounting of major versus small conventional weapons, a fact which causes obvious problems for any analyst attempting to draw conclusions. And H. St. John B. Armitage, a retired British diplomat specializing in Middle East affairs, observes that Grimmett's numbers "suffer from different methods of calculation and estimates, guesstimates and speculation, and delays in release of data for security reasons."[6] Still, these statistics provide a framework and a point of departure for this discussion.

The spread of "small" conventional arms is of concern because it also is a destabilizing influence. Aaron Karp provides the following taxonomy of small arms:

> First is defining small arms by exclusion, as those weapons not covered in existing data collections . . . [Second is] Small arms defined as weapons carried by . . . a normal infantry soldier. [Third is] Small arms defined as those transported by animals and light vehicles. This standard permits extension of the definition to include heavy machine guns and some light artillery. [Fourth is] The empirical definition of small arms . . . defines(s) the weapons of ethnic war empirically, listing all the weapons actually used in internecine conflict.[7]

For purposes of this study, Karp's is accepted as the most complete taxonomy. But since there is no comprehensive accounting of "small" conventional weapons, there has been no attempt to quantify the transfers of these weapons.

The impact of small arms can be described in economic terms. For example, it costs approximately $112,000 (fiscal year 1995 dollars) to outfit a "generic" platoon with everything necessary to fight, but this figure does not include support equipment such as spares, training, and so forth.[8] A third world country, substate, or terrorist group could outfit 300 combat troops for the relatively low cost of $1 million. Where would a group obtain these weapons? They are easily obtained on the international arms market. For example, Sam Cummings, a British subject born in Philadelphia, runs Interarms, a firm that is over 30 years old. "Cummings sells over $80 million worth of pistols, rifles, submachine guns, hand grenades, and other weaponry every year to customers ranging from Guatemala to the People's Republic of China."[9] *Jane's Infantry Weapons 1994-95* lists over 250 manufacturers of infantry weapons. Some of the products made by firms listed in *Jane's* are antitank ammunition, antitank grenades, antitank launchers, antitank systems, automatic pistols, automatic rifles, night vision systems, grenade launchers, hand and rifle grenades, and machine guns.[10] It is appropriate to say that "major systems cost millions of dollars, but millions of people are killed very cost-effectively by small arms."[11]

Current and Future Armed Conflict

Conventional warfare since the cold war has been primarily intrastate, nationalistic, ethnic, political, and/or religious in nature. According to the *Stockholm International Peace Research Institute (SIPRI) Yearbook 1994*, there were "34 major armed conflicts in 28 locations in 1993."[12] The institute defines major armed conflicts as, "prolonged combat between the military forces of two or more governments or of one government and at least one organized armed group, and incurring battle-related deaths of at least 1,000 persons during the entire conflict."[13] Each of these conflicts features the use of conventional arms. Conventional weapons proliferation has contributed to numerous conflicts in the 1990s (e.g., the Gulf War, Somalia, the drug war, and Bosnia).

Proliferation of conventional arms was a factor in the Gulf War. The Iraqi army ballooned from 180,000 to 900,000 troops in the 1980s. Iraq's conventional weapons inventories also jumped dramatically: tanks increased by 211 percent (from 2,700 to 5,700); artillery increased by 161 percent (from 2,300 to 3,700); combat aircraft increased by 286 percent (from 332 to 950).[14] Saddam Hussein's armed forces were equipped primarily by the Soviet Union, but the French were also major suppliers. The Soviets supplied "thousands of tanks, hundreds of aircraft, and at least 819 Scuds."[15] Iraq's purchases from the Soviet Union totalled approximately $23.5 billion from 1982 to 1989. France provided technical assistance: "French technicians reputedly made guidance modifications to Iraqi Scuds, and married the French Thomson-CSF Tiger radar to a Soviet-built Il-76, creating the Iraqi Adnan AWACS."[16]

Lebanese businessman Sarkis Soghanalian also assisted the Iraqis in their arms buildup as a "middleman" in arms negotiations. He made his fortune by brokering arms deals with Saddam Hussein. Soghanalian engineered a sale of 26 Hughes

MD-50 helicopters to Iraq as civilian aircraft; the helicopters were later outfitted with machine guns.[17] Also involved in the Iraqi arms trade was Chilean arms dealer Carlos Cardoen. Cardoen supplied Iraq with cluster bomb technology worth $400 million. He was finally charged in 1992 (by the US government) with "money laundering and illegal shipment of weapons-grade zirconium from the United States to cluster bomb facilities in Chile and Iraq."[18]

Also involved in Iraq's arms buildup was James Guerin, who headed International Signal and Control, operating out of Lancaster, Pennsylvania. Guerin "engaged in a pattern of financial fraud and money laundering . . . [he] routinely violated the international arms embargo against South Africa and smuggled hundreds of thousands of critical electronic components to Iraqi military factories."[19] Finally, convicted of violating US arms export control laws in 1992, Guerin was sentenced to 15 years in prison.

On the surface, it is obvious that the Iraqi invasion of Kuwait led to the Gulf War. However, it can be argued that Iraq's arms buildup in the 1980s contributed to Saddam's inflated confidence and his decision to invade. By August of 1990, Hussein possessed a "powerful and combat-tested military equipped with first-rate military systems, and he had embarked on a vigorous weapons development program."[20] Therefore, conventional arms proliferation was an important factor in the Gulf War, leading, at least indirectly, to American and coalition involvement.

The situation in Somalia also demonstrates the problems associated with the proliferation of conventional arms. American support of former Somali ruler Siad Barre contributed, at least in part, to weapons proliferation in Somalia. The US "supplied nearly $300 million in military aid [to Somalia]. . . . When Barre was overthrown in 1991, a portion of his stockpile of US-supplied military trucks, armored vehicles, antitank weapons, rifles, and ammunition found its way into the hands of the armed gangs. . . ."[21] Thus, the proliferation of major and small weapons contributed to anarchy as the warlords, including Mohamed Farah Aidid, competed for power and brought starvation and hardship to the Somali people. This, in turn, brought the attention of the world press, and ultimately the involvement of the United States in a United Nations peacekeeping effort. Once again, conventional weapons proliferation played a role in American military involvement.

The drug war is perhaps a nonpolitical example of armed conflict. Central and South American nations, as well as the United States, are employing conventional military forces to counter the drug threat. One reason for the use of military force is the weaponry possessed by the Medellín and Cali drug cartels—the two largest. Drug arrests and information from the US Customs Service provide insight into the type of arms possessed by the cartels. Upon the arrest of two drug smugglers in 1988, the Customs Service recovered:

> 100 pounds of C-4 explosive, 25 . . . machine guns, 20 AR-15 rifles and five M-60 . . . machine guns. Agents were able to identify two previous shipments that contained the following: 25 pounds of Tovex plastic explosives, 30 AR-15 rifles, five 50-caliber rifles, 25 silencers for . . . machine pistols, two . . . sniper rifles and night vision equipment.[22]

Additionally, Mexican authorities seized "360 AK-47 rifles, 145,000 rounds of ammunition, six US-made military rifles, metal detectors, infrared rifle scopes, [and] 92 bayonets . . . [in 1988]."[23] These weapons were bound for the drug cartels in Colombia. In addition, US officials apprehended individuals representing the cartel who were attempting to buy 24 Stinger surface-to-air missiles. This data indicates the types of weapons favored by the cartels as well as their firm resolve to defend their drug empires. It is also an excellent example of how nongovernmental organizations can impact the policies of nations.

American and United Nations peacekeeping or peace-enforcement engagements in the Bosnian civil war are fraught with danger because the war has the potential for ensnaring participating nations in a major armed conflict. Conventional weapons are playing a critical role in Bosnia. The Bosnians have an army of approximately 60,000 troops with a reserve of 120,000 more, about 40 T-55 main battle tanks, 30 armored personnel carriers, and nearly 400 artillery pieces. The Serbians, on the other hand, possess an army of approximately 80,000 troops. They have an estimated 330 main battle tanks, including the M-84 and the T-72. They also have 800 artillery pieces, various surface-to-air-missiles, and approximately 40 aircraft.[24] Qualitatively, the Serbs have better leadership than the Bosnians, having inherited the Yugoslav general staff. Also, the Serbs have a two-to-one margin in artillery to go with their almost ten-to-one margin in tanks. The suffering and deaths in that region (casualties are estimated at 20,000–50,000 through 1993), and the unrelenting ethnic nature of the war, make Bosnia highly unstable.[25] The presence of conventional arms in great quantity exacerbates the instability. Resolution of that conflict is not imminent; therefore, American and European involvement in a conventional war there must not be ruled out.

A related area of global security concern is the military-industrial base in the third world. Approximately 40 third world countries now possess the ability to manufacture weapons.[26] "In 1950, defense industries in the developing world produced just $2 million worth of goods; in 1984, the figure was $1.1 billion. [Currently], at least 19 [countries] build submarines. Ten to fifteen countries are [currently] producing cruise missiles."[27] Third world weapons producers are not going to displace the traditional Western suppliers, but they can fit into "niche" markets because they offer "a combination of low prices, good customer service, and guaranteed availability."[28] Examples include China, which exported missiles to the Middle East and is "now offering an advanced fuel-air explosive to international buyers."[29] Other producers in the developing world ranking in the top 15 of world arms suppliers in 1991 include Israel, North Korea, Brazil, and Bulgaria.[30] In 1991, conventional arms exports of these nations amounted to: China $925 million, Israel $380 million, North Korea $160 million, Brazil $70 million, and Bulgaria $70 million.[31] The primary contribution of third world arms producers is to increase the firepower available to states or substate groups engaged in regional conflicts, and to increase the cost of intervention by the developed nations.[32]

Some relevant observations about future armed conflict confronting the world community may now be offered. The primary threat in most of the third world concerns either ethnic conflict, civil war, political/ideological war, or revolutionary/terrorist activity. The developed nations of the world may also become involved in conflict, as the Gulf War, Somalia, the drug war, and Bosnia indicate. In the early 1990s, 28 regions in the world experienced major armed conflicts. Many states in the third world have the capability to wage wars with weapons provided by a sponsor state, captured stockpiles of weapons, weapons bought on the international market, or weapons produced in their own country. These facts should interest the global community in pursuing more thorough arms control policies, especially in the third world.

Prospects for Peaceful Solutions

Prospects for peaceful solutions to the third world's armed conflicts, and those likely to arise in the near future, depend on many factors. That the world community needs more focus on solutions to the proliferation of conventional weapons is evident, but "how" is problematic. The 1994 US National Security Strategy (NSS) contains American policy on the proliferation of conventional weapons. This strategy document provides the overarching military and political objectives for our nation with respect to conventional arms, and offers the following:

> We will continue to seek greater transparency, responsibility and, where appropriate, restraint in the transfer of conventional weapons. . . . The UN register of conventional arms transfers is a start in promoting greater transparency of weapons transfers and buildups, but more needs to be done.[33]

This document is particularly important because America, as the sole remaining superpower, will be an integral player in negotiating worldwide arms control agreements. The NSS underscores this position: "The US is prepared to promote, help negotiate, monitor and participate in regional arms control undertakings compatible with American national security interests."[34]

One area with the potential to resolve conflicts peacefully, or with minimal casualties, is the use of nonlethal weaponry. In fact, using nonlethal weapons to combat the effects of conventional weapons poses an interesting paradox. The *SIPRI Yearbook 1994* defines nonlethal weapons as: "both old measures and new technological initiatives aimed at producing disabling effects without necessarily causing significant harm to persons."[35] The US Departments of Defense and Energy are currently pursuing technologies to develop a nonlethal capability.[36] So far, the most promising uses for this technology appear to be in peacekeeping or peace-enforcement operations.

One of the main difficulties this program will face in the coming years is funding. In an era of tight budgets, with the military services fighting over a shrinking share, the competition for nonlethal research dollars will be ferocious. Nevertheless, the Army's Armament Research, Development, and Engineering Center in New Jersey has been working on this type of weapon for years. Other agencies involved include Sandia National Laboratories in New Mexico and Lawrence Livermore Laboratories in California. The primary value of nonlethal weapons is that they may reduce the deaths caused by conventional arms. Their use may be particularly effective in those third world nations where conflicts are limited and the armed forces are relatively small.

Many nonlethal technologies are being developed in the United States. One is a "sticky foam" that will quickly incapacitate a person. Others include antisensor weapons that temporarily disable human eyes or other sensors.[37] High-power microwave technologies may generate an electromagnetic pulse that stops electronic systems from operating and disables radar and communication devices.[38] Also being developed are liquid metal embrittlement agents and Teflon lubricants that will render concrete pavements useless. Other possibilities are chemical agents that will change fuel to jelly and sleep-inducing chemicals that can turn an unruly mob into "sleeping babies."[39]

These are only some of the nonlethal technologies being developed. Many are years away from deployment, but *USA Today* and CNN News reported that US troops carried nonlethal weapons as they assisted in the "withdrawal of United Nations forces from Somalia."[40] Lt Gen Anthony C. Zinni, commanding a force composed of troops from six nations, selected "guns that fire tiny beanbags, rubber bullets, and two kinds of sticky foam."[41] These weapons helped to avoid a situation similar to that which occurred in June 1993 when 24 Pakistanis and 20 Somalians were killed during an exchange of gunfire. "We took a look at what we could use to break up a crowd formation before they became dangerous to troops. The idea was if you don't have to hurt people, don't do it."[42] Officials at the Department of Defense elected not to use experimental lasers because they have the potential to cause serious injury.

International Control Efforts

Many diplomatic initiatives have addressed the problem of conventional arms. Some of the more important agreements include the Conventional Armed Forces in Europe (CFE) Treaty, the Missile Technology Control Regime (MTCR), the Organization of Security and Cooperation in Europe (OSCE), Forum for Security Cooperation, Confidence and Security Building Measures, the Permanent-Five Guidelines, and the UN Register of Conventional Weapons. Each initiative attempts to put limits and/or controls on the acquisition and delivery of conventional armaments. Each is successful to a certain extent, but each also has limitations. These initiatives should be examined to determine their strengths, weaknesses, and prospects for the future.

The CFE treaty entered into force in 1992. Signed in 1990 by 22 NATO and Warsaw Treaty Organization (WTO) countries, it is now recognized by 30 nations. The agreement limits conventional armaments in the Atlantic-to-the-Urals (ATTU) region of Europe.[43] According to Amy Woolf, "Each group of [CFE] states (NATO countries on the one hand and former members of the now-defunct Warsaw Pact on the other) will be permitted to keep in the Atlantic-to-the-Urals geographic area a maximum of 20,000 tanks, 30,000 armored combat vehicles, 20,000 artillery pieces, 6,800 aircraft, and 2,000 attack helicopters."[44] Adjustments in accordance with this treaty must be carried out by 17 November 1995.[45] The CFE treaty, while containing some rough spots, is operating successfully. Even the fall of the Soviet Union did not cause a crisis, since many of the political changes in Europe are now incorporated in the agreement. The goal of the treaty is cooperation by the member nations on matters of security, so there is a strong motive for compliance.[46] On the other hand, CFE has not prevented or ameliorated any conflicts, such as that in Azerbaijan.

One problem currently faced by CFE has to do with the "flank zones."[47] These flank zones surround Russia, and the CFE agreement dictates sublimits on the equipment that forces placed in these areas may have. Russia has objected to these sublimits for four reasons:

> First, the flank limits are "old think," reflecting a cold war military balance that now exists only in history books. Second, . . . the flank limits will force Russia to cram its equipment in Kaliningrad—the small Russian enclave sandwiched between Poland and Lithuania. Third, . . . potential conflicts in the Transcaucus require an additional deployment of forces . . . Fourth, . . . Russia would like to use existing garrisons in its northern flanks to house troops . . . from other parts of the former Soviet Union. . . .[48]

While the Russians have some good points, the US is reluctant to agree for fear that this type of change will "open the floodgates," thus undermining the treaty.[49]

NATO's primary benefit from CFE is the massive reduction in Warsaw Pact military equipment. The treaty was "a reflection of and a contribution towards a hugely diminished Soviet military threat to Western Europe, and military presence in Eastern Europe."[50] Figure 7 shows the adjustments to treaty-limited equipment that each major "group of states" must make to reach the required goals. The "zero" (0) line represents the level of equipment allowed the various forces. Columns running downward from zero represent mandatory reductions in equipment; NATO's upward column indicates that it may add 1,966 pieces of equipment (but is not required to do so).[51]

The MTCR includes 23 member nations.[52] The original agreement seeks to control missile delivery systems exports. Although the MTCR is not a treaty, signatories mutually agree to follow its guidance. (There is no enforcement mechanism). The MTCR classifies weapon systems into two categories. Category I includes delivery systems with a range greater than 300 nautical miles and a payload greater than 500 kilograms.[53] Examples of these delivery systems include intercontinental ballistic missiles, drones, cruise missiles, and remotely piloted vehicles. Sales and transfers of delivery systems in category I must overcome a "strong presumption of denial." This means that members of the MTCR cannot complete a sale of category I systems unless they have an acceptable rationale

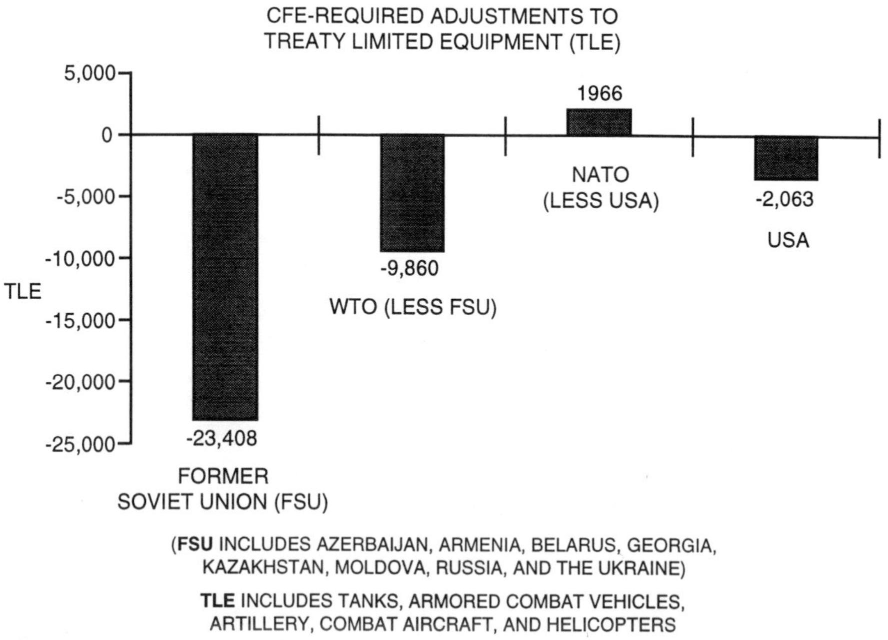

Source: Adapted from data contained in Stuart Croft, "Negotiations, Treaty Terms and Implications," in Stuart Croft, ed., *The Conventional Armed Forces in Europe Treaty* (Aldershot, England: Dartmouth Publishing Company Limited, 1994), 32–34.

Figure 7. CFE-Required Force Structure Adjustments

to overcome the presumption of denial. Category II systems include guidance sets, propellants, and other materials used by delivery vehicles. Category II systems are easier to sell or transfer because there is no presumption of denial. The MTCR stems the flow of weapons of mass destruction; and since many of these systems deliver conventional munitions, the MTCR applies also to the proliferation of conventional weapons.

Expanding the MTCR globally could provide some additional progress in conventional arms control. The positive side to this argument is that the inclusion of all governments increases delivery system transparency. On the negative side, there will always be rogue states that will never comply with any arms control initiative. These states could undermine a global agreement. Yet an expansion of the MTCR would be useful and appropriate because the benefits of transparency outweigh the negative impact of renegade nations. Indeed, the national security strategy states: "To combat missile proliferation, the United States seeks prudently to broaden membership of the Missile Technology Control Regime (MTCR)."[54]

The Organization on Security and Cooperation in Europe, which began in 1975 with the passage of the Helsinki Final Act, currently includes 53 states in Europe, along with Canada and the United States.[55] The membership of Serbia/Montenegro (the former Yugoslavia) has been suspended due to aggression in Bosnia. The primary functions of the OSCE relate to "early warning, conflict prevention, and crisis management."[56] Helsinki, Finland, was the site of a cardinal meeting in July 1992 to determine the future of OSCE. That summit produced the Helsinki Document, which was agreed to by the heads of state of the member nations. The document sums up the purpose of OSCE:

> The OSCE is a forum for dialogue, negotiation, and cooperation, providing direction and giving impulse to the shaping of the new Europe. We are determined to use it to give new impetus to the process of arms control, disarmament, and confidence and security-building.[57]

The central question facing the OSCE is whether it will be successful in arbitrating future conflicts. Toward that end, the Forum for Security Cooperation (FSC) was formed in 1992 to deal with OSCE security issues. Its task is, "trying to address arms control negotiations, security enhancement, cooperation, and conflict prevention."[58] The FSC has established a "Program of Immediate Action" to achieve its objectives of "preventive diplomacy, peacemaking, peacekeeping, peace enforcement and peace building."[59] The program has 12 items on its agenda, divided into track A and track B. Track A items include "arms control and Confidence and Security Building Measures, enforcement, force generation capabilities, global exchange of military information, cooperation in nonproliferation efforts, and regional measures."[60] Track B items are "force planning, cooperation in defense conversion, cooperation on nonproliferation (excluding track A items), military cooperation and contacts, regional security issues, and security enhancement consultations."[61] The FSC has promise in the area of arms control if consensus is achieved on the track A and track B agenda items. Expanding the FSC globally could provide the framework necessary for worldwide conflict resolution.

Related to the OSCE and the FSC are confidence and security building measures (CSBM). Guidelines regarding CSBMs were agreed to by all the OSCE states at the Stockholm 1986 conference. These guidelines "increase openness and predictability about military activities in Europe, with the aim of reducing the risk of armed conflict in Europe."[62] Vienna Conferences in 1990 and 1992 revised the guidelines, which now include requirements for 42 days' prior notice for exercises containing 9,000 troops and 250 tanks.[63] Additionally, participating states must provide at least a one-year notification for exercises involving more than 40,000 troops.[64] The guidelines also provide exercise observation privileges for member states; and in 1993, four reportable exercises were conducted.[65] CSBMs provide transparency and build confidence between European nations due to exercise observation and notification requirements. However, CSBMs do not resolve conflicts; for this the FSC has greater potential because it is consultative and does not operate under a rigid set of guidelines.

The first international diplomatic attempt to quantify the conventional arms trade resulted in the UN Register of Conventional Arms. Established by Resolution 46/36 L on 9 December 1991,[66] the register was first published in 1993. The resolution provides for the voluntary reporting of arms transfers—of battle tanks, armored combat vehicles, large-caliber artillery systems, combat aircraft, attack helicopters, warships, and missiles/missile launchers. The goal of the resolution is to increase the visibility of conventional weapons.

The UN register is entirely voluntary, however, and there is no adequate method for cross-checking the submissions of member nations. Expanding the register to include small arms is one potential avenue of improvement. It would offer more visibility into the small arms trade and would be a positive, stabilizing step.

The permanent-five nations of the UN Security Council—the United States, Britain, France, Russia, and China—agreed to guidelines in 1991-92 that would "restrain the flow of arms to other nations, particularly those in the Middle East."[67] The principles agreed to are: "Increased transparency in arms sales; consultations among arms suppliers; implementation of existing arms control regimes; restraint in conventional arms transfers; and establishment of a zone free of weapons of mass destruction in the Middle East."[68] An additional recommendation was to establish the UN Register on Conventional Arms, which was subsequently adopted and is probably the most positive result stemming from these negotiations. Although these principles represent a positive step, consultations with respect to conventional arms control have stalemated since China objected to the sale of F-16s to Taiwan.[69]

These forums do not by any means control all elements of the arms trade. Significant gaps remain, especially with respect to small arms. Diplomatic efforts can resolve conflicts between developed nations, but most of the governments that belong to the OSCE, CFE, and MTCR are not in imminent danger of major armed conflict (exceptions include Bosnia and the new republics surrounding Russia). Therefore, the focus of future arms control diplomacy should be in the third world. The emotionally intense nature of most third world armed conflicts almost ensures that diplomacy will be slow to resolve them. Nevertheless, the developed nations should pursue stronger diplomatic options.

The preceding discussion might lead one to believe that the flow of conventional weapons is uncontrollable; but while control will be difficult, the world community can make inroads into the trade. Specifically, pressure must be brought to bear on nations that sponsor terrorist or substate groups. Such pressure can be applied through the United Nations as well as through economic sanctions, most-favored nation status, judicious application of foreign aid, and regional alliances such as NATO. This will require cooperation between all involved nations, and the United States bears considerable responsibility as the sole remaining military superpower. However, the American paradox is to exercise world diplomatic leadership in arms control while continuing to lead the world in conventional arms deliveries.

Conclusion

The issue of conventional arms proliferation remains highly complex. These weapons are the armament of choice in every major conflict, and that trend will likely continue. Research shows that many third world nations are engaged in armed conflict of one form or another. Furthermore, the likelihood of

American or Western European involvement in third world conflicts over the next 10 years has not disappeared. To see this, one has only to look at the Gulf War, Somalia, Bosnia, and the drug war.

The bottom line is that the United States and the responsible world community must strengthen international diplomatic measures and expand export controls in the third world to prudently limit the trade in arms—at least in "major" conventional arms. Small arms remain extraordinarily difficult to control, since they "are readily and cheaply available on the international arms market."[70] Conventional weapons proliferation may be likened to an enzyme in a chemical reaction; that is, conventional weapons proliferation is the enzyme serving as the catalyst in armed conflict. Conventional arms will not cause a war, but they may speed up the pace and intensity of an armed conflict.

The challenge facing the international community in the next 10 years is to reduce the proliferation of conventional arms. The developed nations must take prudent measures to positively impact this important task.

Notes

1. Richard F. Grimmett, *Conventional Arms Transfers to the Third World, 1986–1993* (Washington, D.C.: Congressional Research Service, 1994), 89.

2. Ibid., 86. I have chosen 1993 because it shows the decline in Soviet/Russian conventional arms sales. Indeed, the Soviet Union ranked first in the world from 1986 to 1990. For example, the Soviets delivered 45 percent of conventional arms in 1986. By 1993 that had dropped to 10 percent. Conversely, the United States had a 16 percent share of arms deliveries to the third world in 1986, but their share had risen to 51 percent by 1993. Furthermore, Grimmett's numbers show that there has been a dramatic decrease in the flow of weapons into the third world. In terms of constant 1993 dollars, the value of weapons transferred was $64 billion in 1986 but had declined to $22 billion in 1993.

3. John F. Burns, "New Afghan Force Takes Hold, Turning to Peace," *New York Times*, 16 February 1995; William D. Hartung, *And Weapons for All* (New York: HarperCollins, 1994), 2–4.

4. Grimmett, 70. Overall rankings for the period 1986–1993: Saudi Arabia, Iraq, India, Afghanistan, Iran, Egypt, Cuba, Vietnam, Angola, Syria.

5. Ibid., 71.

6. H. St. John B. Armitage, CBE, "Trends in the Conventional Arms Market: The Middle East," *Royal United Services Institute Journal*, February 1994, 60.

7. Aaron Karp, "The Arms Trade Revolution: The Major Impact of Small Arms," *Washington Quarterly*, Autumn 1994, 71.

8. Ibid., 69.

9. Hartung, 190.

10. Ian V. Hogg, ed., *Jane's Infantry Weapons 1994–95* (Guildford and King's Lynn, England: Biddles Ltd, 1994), 7–9, 697–704.

11. Michael M. Zanoni, "The Shopping List: What's Available," in Peter C. Unsinger and Harry W. More, eds., *The International Legal and Illegal Trafficking of Arms* (Springfield, Ill.: Charles C. Thomas, 1989), 63.

12. Peter Wallensteen and Karin Axell, "Major Armed Conflict," in *Stockholm International Peace Research Institute (SIPRI) Yearbook 1994* (New York: Oxford University Press, Inc., 1994), 81. To put these numbers into context, the number of armed conflict locations in 1989 was 32; in 1990, 31; in 1991, 30; and in 1992, 30. This shows that the number of conflicts has been in slight decline since 1989. The 28 locations with major conflicts in 1993 were: Azerbaijan, Bosnia, United Kingdom, Croatia, Georgia, Iran, Iraq, Israel, Turkey, Bangladesh, Cambodia, India, Afghanistan, Indonesia, Myanmar, the Philippines, Sri Lanka, Tajikistan, Algeria, Angola, Liberia, Rwanda, Somalia, South Africa, Sudan, Colombia, Guatemala, and Peru. Final numbers for major armed conflicts in 1994 are not yet available, but one more notable conflict in 1994 concerns Chechnya.

13. Ibid., 81.

14. Richard P. Hallion, *Storm Over Iraq: Air Power and the Gulf War* (Washington, D.C., and London: Smithsonian Institution Press, 1992), 128.

15. Ibid., 127.

16. Ibid., 128.

17. Hartung, 236.

18. Ibid., 194.

19. Ibid., 192.

20. Hallion, 133.

21. Hartung, 2.

22. Eradio E. Uresti, "The Guns-for-Drugs Trade: Implications for US Foreign Policy," (Unpublished thesis, Naval Postgraduate School, Monterey, Calif., 1991), 30.

23. Ibid.

24. *The Military Balance 1993–1994* (London: Brassey's [UK] Ltd, 1993), 74–75.

25. Wallensteen and Axell, 88.

26. Brad Roberts, "From Nonproliferation to Antiproliferation," *International Security* 18, no. 1 (Summer 1993): 146.

27. Ibid.

28. Amit Gupta, "Third World Militaries: New Suppliers, Deadlier Weapons," *Orbis* 37, no. 1 (Winter 1993): 57.

29. Ibid.

30. David Silverberg, "Global Trends in Military Production and Conversion," *The Annals of the American Academy of Political and Social Science*, September 1994, 124–25.

31. *World Military Expenditures and Arms Transfers 1991–1992*, US Arms Control and Disarmament Agency, 1994, 18.

32. Gupta, 68.

33. *A National Security Strategy of Engagement and Enlargement* (Washington, D.C.: The White House, July 1994), 12.

34. Ibid.

35. Richard Kokoski, "Non-lethal Weapons: A Case Study of New Technology Developments," *SIPRI Yearbook 1994* (New York: Oxford University Press Inc., 1994), 368.

36. Barbara Starr, "Pentagon Maps Non-Lethal Options," *International Defense Review* 27, no. 7 (July 1994): 30.

37. Arthur Knoth, "Disabling Technologies, A Critical Assessment," *International Defense Review* 27, no. 7 (July 1994): 33.

38. Kokoski, 374.

39. Ibid., 377.

40. "Marines' Mission to Somalia Non-Lethal," *USA Today*, 15 February 1994.

41. "Now to the Shores of Somalia with Beanbag Guns and Goo," *New York Times*, 15 February 1994.

42. Ibid. Quote attributed to an unnamed senior American general.

43. *SIPRI Yearbook 1993* (New York: Oxford University Press, Inc., 1993), xx.

44. Amy F. Woolf, *Arms Control and Disarmament Activities: A Catalog of Recent Efforts*, Congressional Research Service, 17 January 1993, 25; Stuart Croft, "Negotiations, Treaty Terms and Implications," in Stuart Croft, ed., *The Conventional Armed Forces in Europe Treaty* (Aldershot, England: Dartmouth Publishing Co., Ltd., 1994), 30.

45. *The Military Balance 1993–1994*, 246.

46. Lee Feinstein, "CFE: Off the Endangered List," *Arms Control Today*, 1 October 1993, 4.

47. Ibid., 5.

48. Ibid.

49. Ibid.

50. Colin McInnes, "The CFE Treaty in Perspective," in Stuart Croft, ed., 12.

51. Croft, 32–34.

52. Richard Boucher, "Missile Technology Control Regime Guidelines Revised," US Department of State *Dispatch*, 18 January 1993, 41. Member nations include: Australia, Austria, Belgium, Canada, Denmark, Finland, France, Greece, Germany, Ireland, Iceland, Italy, Japan, Luxembourg, the Netherlands, New Zealand, Norway, Portugal, Spain, Sweden, Switzerland, United Kingdom, and the United States.

53. Ibid.

54. *National Security Strategy*, 11.

55. John Borawski and Bruce George, MP, "The CSCE Forum for Security Cooperation," *Arms Control Today* 23, no. 10 (October 1993): 13.

56. "Helsinki Document 1992," *SIPRI Yearbook 1993*, 179.

57. Ibid., 192.

58. Borawski and George, 13.

59. Ibid.

60. Ibid., 14, 15.

61. Ibid., 15.

62. *Arms Control and Disarmament Agreements* (Washington, D.C.: United States Arms Control and Disarmament Agency, 1990), 319.

63. "Vienna Document 1992 of the Negotiations on Confidence and Security Building Measures," *SIPRI Yearbook 1993*, 642.

64. Ibid., 646.

65. Wallensteen and Axell, 596.

66. Ibid., 533.

67. Woolf, 31.

68. Ibid.

69. Ibid., 32.

70. Jeffrey Lefebvre, "Fueling the Fire: The Arming of the Horn of Africa After the Cold War" (Paper presented to African Studies Association, Toronto, Canada, 3–6 November 1994), 2.

14

Regional Impacts of Civil Wars

Kurt A. Stonerock

Not long after the Gulf War, Jimmy Carter stated that of the 116 wars since World War II, all but the Iraqi invasion of Kuwait were civil wars.[1] While the exact number is subject to how one defines civil war, study after study shows that indeed the predominant form of warfare, both during and subsequent to the end of the cold war, has been civil war. Many excellent analyses have been written over the past several years on the nature of civil wars. Several of these writings have defined both the term and overall nature of civil war. Other writings have searched for explanations for the beginnings of civil wars and ways to end them.

This study explores a seldom-studied aspect of civil wars. It analyzes the extent to which civil wars take on a regional impact, the nature of such impact, and what to expect in the future. This inquiry has much relevance, given both the above-mentioned frequency of civil wars today and the potential for more civil wars as we move into the twenty-first century. We need to understand the degree to which states get involved in the civil wars of their neighbors. More significantly, we must appreciate the extent to which that involvement is involuntary.

Civil wars are often the most ruthless types of war. They pit neighbor against neighbor within a state and frequently result in enormous civilian suffering. They often involve extreme acts of savagery, as the belligerents know that the victor will govern the loser. Finally, they tend to create lasting animosities among people who must then learn to live together after the fighting has ended.[2] Given these attributes, post–cold war politicians the world over may find it desirable to stand clear of the civil wars of their neighbors rather than risk the lives of their own people.

Many Americans associate a certain sensitivity with the term *civil war* that is rooted in our own history. This association reinforces the desires of politicians who let other countries sort out their internal problems without US interference. One could argue that this association was the dynamic at work in January 1995 when State Department spokesman Mike McCurry discussed Washington's position on the Chechnya revolt. The *Washington Post* reported that "the United States yesterday tempered its concerns over continued Russian army attacks on the breakaway region of Chechnya by citing its own violent experience containing secessionism during the Civil War." McCurry was quoted as saying,

> We have a long history as a democracy that includes an episode in the history of our own country where we dealt with a secessionist movement through armed conflict called the Civil War and so we . . . need to be conscious of those types of issues when we look at a new democracy in the former Soviet Union, in Russia, dealing with what has already provided enormous political debate within Russia. We have to, you know, look at the full scope of issues that define (the relationship).[3]

This study analyzes the degree to which prudent leaders can afford to turn a blind eye to civil wars in their region. It reviews the extent to which observers believe civil wars will affect regional or global security concerns into the next century. The study also analyzes the nature of several ongoing civil wars and projected regional hot spots around the world. The reader may contend that focusing on the here and now precludes lessons learned from many notable civil wars throughout history. This focus is intentional. The civil wars of history still offer tremendous insight into their nature, how they start, and how they end. But, the ready access to and the capabilities of modern conventional weapons throughout the world inject a level of violence and speed into the destructive dimension of modern civil wars which, in turn, greatly accelerate the tendencies of civil wars to expand to the regional level. Furthermore, the relative and global connectivity of even the most remote portions of the world today, particularly in terms of trade and communications, also has significantly escalated the regional ripple effect of civil wars. For these reasons, the author restricts the data to modern civil wars to attain the most accurate picture of the expansive nature of tomorrow's civil wars.

This examination also suggests that in all probability civil wars will continue to be the most common type of war well into the next century. Finally, while this study does not propose means to end civil wars, it offers possible courses of action to limit the adverse effects of civil wars on regional neighbors.

Civil War Defined

Studies have defined the term *civil war* in various ways. This study relies on the definition of Roy Licklider as outlined in *Stopping the Killing*. Licklider defines civil war as "large-scale violence among geographically contiguous people concerned about possibly having to live with one another in the same political unit after the conflict." His definition incorporates two important criteria. First, there must be "multiple sovereignty" in that the people "pay taxes, provide men to its armies, feed its functionaries, honor its symbols, give time to its service, or yield other resources despite the prohibitions of a still-existing government they formerly obeyed," thus differentiating civil wars from other types of domestic violence such as riots.[4] Second, physical violence to people is involved. Licklider has used the operational definitions of the Correlates of War project: "a) 1,000 battle deaths or more per year and b) effective resistance" (either, at least two sides must have been organized for violent conflict before the war started, or the weaker side must have imposed casualties on its stronger opponent equal to at least 5 percent of the number of casualties it suffered at the hands of that opponent). This last criterion distinguishes civil wars from political massacres.[5]

Under this mainstream definition then, this writer classifies such wars of secession as Chechnya's war with the Russian Federation as a civil war. Similarly, this definition classifies wars to overthrow current governments, like the war in Algeria, as civil wars. Hit and run guerrilla wars, acts of terrorism, and most coup attempts do not conform to this definition. Observers have labeled conflicts like those in Somalia as civil wars, even though these conflicts do not adhere completely to the definition outlined earlier in this analysis. More specifically, in the conflict in Somalia it is difficult to identify the government in charge. Similarly, although President Bill Clinton's chief of staff recently referred to the Serbian war of aggression as a civil war, this writer found it difficult to identify a government in charge.[6] These borderline definitions of civil war are not critical to the focus of this study, however, since the ramifications of their internal strife to the neighboring countries do not vary markedly from the types and degrees of strife caused by more conventionally structured civil wars.

Historical Trends

Numerous studies have documented the growing frequency of civil wars. Figure 8 shows the annual number of wars under way from 1816 to 1992.

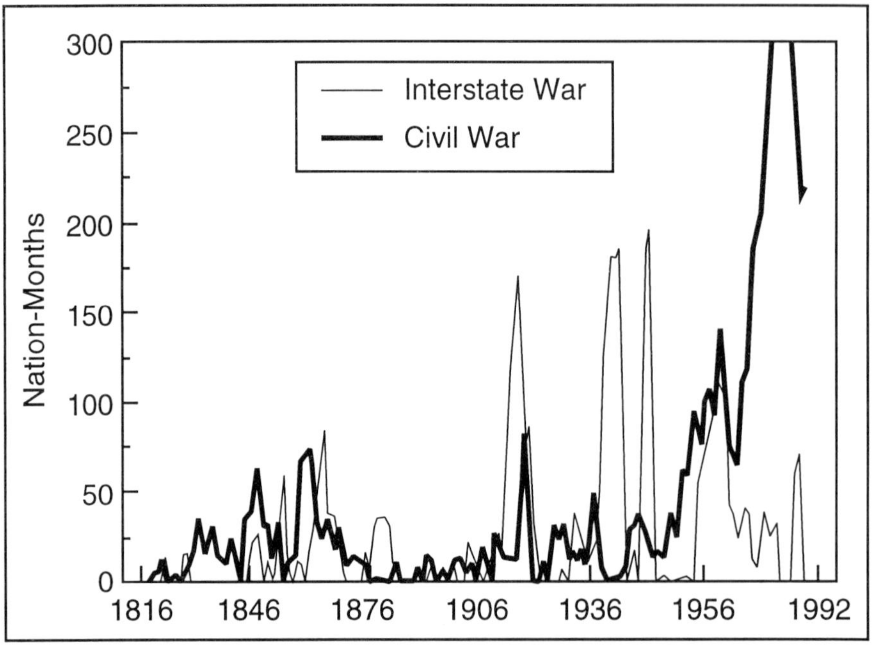

Source: Courtesy of the Correlates of War Project and J. David Singer

Figure 8. Annual Number of Wars Under Way, 1816–1992

The cold war witnessed the competition of the two superpowers for regional influence throughout the world by sponsoring either state governments or rebellious factions within those states. Angola and Nicaragua encompass only two examples of such cold-war-sponsored civil wars. More significantly, however, with the end of the cold war the world has seen an increase in the number of civil wars. This increase occurred as states, perceiving themselves as unrestrained by superpower influence, began to settle long-festering internal scores related to race, religion, regionalism (to include imbalanced economic distribution between classes or regions), ethnicity, or language.[7]

The enormity of the human suffering illustrates the size of the problem. According to two independent studies, civil wars constituted 14 of the 16 wars raging in 1990. These 14 wars have accounted for more than 2.5 million deaths. Civilian casualties comprised more than 90 percent of these deaths.[8] Civil wars have produced a large number of the estimated 41 million refugees in the world today.[9] Readers can visualize easily the magnitude of this carnage by sampling a few of the countries recently involved. Observers have estimated that civil wars caused the deaths of 500,000 and the displacement of about 2 million recently in Rwanda.[10] Sudan's 11-year civil war resulted in the deaths of up to 1 million and the displacement of 3 million.[11] The 15-year-old civil war in Mozambique had caused more than 650,000 deaths by the time a peace treaty was signed in 1992.[12] More than 150,000 deaths resulted from the civil war in Liberia, and 1 million remain displaced.[13] Sri Lanka's ongoing 15-year civil war has killed 40,000 and has displaced thousands more.[14] Unrest in Algeria in 1994 caused 25,000 to die.[15] The 34-year-old civil war in Guatemala has accounted for more than 100,000 deaths and the displacement of 1 million.[16] Finally, over 20,000 have died in Afghanistan's two and one-half-year-old civil war.[17] Even if one sets aside the human suffering, the treasure spent and productivity lost by these states are clearly enormous.

This study, however, focuses particularly on the degree to which civil wars have crossed political boundaries, thereby causing regional problems. We can turn first to situations wherein leaders voluntarily involved their states in the affairs of neighboring civil wars. We can classify these situations as largely humanitarian involvement, involvement for regional stability, or opportunities for parochial gains.

Realists contend that no state involves itself in a humanitarian mission without expecting such gains as goodwill or future access to a region and its assets. Most analysts hold that America's intervention in Somalia fell into the category of voluntary humanitarian and goodwill participation. However, one state may not perceive another state's motive as altruistic. For example, Daniel Pipes, editor of *Middle East Quarterly*, points out that "many groups and governments accused Washington of establishing a new colonialism in Somalia." He cites a Beirut newspaper that considered the United States' involvement in the tragedy as an "excuse to intervene to reshape the political situation in the Horn of Africa and the entire center of Africa."[18]

Examples abound of states involving themselves in the civil wars of other states primarily to maintain the stability of a region; however, states need not be neighbors in today's "global community" to want to ensure the stability of a particular region. In today's interconnected world, these interests often have economic implications, but they also may have a military nature, particularly if the warring neighbors control weapons of mass destruction. This search for stability motivates many states to contribute forces and materiel in UN, regional, or coalition peacekeeping efforts.

Finally, states may involve themselves in the civil wars of their neighbors for less than altruistic reasons. Declared or covert third-party sponsorship of either side in a civil war is still common despite the end of the cold war. For example, the Algerian government has accused Sudan of assisting Algerian guerrillas by permitting Iran to use Sudanese territory as a transit point for weapons.[19] Similarly, Nigeria contends that France wants to prevent Nigeria from becoming a regional power by using Sierra Leone, a French ally, as a conduit for weapons into civil war-torn Liberia.[20] As evidenced by these examples, third party involvement can get complex as states seek gains at the expense of a state embroiled in civil war.

More significant to this study, however, is the degree to which conditions draw states involuntarily into conflicts. For the purposes of analysis, this study groups these forces into three categories: refugee problems, internal security problems, and regional environmental ramifications.

Civil wars often ruthlessly "displace" large numbers of people by forcing them to flee their countries, thereby becoming refugees. Estimates show that up to 1.8 million refugees escaped from Rwanda into neighboring Zaire, Burundi, and Tanzania in the space of just two months.[21] Depending on the course of events of a given conflict, the refugee problem generated by a civil war often becomes a tremendous security burden to neighboring countries who find themselves hosts to the flood of refugees, often on short notice. For example, the government of Zaire has involuntarily become deeply embroiled with the tragedy of the Rwandan civil war. The population of the Zairian town of Bukavu has swollen from 60,000 to 800,000.[22] The international media recently reported that Zairians were taking "brutal measures" to crack down on rampant crime in a refugee camp of 200,000 Rwandans that included a riot that killed 18 Rwandans and one Zairian soldier.[23] Several sources have reported that former Hutu government and military officials virtually run the Zairian refugee camps. These officials are accused of causing gross distribution problems with international aid sent to the camp as they funnel the food and supplies from the refugees to the estimated 30,000 Hutu soldiers resting, training, and rearming in the Zairian hills for another attack on the new Tutsi-led Rwandan government.[24]

A different type of internal problem has arisen from the Rwandan tragedy in neighboring Tanzania. There the 200,000 Rwandan refugees received far better rations and care than the Tanzanian people themselves due to the flood of earmarked international aid. Fiona Terry, the coordinator for the French branch of the charity group Doctors Without Borders, told a news conference, "The obvious way to tell the difference between a Rwandan and a Tanzanian is by their health." She added that the malnutrition rate among Rwandan refugees ranged between 2 and 4 percent as compared to about 7 percent for Tanzanians.[25] The disruptive effect this difference could have on the Tanzanian people is obvious.

Refugee problems are not necessarily short-term or restricted to less developed or even neighboring nations. For example, in 1990 the US government granted 200,000 Salvadorans "temporary protected status" under legislation that allowed them to remain in the United States and work legally, but this legislation did not advance them toward permanent residency as immigrants. Many observers agree that these Salvadorans no longer need protection, given the stable political situation in their country since the 1992 Salvadoran civil war truce. However, most of these refugees want to remain in the United States, where they have put down roots. As late as November 1994, the US government has continued to work through the political controversy surrounding this issue.[26]

The security concerns a neighboring civil war can bring to a state has many forms. For example, security concerns can have enormous economic effects in the form of lost revenues, destroyed or nationalized assets in-country, a weakened trading partner, and lost access to needed resources. A relatively small but clear case demonstrates this point. In December 1994 Indian rebels and Mexican government forces fought for 12 days. Although not a full civil war, this limited action contributed to the Mexican peso's plunge of 38 percent against the dollar. Foreign investors lost millions due to the crash, according to one Latin American investment analyst.[27]

In addition to economic concerns, states also suffer physical security problems due to neighboring civil wars. Some observers expect Burundi, on the border with Rwanda, to tumble into civil war in Rwanda's wake, given that these countries have a similar geography, language, and ethnic mix of Tutsis and Hutus.[28] At the hands of Islamic fundamentalist groups, France has recently seen many of its citizens in Algeria murdered, one of its planes hijacked, and terrorist recruiting and training cells established on French soil. According to Gilles Kepel, a French expert on north African affairs, "It is clear that the fundamentalists are trying to create a large social base to solidify their movement in France. We can no longer escape the consequences of Algeria's turmoil."[29]

Finally, observers cannot ignore the regional environmental ramifications of civil wars any longer. Sources in Zaire report that Rwandan refugee camps impede a critical corridor between two parts of a Zairian national park. These same sources recognize the corridor as a "critical biological link" in the ecosystem of the park because of the variety of animals that transit there. According to the *New York Times*, "The refugee camps pose threats to the animals in several ways. The human presence discourages the animals from entering the corridor. Those animals that do venture forth are at risk of catching human diseases. And the refugees are exploiting the forest for food and firewood."[30] Elsewhere in Africa, civil wars have forced settled populations to leave the land, resulting in its neglect and exacerbating desertification. These wars also have frequently targeted animal reserves and water resources.

Future Projections

As we look beyond the turn of the century, we see no indication that civil wars will diminish either in terms of sheer numbers of conflicts or the magnitude of their destruction. The previously mentioned factors spurring current civil wars will remain obvious in a monopolar world 10 years hence. We can defend this assertion best by analyzing various regions of the world which either currently are or show indications of becoming "hot spots" for civil wars to break out. These potential civil wars would have significantly adverse regional and global implications.

The 89 ethnic republics and regions of the Russian Federation can serve as a tinderbox of internal conflict. Given the precedent-setting dissolution of the Soviet Union and the substantial military action in Chechnya, a distinct possibility exists for that conflict to spill into neighboring republics of the North Caucasian region, which is "a volatile melting pot of ethnic groups that share Chechen suspicions of Kremlin intentions."[31] According to a recent analysis by Leon Goure (of the Science Applications International Corporation), while non-Russian ethnic elements represent only 18 percent of the total population and therefore lack the "critical mass" to bring about the disintegration of the Russian Federation, these non-Russian ethnic elements "do not lack for geographic concentration and potential conflicts in certain parts of Russia, and this raises concern that secession by such areas may set in motion a widening movement unless effectively resisted by the central authorities."[32] A Russian Federation that perceives itself in a state of dissolution could conceivably return to much more authoritarian leadership to stem the tide. This new direction could thrust the rest of the globe into a new cold war. At a minimum, chaos in the nuclear-armed Russian Federation would be a significant security concern for other states.

China also may face growing internal unrest in the near future, but for economic rather than ethnic reasons. Futurists Alvin and Heidi Toffler paint a chillingly realistic scenario wherein the economically booming coastal provinces escalate their current defiance of the central government in Beijing. The Tofflers foresee the day when these provinces refuse to contribute the funds the central government needs to improve distant rural conditions or put down agrarian unrest. They state:

> Unless Beijing grants them (the coastal provinces) complete freedom of financial and political action, one can imagine the new elites insisting on independence or some facsimile of it—a step that could tear China apart and trigger civil war. With enormous investments at stake, Japan, Korea, Taiwan, and other countries might be compelled to take sides—and thus find themselves sucked unwillingly into the conflagration that might follow.[33]

Future regional security ramifications stemming from the blossoming Algerian civil war extend well beyond France. Peter Rodman (director of Middle East Studies at the Center for Strategic and International Studies) sees high stakes for the Mediterranean region. "A civil war could destabilize the region and trigger a mass exodus spilling over into Europe."[34] Given their own increasingly radical Islamic movements, Egypt, Tunisia, Morocco, and Libya are particularly nervous when they consider the destabilizing effects on their own governments of a successful Islamic revolution in Algeria.[35] Along with France, Spain and Italy are concerned about the hundreds of thousands of immigrants likely to be generated by a fundamentalist Islamic government coming into power in Algeria.[36] Finally, an anti-Western government in Algeria could jeopardize trade, especially the important supplies of oil and gas Algeria currently exports to Europe.[37]

Other potential hot spots abound in the world. To C. Payne Lucas (president of Africare, a Washington-based development and relief organization) the 1994 truce in the civil wars of Angola and Mozambique hold vital importance to the region. He states:

> Without sustained peace, notably in Angola and Mozambique, there cannot be effective economic integration and growth in the region. And without growth, Western democracy could prove too fragile and exotic

to survive. That is why, beyond the humanitarian imperative, keeping the peace in Angola is so critical. Angola is the region's last remaining element of destabilization. A peaceful Angola, with its enormous oil, mineral, and agricultural resources, becomes a keystone to regional growth. An Angola in conflict poisons the southern African well, encouraging foreign investors to avoid the region and political dissidents to resort again to violence.[38]

Prospects for Resolution

Having analyzed the propensity of civil wars to affect their neighbors adversely in a variety of ways, it is appropriate to end this study with a brief look at possible ways an external state could employ its diplomatic, economic, informational, and military instruments of power to at least "contain" the regional impact of a given civil war.

Peaceful Containment

The first consideration shows an appreciation for the uniqueness of every civil war and thus, in true Clausewitzian fashion, emphasizes that the state needs to focus first on quickly attaining and correctly analyzing sufficient intelligence to allow for the formulation of an accurate assessment of the "nature" of a particular war. Such an analysis provides good clues about the potential regional impact of that war in terms of such important areas as potential refugee management requirements, possible environmental effects, or potential destabilizing results from the fighting on neighboring states.

To contain a civil war diplomatically a state could, either unilaterally or through an international body, put the warring parties in the civil war on notice that it will deal with both sides harshly should either party allow the war to extend beyond its own borders. A state also could use its diplomatic machinery to assemble any coalitions it may need to coordinate men and materiel for refugee relief efforts.

Economically, a state could, depending on its needs in a given conflict, assemble or solicit economic assistance in the form of supplies needed to care for large influxes of refugees and organize other forms of economic aid to help ensure the stability of regional economies likely impacted by the warring state. This assistance, in the form of money or such system essentials as oil, could be particularly important to a state whose economy is normally heavily dependent upon trade with the warring state.

A liberal movement of information between states concerning progress of the war, refugee flows, or imminent environmental impacts could be extremely helpful in the proactive posturing of neighboring states' resources to mitigate the effects of a civil war's expansion.

Military Containment

If an external state decides to use military power to help contain the civil war of a neighboring state within its borders, the military should respond rapidly and with "overwhelming force." The US did as much in Somalia and Haiti. Such actions help to preempt new problems and ensure that adversaries understand the imprudence of resistance. These principles apply irrespective of whether a state uses military force unilaterally or as part of a coalition or regional or UN force.

In December 1994 UN forces broke with their traditional roles as peacekeepers and joined Zairian government troops in a sweep of one Rwandan refugee camp to remove weapons and criminal elements.[39] Thus, precedent exists for an aggressive military response to contain refugee problems that emanate from civil wars. The rapid and powerful force strategy recommended here applies particularly well to the type of activity found in the beginning stage of a refugee camp's existence, thus preempting the chaos experienced in the Rwandan refugee camps in Zaire.

To use the military instrument to provide rapid relief supplies and personnel to support these refugee camps could continue as a viable mission. Similarly, accelerated security assistance efforts (small arms, Airborne Warning and Control System surveillance, and Patriot missiles, etc.) to neighboring states could help to alleviate concerns within those states and send a message to the warring parties not to let the conflict spill across borders.

"Shows of force" also may be a highly effective mechanism to contain civil wars. Such efforts might entail stationing troops on a warring state's borders as the US is currently doing in

Macedonia to contain the Bosnian conflict. Similarly, troops may be stationed in nearby coastal waters as the US recently did via a "float reserve" of 2,000 Marines off the Haitian coast.

Clearly, irrespective of the roles it may play to prevent or terminate civil wars, the military power of a nation certainly can play an important role in containing these most disruptive of all wars.

Notes

1. Roy Licklider, *Stopping the Killing, How Civil Wars End* (New York: New York University Press, 1992), 7.

2. Robin Higham, *Civil Wars in the Twentieth Century* (Lexington, Ky.: The University Press of Kentucky, 1972), 6.

3. "U.S. Compares Chechnya Revolt with American Civil War Issues," *Washington Post*, 4 January 1995, 20.

4. Charles Tilly, *From Mobilization to Revolution* (Reading, Mass.: Addison-Wesley, 1978), 192.

5. Licklider, 9.

6. "A Civil War," *New Republic*, 19 December 1994, 7.

7. John Spanier, *Games Nations Play* (Washington, D.C.: CQ Press, 1993), 267-70.

8. "Civilians Often Bear War's Brunt," *St. Petersburg Times*, 17 February 1991, 7A.

9. "Current Policies About Refugees Leave Bosnians and Others Out in the Cold," *Wall Street Journal*, 1 March 1993, 11.

10. "U.N. Considers Action on Rising Violence in Rwandan Camps," *New York Times International*, 3 November 1994, A5; and "U.S. Forces to End Rwanda Mission on Schedule by Oct. 1," *Boston Globe*, 23 September 1994, 7.

11. "Sudans Long Civil War Threatening to Spread," *New York Times*, 22 November 1994, 3.

12. "Mozambique Party Quits Voting Process," *Washington Times*, 28 October 1994, 17.

13. "U.S. Officials End Liberia Mission," *Dallas Morning News*, 16 November 1994, 26.

14. "After the Sri Lanka Violence: A Sense of Despair," *New York Times International*, 30 October 1994, 3.

15. "Attention is Focused on Algeria's Hidden War," *Financial Times of London*, 28 December 1994, 2.

16. "U.N. Steps Up Human Rights Watch in Civil-War-Plagued Guatemala," *Washington Times*, 28 November 1994, 18; and "Guatemala's Plight," *Boston Globe*, 26 November 1994, 15.

17. "Forgotten War Rages in Afghanistan," *Washington Times*, 26 November 1994, 8.

18. "The Paranoid Style in Mideast Politics," *Washington Post*, 6 November 1994, C4.

19. "Sudan Linked to Rebellion in Algeria," *New York Times*, 24 December 1994, 3.

20. "War Engulfs Liberia, Humbling the Peacekeepers," *New York Times International*, 7 October 1994, 4.

21. "Burundi Wants Rwandans Out," *Washington Times*, 20 October 1994, 14; and *New York Times International*, 3 November 1994, A5.

22. "Zaire's Premier Confident About Recovery," *Washington Times*, 11 October 1994, 11.

23. "Zaire Cracks Down on Refugee Camp," *Baltimore Sun*, 29 November 1994, 12.

24. "Refugees: Relief Effort in Rwanda Turns Nightmarish," *Los Angeles Times*, 15 November 1994, A4.

25. "Doctors Quit Refugee Camp, Refuse to Aid Mass Killers," Reuters News Agency, *Early Bird Supplement*, 29 December 1994, A2.

26. "U.S. to Alter Status of Salvadorans," *Washington Post*, 24 November 1994, 1.

27. "Mexican Rebels Agree to Attend Peace Talks," *Washington Times*, 29 December 1994, 13.

28. "Efforts Under Way to 'Change Hearts' of Burundians," *Dallas Morning News*, 13 November 1994, 28A.

29. "Algeria's Problems Spilling into France," *Washington Times*, 28 December 1994, 13.

30. "Rwanda Refugee Crisis is Threatening Gorillas in Neighboring Areas," *New York Times*, 25 October 1994, C4.

31. "Fire in the Caucasus," *Time*, 12 December 1994, 6.

32. "The Russian Federation: Possible Disintegration Scenarios," *Comparative Strategy* 13, no. 4 (October/December 1994): 409.

33. Alvin Toffler and Heidi Toffler, *War and Anti-War, Survival at the Dawn of the 21st Century* (Boston: Little, Brown and Co., 1993), 214–15.

34. "The Time Bomb in Algeria," *Washington Post*, 1 January 1995, C1.

35. "Algeria: Islamic Militants Threaten More Than This N. African Nation," *Christian Science Monitor*, 27 December 1994, 11; and "The Maghreb Cauldron," *Armed Forces Journal International*, October 1994, 54.

36. "Algeria's Instability Has Potential to Spread," *Baltimore Sun*, 29 December 1994, 1.

37. "A Vote Nullified Becomes Terrorism," *Los Angeles Times*, 29 December 1994, 11.

38. "Angola's Rescuer: Angola," *Washington Post*, 30 December 1994, 17.

39. "U.N. Troops Help Rwanda to Strip Camp of Weapons," *New York Times*, 15 December 1994, 6.

15

Threats from Third World Regional Hegemons

James E. Overly

The cold war paradigm that encompassed world politics from about 1945 to 1989 was characterized most strongly by global competition between the United States and the former Soviet Union. A part of that rivalry involved the contest for influence among third world states. That contest was marked by a larger degree of intercourse between the two superpowers and nations of the third world than otherwise would have been the case had the intercourse been based strictly on classic realpolitik bilateral interests. Indeed, that degree of superpower involvement with third world affairs was not present previous to the cold war.

In the cold war bipolar environment, the political actors of the third world came to understand a most important unwritten rule of the game: A regional conflict could not lead to a direct confrontation between the two superpowers as it did during the Cuban missile crisis, for such a conflict had obvious dimensions of nuclear danger. This unwritten rule served to contain or depress regional conflicts or chronic antagonisms among or within nation-states and to limit or moderate them when they did occur.

It is now obvious—since the fall of the Berlin Wall and the breakup of the former Soviet empire—that the bipolar framework for the moderation of regional conflicts has crumbled. Moreover, the framework crumbled without replacement by a comparable new order. (Pundits have more accurately described the new world order proclaimed by President George Bush as the new world disorder.) The implosion of the former Soviet Union caused a precipitous decline in Russia's subsequent influence and diminished the scope of her dealings with other nations. For its own reasons, the United States has evidenced a slower, more hesitant withdrawal from intense involvement in world affairs.

As superpower involvement in world affairs diminished, third world powers aspiring to increase their influence in several areas of the world have been testing the will of the great powers—and in some cases, neighboring countries in their own region—to draw lines of tolerance pertaining to regional conflicts. These conflicts have ranged from Iraq's invasion and occupation of Kuwait in 1990, to the dissolution of countries formerly held together by military forces such as the former Yugoslavia and the former Soviet Union's Caucasus republics, to the internal collapse of Somalia, Rwanda, and Haiti. Thus, many academics and political analysts have concluded that the world has become more dangerous, not less, in the wake of the collapse of the cold war order.

These post-cold-war conflicts elicited varying responses from other nations. The United States and its allies responded overwhelmingly to turn back Iraq's aggression in Kuwait. Contrast this response to their being much more muted in their reactions to the wars erupting in the former Yugoslavia and the states emerging from the ruins of the defunct Soviet Union. On the other hand, the United States deployed sizable numbers of military forces to address internal problems in Somalia and Haiti that represented no threat outside their borders.

These situations and the reactions to them by other powers beg the question: Is there a systematic way to predict likely applications of military force by anyone that might give rise to security concerns on the part of other nations? That is, can we predict the nations likely to employ military forces to embark upon regional hegemony during the next five to 10 years? If so, then we will be able to identify likely security concerns around the globe more easily and use their predictions to enhance the prospects for stability.

To begin the search for the answers to these questions, we must define *hegemony* more precisely. There is extant a variety of definitions of hegemony that must be winnowed, ranging from the generic to specific applications of the term as a characteristic primarily applicable to super or great powers. Most definitions, nonetheless, contain elements of the useful but general definition espoused by Jack C. Plano and Roy Olton:

"Hegemony is the extension by one state of preponderant influence or control over another state or region. A policy of hegemony may result in a client-state or satellite relationship and the creation of a sphere of influence."[1] David J. Myers defines *regional hegemons* as "states which possess power sufficient to dominate a subordinate state system."[2] He describes three relevant dimensions of power: the material, the military, and the motivational.[3] For our purpose, we focus on the military aspect and modify these definitions of hegemony as follows: A state establishes hegemony (i.e., it extends preponderant influence or control) militarily over another state or region, normally against a neighbor or in its immediate region, through the application of the military instrument of power.

A state's mere use of the military, however, may or may not constitute a "threat" to another. A clear threat exists when a state uses military force in such a way that another state perceives its sovereignty or physical survival—its core interests—at risk. Further, if one country's military action should threaten another country's important socioeconomic interests, the risks may be classified at the intermediate level. Interests at the intermediate level are not considered vital or critical to the nation's survival as a sovereign entity, but they do consider them important to the way or quality of life in that nation. Finally, the risks may be to another nation's peripheral interests, which concern ideological, humanitarian, or attitudinal matters.

Traditionally, the reaction of a nation to a perceived threat has varied directly according to the perceived degree of danger to the nation's core interests. During the cold war, the two superpowers analyzed every third world military action according to the perceived effect on their strategic interests. But another unwritten rule of the cold war framework outlined that only in unusual, clearly defined instances did superpower military forces intervene; elsewhere, the preferred form of superpower intervention came through proxies or nonmilitary means. More recently, however, super and great powers with ability to project military force to distant corners of the world have at times exercised that capability when a far-removed aspiring regional hegemon employed military force to threaten its neighbors. Thus, hegemony as a threat to world security has become doubly dangerous. On the one hand, restraints on aspiring regional hegemons have been loosened; while on the other, the question of whether or how other nations may react has become less predictable. Michael T. Klare, professor of peace and world security studies at Hampshire College, sardonically describes the course of post-cold-war American foreign policy thinking:

> Republicans and Democrats do not agree about much, least of all in the foreign policy area, but on one key point they seem to share the same delusion: that America's national security interests are best secured by preparing for an unending series of conflicts with "rogue states" in the Middle East and Asia.[4]

Historical and Present State of the Problem

Few broad studies of international affairs have focused on regional hegemony systematically and analytically. Instead, in some cases, observers have arbitrarily chosen countries based on empirical observations of "likely suspects" in certain geographic regions and written about them as historic or potential military threats. Others have focused primarily on the history of great power reactions to the activities of regional hegemons. But let us identify the aspiring hegemons in the third world who could raise a military threat against another nation and thereby create a regional, if not a global, security concern during the next decade. The potential number of hegemons is large, for analysts might characterize most of the approximately 180 nations in the world as still developing their political, economic, and social institutions and infrastructures; most have military forces; and most are not geographically isolated island nations.

Karl P. Magyar advances an analytical methodology for analyzing hegemon-driven security concerns when he posits that states develop as international actors in stages.[5] First, the formative stage occurs at the inception of a state. Second, the consolidative stage of building legitimate political and administrative institutions develops in a long process after a state attains independence. Indeed, the consolidative stage may be subdivided into an early, aggressive, "forced" phase and a later, perhaps an enduring or mature phase. Third, the expansive stage occurs when states attempt to export their power into neighboring lands. Having attained internal consolidation and a dominant regional position, Magyar argues the states then qualify as great powers and enter the global or imperial stage. This stage is characterized by the projection of power and expansion of political influence to distant areas. Fifth, the compulsive stage accentuates a growing imbalance between a great power's resources and ambitions, leading to the power's precipitous weakening, if not collapse.

Magyar places the great bulk of states in the world today in the consolidative stage, with about half in the early phase of this stage. A number of the states in this consolidative stage, Magyar argues, are among the most unstable states in the international system. Into this category he places some established but perennially volatile Latin American states, most African states, post-cold-war Russia and the Confederation of Independent States (CIS), and a number of other third world states with greatly disproportionate arms acquisition policies, including North Korea.

Combining the phenomenon of aspiring regional hegemons with greater freedom to maneuver after the collapse of the cold war structure with Magyar's state classification system and its attributes of states in the volatile, forced, and consolidative phase seems to depart from a more systematic identification of the states in each region potentially prepared to use military force to expand or otherwise increase their regional or global influence. A tour d' horizon of each region follows. Each section discusses nations which have acted as hegemons in the recent past or which are aspiring hegemons. Most of these regions are presently in the consolidative or expansionist stages of national development.

Latin America

Peru and Ecuador revived an old border dispute in early 1995 when clashes broke out between army units on the frontier. This clash is the most recent transnational border confrontation on the South American continent, but many similar skirmishes from the past could be revived. For example, Ecuador also has had border clashes with Colombia, and Bolivia dreams of a path to the sea. With territorial acquisition in mind, these conflicts also may portend expansionist ambitions.

One must keep an eye on Cuba, Guatemala, and Nicaragua, all of whom have actively employed their military forces or extended military support in regional conflicts in the past. Today Cuba's economy continues to deteriorate and Nicaragua is deeply immersed in building a democracy and market economy; nonetheless, the political operatives in both countries are the same powers who fueled past conflicts in their regions. They are either still in power or have retained powerful influence over their new governments. The point becomes pertinent in considering allusions to ties between rebel leaders and the Sandinistas of Nicaragua contained in early 1995 news reports of renewed fighting in the Chiapas region of Mexico.

Western Europe

Western Europe is comprised of mature states, all of whom now have democratically elected governments with free, integrated markets or mixed government-private sector economies. Thus, with a possible exception discussed later, in the main they are not candidates to repeat the deeds of past regional hegemons. Instead, the fundamental question for Western Europe throughout the remainder of the twentieth century, and probably into the next century, focuses on the role of the United States in European security affairs. That role has significantly and rapidly decreased since the demise of the Warsaw Pact. Analysts have debated the issue under the guise of discussions about future roles of the North Atlantic Treaty Organization (NATO). More importantly, they have debated it under the rubric of developing the European Union (EU) as an extensive political entity with its own defense capability exercised through such principally European security organizations as the Western European Union (WEU) and the Organization for the Security and Cooperation of Europe (OSCE). Thus, the EU (even though several of its largest and most important members are mature major powers) itself may be considered as being in the early stages of a consolidation phase as a transnational political unit, with the establishment of regional hegemony as a potential objective.

This suggestion does not imply in any way that the EU will suddenly become aggressive. Indeed, all major European powers are currently decreasing the size of their military forces; most of them still want the US to play a strong role in European security affairs; and most appear willing to join with the US to react militarily to third world crises when necessary. Nevertheless, to further the end of "europeanizing" regional security, Western European governments are likely to feel increasing political pressure to use their own military forces—either nationally or through their regional security organizations—to intervene in small regional conflicts on the borders of Europe when it appears to Europeans' political advantage to act independently or ahead of the United States.

Greece and Turkey, two nations straddling the border between Europe and Asia, show no signs of definitively resolving old disagreements that have deteriorated into conflicts. In the breakup of the former Yugoslavia into several nations, Greece has resurrected an old difference with the Republic of Macedonia that portends military conflict, and has held hostage the policy of the EU and other nations vis à vis that emerging nation. Turkey, on the other hand, has had to deal with a resurgence of historic Kurdish attempts to forge an independent nation from areas the Kurds populate in Turkey, Iraq, and Syria. Turkey also has found itself presented with an opportunity to expand its influence, albeit so far not militarily in some of the new Moslem republics emerging from the former Soviet Union (discussed in a later section) and in Bosnia.

Middle East and North Africa

A plethora of actual or aspiring regional hegemons are emerging in the volatile Middle East and North Africa region. As Magyar points out, Israel expanded into lands belonging to Jordan and Syria, and the recent Israeli-Jordan peace treaty and the Israeli-Palestine Liberation Army peace agreement have not settled the land-ownership issues.[6] One needs only to recall the eight-year Iran-Iraq war, the Iraqi invasion of Kuwait and the ensuing Gulf War, the battles between North and South Yemen, the Yemeni rivalry with Saudi Arabia, and

Syria's occupation of Lebanon to be aware of the aspirants for regional hegemony in the area.

Closely associated with these states are the fragile states of North Africa. The most unpredictable state in that area has been Libya, which acted militarily against Egypt and Chad, supported terrorism against the US and Western Europe, and fostered insurgent movements in sub-Saharan Africa and in countries as distant as the Philippines. While the Muammar Qadhafi regime's expansionist activities may have been less visible after the US raid of April 1986, there is no guarantee that the regime's hegemonial ambitions have abated or that the region will remain relatively quiescent in the future.

If Libya is the most disruptive country in the region, Algeria's current internal struggle with the forces of political Islam presents the most volatile situation.[7] The outcome of that struggle is potentially disruptive to the region and beyond, as has been Algeria's support of the Polisario Front in neighboring Western Sahara. Morocco, also, has demonstrated expansionist aims with its attempted absorption of Western Sahara, its occasional military involvement in sub-Saharan Africa, and its participation in the liberation of Kuwait in 1991.

A "bridge" state from the Arab world to Black Africa because of geography and its Arab and Black African populations, Sudan remains locked in a vicious civil war. At the same time, the central government is harshly implementing political Islam and aligning itself with the terrorist-supporting states of Iran and Libya to expand its influence in the wider region that includes Chad, Ethiopia, Eritrea, Somalia, and most notably Egypt.

Sub-Saharan Africa

As the continent with the greatest proportion of its states in the formative or early consolidative stages, Africa likely will witness more wars in its sub-Saharan region than any other region of the globe. The mostly internal conflicts in African countries can be exploited now by emerging regional hegemonic neighbors who are aware of the traditional great powers' declining interest in interfering on the continent. Examples of such emerging regional hegemons include Nigeria (acting most recently in the Liberian civil war) and Tanzania (acting in

Uganda, the Comoros, and the Seychelles). One example includes Uganda, where the government, despite its denials, clearly used its own military resources to support the Rwandan Patriotic Front's overthrow of the Rwandan government. Another example includes Zaire's military actions in Rwanda and Angola.

President Nelson Mandela initially has directed South Africa away from the interventionist and hegemonic policies of the preceding white governments. Nevertheless, he will find it difficult for South Africa, as powerful as the country is militarily, to avoid involvement in future southern African conflicts, even if only in peacemaking or peacekeeping roles.

Ranging over Africa with an eye toward the future, Magyar succinctly describes the continent as a major source of global security concerns: "Formative conflicts are underway or perhaps may be expected in Somalia, Djibouti, Eritrea, Ethiopia, Sudan, Chad, Western Sahara, Nigeria, Zaire, Tanzania, and South Africa. Africa also experiences several expansionist efforts initiated by Nigeria, Morocco, Sudan, Libya, Tanzania, Ivory Coast, and Zaire."[8] Such a tumultuous conflict environment offers ample opportunity to emerging hegemons.

Russia, the "Near Abroad," and Eastern Europe

Paul Hacker sums up some of the most significant problems facing the region once dominated by the former Soviet Union and the Warsaw Pact:

> These include . . . (1) most crucially, how to consolidate democracy in Russia and to promote a new set of relations with the former Soviet republics in conditions of internecine wars, perceived threats from Islamic extremists, and economic breakdown; (2) how to achieve the coexistence of different nationalities occupying the same territory in many countries in the region; and (3) how to overcome the legacy of over four decades of communist rule and subservience to the former USSR in Eastern Europe while developing a new set of ties to the West that will enhance security throughout the Continent.[9]

In early 1995 Russian troops quashed the Chechnyan bid for independence. As Hacker points out, "A major problem for the Russian military has been to restructure for a world of peace and to find a new mission. The prospect of fighting a war in Western Europe or of using military force to keep control of

Eastern Europe has been superseded by the need to protect Russian interests in the former Soviet republics."[10] Moreover, other vital questions remain relating to the degree of Russian civilian control over the military, the control of ex-Soviet nuclear weapons and other weapons of mass destruction deployed in the newly independent states, and the division of ex-Soviet military assets between Russia, the Ukraine, and other new republics—including the territorial problems of ports.

One could argue that prior to 1989, the former Soviet Union was, according to Magyar's classification system, a declining global/imperial state in the compulsive stage. It is clear now that Russia has joined its new republics in the consolidative stage. With the region's vast amount of lethal weaponry, a Russian military without a mission, and upheavals that have yet to run their course, many observers would argue that the situation in this area is of the gravest concern as the world enters a new millennium. The opportunities this region provides to such other would-be hegemons as Iran and Afghanistan, and perhaps even Turkey, are ominous.

South Asia

South Asia is another area of the world with bitter rivalries between competing regional powers, with some of them becoming more dangerous because of advanced efforts to develop nuclear weapons. India, the largest country and also one with the largest military in the region, continues its quest to dominate the region's affairs through its military forces. Added to a lengthy list of past regional military interventions on virtually every border, the recent dispatch of military troops by India to intervene in Sri Lanka's civil war amply illustrates its proclivity to enhance its regional hegemony through forcible means.

In Pakistan the military remains the "power behind the throne." The military's activism in pushing the government to acquire nuclear weapons and other sophisticated weapons systems, makes Pakistan an unsettling neighbor to India and other regional states. Moreover, the military's willingness to be deployed in United Nations (UN) peacekeeping missions in distant areas manifests its readiness to see its military employed as an instrument of national power and influence. Pakistan also played a key role in neighboring Afghanistan's internal war.

The grip of an unending civil war that keeps it in an early consolidative stage continues to hold Afghanistan. Nonetheless, partly because of its bent toward fundamentalist Islam, it seeks influence in the newly independent states of the former Soviet Union, which might presage Afghanistan's expansionist ambitions.

Southeast Asia

Events seem to be quieting in the Southeast Asian subcontinent. However, even this geographic area has had more than its share of small but expansive powers willing to employ military force to gain regional influence. Vietnam, although having to concentrate on rectifying the wretched state of its economy, retains the historical will to be a regional power. Thailand, forced to develop a capable armed force because of its defense needs, now helps to maintain its image as a regional power by offering its troops for international peacekeeping duty. Also in this region, the 1975 invasion by Indonesia and its subsequent occupation of East Timor vividly demonstrate that it will not hesitate to employ its military to acquire additional influence and territory.

The Far East

China remains the enigma of the Pacific rim, particularly in reference to the future. China's military history, the size of the country, its population, and its military suggest that analysts consider the country as a classic regional hegemon. However, although historically China has aggressively defended its borders, it has not often sought to project itself beyond its historic region. China even defends its involvement in the 1950s in Korea, the 1960s war with India, and its incursions into Vietnam in the 1970s as extensions of border defense rather than outright expansive military action. Its military behavior and intentions in the first years of the next century likely will be, once again, functions of internal political struggles among powerful political factions—most of which would probably agree on retaining regional but not global domination.

If China is the most enigmatic regional hegemon in the Pacific, North Korea is the most unpredictable. Because of North Korea's large numbers of well-equipped, highly trained and fanatically committed troops, and what is believed to be a nascent nuclear weapons development program, analysts must continue to consider it as a potential hegemon capable of using military power to gain influence in the region as long as its authoritarian regime remains in power.

Consequences

With the end of superpower rivalry throughout the globe and the precipitous decline in Russian activity and influence, the United States is also (albeit more slowly) reducing its major global military commitments, its provision of economic development aid, and its diplomatic activities. Similarly, so have many other Western powers. This collective decline in all these great powers' international activities creates a power vacuum that third world regional hegemons are eager to exploit.

In some cases, the decline in Western or international economic development aid to the third world could lead some countries to exercise military force to gain control of the resources of weak neighbors. In others, it could lead to the military's usurping domestic political power to protect its financing. In both situations, the military's actions are likely to produce threats to existing regional security arrangements and thus become concerns to the immediate region, if not beyond.

Projected Security Implications

As useful as readers might find the preceding discussion in identifying present regional hegemons or hegemonic aspirants on purely historical or topical bases, the issue begs for a more systematic method of analyzing regional hegemony and projecting possible security implications. Magyar's model provides a useful framework for classifying the evolutionary level of any state. Using that model to examine the previously discussed current or potential hegemons, it becomes evident that most of the nations discussed heretofore as potential hegemons are states in the volatile consolidative stage of development. This model narrows the search somewhat, but are there other tools that analysts can use to identify the most likely states to apply military force as a national instrument of power? A useful tool developed in the United States Air Force for planning air campaigns can be modified to serve the purpose.

Col John A. Warden III devised a "five ring" model to analyze a target country as a system and used it to develop the highly successful 1991 Gulf air war strategy. According to Warden, a country's leadership is the center ring of five interrelated concentric circles, representing other "vital parts" of a nation-state—system essentials (e.g., oil, water, food, medicine, and raw materials), infrastructure (e.g., roads, electrical grid, and petroleum distribution), population (e.g., whether supportive of the leadership, the standard of living, the level of education, and homogeneity), and fielded forces (i.e., usually the military).[11]

For our purposes of examining third world hegemons, the elements of leadership, system essentials, and fielded forces are arguably the most germane. For example, the leaders of hegemonial states, for whatever political, economic, or personal reasons, seek domination over their neighbors. That leadership must dominate the state governmental apparatus to implement those policies. The country's economy must be capable of supporting a strong military (even if the government policy is to devote a disproportionate share of gross domestic income to the task). Its military must be capable of projecting force.

Thus, to identify potential hegemons, one looks for a state in the consolidative stage, usually but not necessarily a state with a nondemocratic government (most likely one with a charismatic dictator or otherwise strong leader or clique at the top). A potential hegemon is usually one with an emphasis on the military and military spending that is disproportionate to other social sectors or economic development and social needs. Obviously, the military must be able to project force, but even small, underfunded African military organizations have repeatedly demonstrated the capability of projecting force into neighboring countries.

If the expansionist state has or is developing nuclear weapons, chemical and biological weapons, and missile delivery systems, that aspiring hegemon obviously becomes more dangerous and offers a greater security concern not only for its neighbors but other states beyond the region as well. For example, during a UN conference on renewing the Nuclear Non-Proliferation Treaty (NPT) held in April 1995, foreign ministers from the "north" (i.e., the developed states) and the "south" (i.e., developing or consolidating states) drew "battle lines," according to one account.[12] That report quoted Nigeria's foreign minister, Tom Ikimi, as staking out the position of the "third world hard-liners": "The way forward is to extend the treaty for a fixed period"—and not indefinitely, as sought by the United States.

The NPT recognizes five nuclear states: the United States, Great Britain, France, Russia, and China. In addition to these five states recognized by the treaty, three of the former Soviet Union's newly independent states—Ukraine, Belarus, and Kazakhstan—are heirs to Soviet nuclear weapons, but are obliged to return them to Russia. Three "undeclared" nuclear powers include India, Pakistan, and Israel. Observers suspect at least three other states of harboring nuclear plans—Iraq, North Korea, and Iran. They believe three others to have abandoned nuclear weapons programs—South Africa, Argentina, and Brazil. Analysts have judged another 11 states, all of whom are developed nations or newly industrialized countries (i.e., South Korea and Taiwan) as capable of building weapons. Thus, two of the recognized nuclear powers, the three newly independent states with nuclear weapons belonging to Russia, the three undeclared nuclear powers, and the three others suspected of having plans to develop nuclear weapons are states in the consolidative stage of national development.

This methodology, combining the Magyar and Warden analytical methods, supports our earlier assertion that Russia in the "near abroad" and China in the Far East will be two of the most important states to watch for hegemonic activity as we enter the twenty-first century. So, too, does it identify India and Pakistan. In the case of Libya, this methodology would identify the North African country's wealth and bellicosity, its documented support for international terrorism, and its attempts to develop or obtain weapons of mass destruction (both nuclear and chemical/biological) with the sophisticated weapons platforms to deliver them. The analysis would support the present conclusion that Libya is among the most destabilizing regional hegemons and is likely to remain so, at least as long as the current regime remains in power.

If the analysis compares data for a country against the strengths and weaknesses of its neighbors, other situations portending security concerns for the immediate region and beyond could likely be identified. Such an analysis would identify Iran, Iraq, and Syria as likely hegemons at the ingress into the next century.

The burgeoning attempts by ambitious third world rogue states to establish or enhance regional hegemony through the application of military force presents an ultimate irony. The demise of the cold war and the agreements to destroy sizable portions of the main protagonists' nuclear arsenals should make the world feel safer and imply fewer situations requiring a military presence. Yet the activities of present and future hegemonists will likely make great power military responses ever more frequent and necessary. This eventuality will levy unwelcome requirements on the great powers, who will bear the bulk of the world's responsibility to respond militarily to hegemonic aggression:

- First, and foremost, the great powers will need to maintain large standing military forces and reserves in a high state of readiness, perhaps at higher budget levels than many Western political leaders are currently prepared to support.
- Second, the great powers will need to restructure their military forces to develop the capability to project force rapidly to distant countries where the most basic supporting infrastructure may be nonexistent. That is, the military organizations of great powers must be prepared to bring what they need to do the job because it cannot be assumed to be in place.
- Third, the political unacceptability of any great power acting alone in a regional conflict means that the great powers will need to develop and expand "interoperability." (Interoperability means military organizations arrange command, con-

trol, communications, intelligence, and logistical issues to work together.)

• Fourth, the military activities of regional hegemons disrupt the lives of large numbers of civilians, creating refugees who require immediate humanitarian assistance. In turn, the great powers who bear the brunt of humanitarian relief efforts must enhance the capability of their military forces to transport, deliver, safeguard, and distribute humanitarian assistance. Moreover, they will need to enhance their ability to work together better with nongovernmental organizations and private voluntary organizations, the traditional agent-purveyors of humanitarian assistance.

Prospects for Peaceful Resolution

Globally speaking, regional hegemony presents daunting, if not impossible, challenges to peaceful resolution of the conflicts it creates. Hegemonists who use military force aggressively against their neighbors often can achieve their objectives quickly, for they can act faster than the opposition can react. The traditional choices have included unilateral, regional, or international organization discussion, condemnation, economic sanctions, and diplomatic efforts at mediation in the short run, and such long-run measures as arms control agreements or restrictions on technology transfers. Paradoxically, the most successful efforts at peaceful resolution of conflicts resulting from hegemonial ambitions have included the threat or the use of military force, either unilaterally or collectively. How successful peaceful resolution efforts are likely to be later is questionable; however, a determined regional hegemon is less likely to listen to dissuasive diplomacy when he or she knows that:

• It is politically difficult for the US or any European great power to respond militarily and unilaterally, particularly since the leaderships of many of these countries have renounced those options. It is difficult in a practical sense because of military reductions.

• Analysts believe the alternative, collective action, to be unacceptable absent some kind of international legitimization (e.g., by a regional security organization or approval by the United Nations Security Council [UNSC]). Moreover, UN peacekeeping capabilities already may be overextended.

- Hegemons know they can defy such international authorities easily, for no regional security organization (except for NATO) has standing forces and thus these organizations cannot enforce their decisions. Moreover, the UNSC requires international agreement (in fact, unanimous council agreement) on the establishment and authorization of international peacemaking or peacekeeping operations.

Potential Impact on the US

Other countries will continue to place special responsibilities on the US to lead efforts to deal with hegemons of the world. Moreover, the US has a traditional interest in safeguarding the rights of individuals and small countries. On the doorstep of a new millennium, the US must choose either to accept these responsibilities openly, defer them to others, or tolerate the consequences.

First, whatever the choice, the US needs to develop and implement clear policies. This mandate means the US must first clearly redefine and establish domestic consensus on its core, intermediate, and peripheral interests. It must carefully demarcate those interests where violation will bring about a unilateral military response. Second, as Klare argues, the US must assess comprehensively the world security environment and discuss in an open-ended fashion what overall military policy best advances US interests. Should we, he asks, continue to adopt a military posture designed to provide the US with the capability to fight two Iraq-like "rogue powers" simultaneously? Third, assuming such an exercise confirms a military policy aimed at combating regional hegemonism, agencies of the US government involved in monitoring security issues should develop long-range plans for identifying and analyzing likely hegemonic activities and plan diplomatic, political, economic, and military responses. Fourth, the US should lead regional security organizations of which it is a member to plan for contingencies resulting from disruptive hegemonic activities. Moreover, the US also should urge similar organizations of which it is not a member to do the same.

The earlier discussion implies that military responses—more often collective than unilateral—will remain necessary when hegemonic actions threaten regional security. The great powers of the world seldom will agree in advance on the kinds of threats that would generate near-automatic military action. Thus, the United States must remain prepared to address a variety of force projection needs and applications. It also must develop humanitarian action plans that involve the military, upgrade the military's capabilities to perform humanitarian assistance delivery tasks, and define the rules of engagement for the military services to meet likely future requirements for humanitarian responses.

Notes

1. Jack C. Plano and Roy Olton, *The International Relations Dictionary* (New York: Holt, Rinehart and Winston, Inc., 1969), 216.

2. David J. Myers, "Threat Perceptions and Strategic Response of the Regional Hegemons: A Conceptual Framework," in *Regional Hegemons*, David J. Myers, ed. (Boulder, Colo.: Westview Press, Inc., 1991), 5.

3. Ibid.

4. Michael T. Klare, "US Strategy to Defend Against 'Rogues' Needs an Overhaul," *Christian Science Monitor*, 25 April 1995, 19.

5. Karl P. Magyar, "Conflict in the Post-Containment Era," in *Associate Programs, Seminar and Correspondence Lesson Book*, vol. 9, lessons 36–40 (Maxwell AFB, Ala.: Air Command and Staff College, 1994), lesson 39, page 8.

6. Ibid.

7. *Political Islam* refers to the exploitation of Islamic tenets for political purposes. Diplomatic observers and many analysts prefer it as a more accurate description of the phenomena variously described as *Islamic fundamentalism* or *Islamism.*

8. Magyar, lesson 39, 15.

9. Paul Hacker, "Regional Study 2: Security Issues in the Former Warsaw Pact Region," in *Challenge and Response: Anticipating US Military Security Concerns*, Karl P. Magyar, ed. (Maxwell AFB, Ala.: Air University Press, August 1994), 63.

10. Ibid., 64.

11. Col John A. Warden III, "Air Theory for the Twenty-first Century," in *Challenge and Response*, 316.

12. Charles J. Hanley, "Battle Lines Drawn Over Nuclear Treaty," *Montgomery Advertiser*, 19 April 1995, 3A.

16

International Terrorism in the Twenty-First Century

Frank L. Goldstein

The cold war is over, but international terrorism remains a threat across the globe and especially to the United States and its allies. When looking at the future of international terrorism, several key questions need to be answered: Why won't the terrorist threat go away? Is terrorism truly a serious threat or just Western paranoia to maintain military and police budgets? Where should terrorist actions be expected and for what reasons? What will be the impact of terrorism on individual nation-states and overall global stability? And finally, will peaceful resolution and responses to terrorism be possible? Or, will antiterrorism efforts merely begin another version of arms escalation, punitive actions, and repressive governmental endeavors? This chapter explores the global role of terrorism in the twenty-first century, including antiterrorism responses, and the possible consequences to nation-states when they respond to terrorist acts.

Terrorism—Present and Future

Terrorism is defined in many ways, and in its global context no one definition has gained universal acceptance. However, this chapter uses the definitions found in Title 22 of the United States Code, Section 2656(d). The US government has employed the following definitions since 1983:[1]

> – *Terrorism* means premeditated, politically motivated violence perpetrated against noncombatant (noncombatant is interpreted to include civilians and military personnel unarmed at the time of the incident) targets by subnational groups or clandestine agents, usually intended to influence an audience.
>
> – *International terrorism* means terrorism involving citizens or the territory of more than one country.

– *Terrorist groups* means any group practicing, or that has significant subgroups that practice, international terrorism.[2]

What do these definitions suggest? First, they suggest that the nature of international terrorism has not changed significantly in the past 10 years despite radical changes in world politics. In fact, changes in the recent political balance of global power have generated increased terrorist activity. In 1982 Grant Wardlow, in *Political Terrorism*, states, "Groups with little or no direct political power have demonstrated repeatedly in recent years that by employing certain tactics, central to which is the use of directed terror, they can achieve effects on a target community which are out of all proportion to their numerical or political power."[3] With reference to the Middle East, Wardlow's words have as much meaning today as they did then. Despite the peace process and as a direct result of it, Middle Eastern terrorism today creates unrest and widespread panic among the people of Israel, Egypt, and Jordan and apprehension for the people in the rest of the world. Yet, the world was psychologically ready to mark the end of the cold war as the beginning of global peace.

The world community today is subjected to the terrorism of the inclusive Middle East; to African terrorism in Angola, Ghana, Nigeria, Rwanda, and Somalia; and to Asian terrorism in Afghanistan, India, Sri Lanka, Pakistan, Japan, the Philippines, and South Korea. What many had hoped would be the end of European terrorism is now marked by terrorist activities in eastern Europe and France, Germany, Greece, Italy, Spain, Turkey, the United Kingdom, and the lands of the former Yugoslavia and the Soviet Union. Finally, Central and South American terrorism is waged in Chile, Columbia, Ecuador, Peru, and Nicaragua. Thus, the decline of animosity among traditional enemies, or the decline of traditional/conventional war as described by Martin van Creveld in his book, *The Transformation of War*, does not mean the end of organized violence or a decline in terrorist activity.[4]

Historical Perspectives

Historically, terrorist causes have been classified into two main types, with numerous variations and some overlap between them.[5] One broad type is *nationalist-separatist* terrorism. This category is represented by members of "nations, national minorities, and ethnic or racial groups fighting for freedom from what they regard as foreign rule."[6] Examples include the Irish Republican Army of northern Ireland, the Spanish Basque ETA, the Palestine Liberation Organization, HAMAS (Islamic Resistance Movement), several anti-Turkish Armenian groups, and the Puerto Rican FALN in the United States.

A second type of terrorism is the traditional group, which bases its actions on political ideology, and the more complicated of the two. It represents organizations of both the political left and the right, and newly formed environmental groups with ideologically mixed followers. Traditionally, these groups comprised Trotskyites, Maoists, Castroites, Che Guevara followers, Ho Chi Minh followers, West Germany's Baader-Meinhof Gang and a new offspring, and the Red Army Faction. Also included are Italy's Red Brigades, Argentina's ERP, the Japanese Red Army, and the Turkish People's Liberation Army. These examples of leftist terrorist groups have typically advocated some form of socialism to end "evil and oppression." But the end result of their actions typically has been contempt for authority and a strong leaning toward anarchism.

The "right side" of the political spectrum represents also a terrorist threat to democratic nation-states. Right-wing extremists, like their leftist counterparts, aspire to violently overthrow democratic governments in favor of ultranationalistic states. Jonathan Harris lists the following right-wing terrorist examples: the German Military Sports Group Hoffman; Italy's Black Order, Armed Revolutionary Nuclei, and National Advanced Guard; Croatia's Revolutionary Brotherhood; Spain's Youth Force and Warriors of Christ the King; and the United States' Ku Klux Klan and the American Nazi Party.[7]

There exists within the political ideology type a subcategory of terrorists whose ideology is religion-based and is usually fundamentalist in nature. The oldest such group is the Muslim Brotherhood in the Middle East. Some new antiabortion groups in North America who take responsibility for bombings and assassinations also fit into this category.

State support for terrorism inflicted by Cuba, Iran, Libya, North Korea, Syria, South Yemen, and Iraq continues for many of these groups despite United Nations protests or sanctions.[8] Terrorism still provides a safe strategic weapon for countries with little chance of punishment or reprisal for their sponsorship. Additionally, the distinction between domestic and international terrorism is diminishing, as most terrorist organizations have expanded their operations beyond the borders of their own countries to pursue political change.[9] Operating beyond their borders, terrorists intensify the psychological fear equation by threatening to victimize citizens and interests of target countries anywhere in the world.

Terrorist organizations often resort to major criminal activity and to terrorist actions. Drug and arms trafficking is the current method for raising money for terrorist activities.[10] The recent alliances for mutual benefit between drug traffickers and terrorist organizations in Peru and Colombia—with considerable political impact on their own populations and governments—show an example of this new trend.

Finally, terrorist organizations seek to transform their images to that of more *mainstream* organizations. Two classic examples include Sinn Fein's Gerry Adams (political ally of the Irish Republican Army) transitioning from an outlaw barred from the United States to a welcomed statesman and fundraiser—a tactical change which enhanced his credibility and fund-raising ability. Yasser Arafat has taken the same action and has achieved similar results by joining the peace process and appearing more moderate.

How Serious Is the Problem?

Terrorist incidents around the world continue to increase despite the best efforts of security forces. The United States, long considered invincible against terrorist attacks, has suffered more terrorist acts in the past two years than it did during the height of terrorist activity in 1983, despite the massive counterterrorism effort of the late eighties. The takeover of the Iranian mission at the United Nations in New York in 1992 and the bombing of the World Trade Center in 1993 changed the face of terrorism for most Americans and other people in the world.[11] Not only did America lose its invincibility, but the US found that small, loosely organized groups with radical agendas and insulated sponsorships could act with basic impunity. The bombing of a federal building in Oklahoma City in 1995 reinforced the severity of the problem.

While Americans could take some comfort that the rate of attacks against United States interests and personnel fell in 1993, still terrorists directed one-quarter of their attacks worldwide that year at the United States.[12] It seems that terrorists will continue to target Americans because of their international prominence and the worldwide media coverage experienced when they targeted Americans.

Modern terrorists have changed their tactics as the world has changed. While revolutionary terrorism has prevailed for several decades, the current rise in ethnic and religious groups willing to use terrorist tactics to achieve their ends threatens global security and individual nation-states. The modern developed nation-state, with its sophisticated infrastructure and its advanced technology systems, finds itself completely vulnerable to disruption and terrorist action.

Regardless of terrorist motivation, support, or organizational structure, terrorist behavior should be understood for what it represents. Terrorist acts should be perceived as "war."[13] It is a war built on a strategy of intimidation and fear. Fear is a key to the strategy because it accomplishes the required dissemination of the terrorist's communication. In its simplest form, the terrorist provides a "fear-producing event," which is followed by media distribution of that event to the greatest extent possible. Manipulation of populations and media resources is crucial to the overall impact of the message. The reaction of the Japanese population to the 1995 Tokyo subway chemical attack allegedly by the Aum Shinrikyo religious sect, with plans for additional nerve gas attacks, offers a perfect example of the "war of fear" at work.[14]

Future Areas of Concern

Future terrorism will focus on four specific areas. Each area may impact others, but for the purposes of this paper, each should be considered self-contained and a primary focus for future terrorist acts. Additionally, most experts agree that no *one typical* terrorist threat will destroy a nation's sovereignty or will destabilize the world. However, the extent or scope of individual terrorist acts is unlimited, and as shown in Japan, the self-imposed boundaries of terrorist groups can change quickly. The heretofore avoidance of chemical, biological, and nuclear terrorist acts has been broken now. Depending on the event a violent act of mass destruction could cause such world reaction as national boycotts, suspension of civil rights within countries, or international condemnation of a racial or ethnic group in a manner not previously experienced.

The first area of future terrorism will take place in the economic sphere. As nations become more interdependent in trade blocks, and the gap between prosperous and non-prosperous nation-states widens, the opportunities for economic terrorism will expand. Groups using terrorist tactics will interfere with economies for both financial or political gain. The Chilean Grape Incident of 1989 provides an excellent example:

> In March 1989, at the waterfront in Philadelphia, inspectors of the US Food and Drug Administration, acting on an anonymous tip, examined crates of grapes arriving from Chile and discovered two cyanide-laced grapes. The evidence was that the Chilean fruit had been poisoned. No citizen anywhere reported eating the tainted grapes. However, the world reacted. Chilean fruit was temporarily banned, triggering severe economic and political turmoil.[15]

The Chilean grape incident illustrates an example of traditional revolutionary terrorism, state-sponsored terrorism, or political terrorism. Yet, the underlying motivation for the act appears to have been economic. Economic terrorism is a new *action* in a world where trading between competing economies can include protectionism, dominating markets, and economic ruin. For example, the rise of an insurgent Indian group within Mexico, just prior to the signing of the North American Free Trade Agreement between Mexico and the United States, may be viewed as an issue of economic force and control. Although the group described itself as an economic insurgent movement, some of its actions also were called terrorist in nature.

The second area of future terrorism will emanate from religious fundamentalism. The threat is worldwide and concentrated in the Muslim states, but it is by no means inclusive to those states. Much of the Muslim terrorist movement is supported and motivated by Iran, which, along with Sudan and Syria, considers terrorism a primary instrument of state policy.[16] Iran's support for terrorism can be better understood by looking at Iran's organizing struggle between its secular and religious factions, which have limited its interaction with other nation-states and contributed to its isolation.[17] The ascendancy of the religious extremists has expanded Iran's economic problems. Thus, it may appear logical for the leading mullahs to declare a jihad against the West (particularly the United States, the "Great Satan") to shift away from internal problems, to support Islam in a growing secular world, and to restore the Islamic revolutionary spirit both at home and abroad.[18]

Iran has led the world for the past four years as the most active state sponsor of terrorism. That country has been implicated in terrorist attacks in Italy, Turkey, and Pakistan. Their intelligence services support terrorist acts, either directly or indirectly through extremist groups. Iranian intelligence agents are under arrest in Germany and France for their links to murders of Iranian dissidents abroad. Iran also is the preeminent sponsor of extremist Islamic and Palestinian groups. The country provides funds, weapons, and training to "the terrorist organizations known as Hizballah, the Pakistanian Islamic Jihad (PIJ), the Popular Front for the Liberation of Palestine-General Command (PLP-GC) and HAMAS."[19]

The premise of Iran leading a worldwide terrorist campaign against the West, especially the United States, fulfills two major requirements for the leaders of the Tehran government. First, it provides both a moral and symbolic attack against forces that represent evil to Islam (including the United States). Second, it sends a clear message of fear to both the Iranian people and neighboring nations that no individual or nation stands above the wrath of Iran.

The Iranian leadership may feel confident in this behavior based on earlier terrorist action. Yossef Bodansky illustrates the point:

> Tehran has reason to be confident . . . two major terrorist strikes against the United States: the mid-air explosion of Pan Am flight 103 over Lockerbie, Scotland on December 21, 1988; and, in San Diego, California, on March 10, 1989, the fire-bombing of a van driven by

> Sharon Lee Rodgers, wife of the captain of the USS Vincennes, who had mistakenly shot down the Iranian Airbus commercial flight in July 1988.[20]

Additionally, Iran is a main source of support for the fundamentalist regime in Sudan and for the Kurdistan Workers Party (PKK) which has been held responsible for hundreds of terrorist acts in Turkey.[21] Iranian fundamentalists currently are the most active supporters of terrorist activity worldwide.

Religious ideologies have long been associated with terrorism and the support of violence for religious purposes. The doctrines of Christian (Catholic and Protestant), Muslim (Shi'a and Sunni), Jewish, Hindu, and Sikh religions have all been used to justify terrorism.[22] Religious fundamentalism and dogma have provided individuals the support to carry out their fanatical or terrorist activities. However, it should be clearly understood that the vast majority of those who support fundamentalist religious movements do not become terrorists or even support their violent activities.

The intensity of a fundamentalist terrorist differs little from a political, ethnic, or national terrorist. The added concept of having "God on your side" and the promise of life after death adds a divine variable to the terrorist equation. Some of these groups recently have been called "superterrorists" because of their access to nuclear, chemical, biological, and conventional weapons and computer technology.[23] The true global threat from these terrorists is their willingness to use their new weapons. Since these terrorist targets represent "the unholy or unclean," the traditional terrorist objective of political control is substituted with destruction of "evil." As a result, the terrorists' potential use of nuclear, biological, and chemical weapons is considered ideal.[24]

The terrorism of these fundamentalist groups is ideology and religion driven. It is critical for the leadership of these groups to present in a constant and conclusive way, the *rightness* of their views to their followers. The leaders of these organizations will take unilateral and arbitrary actions. However, these same leaders will attempt to legitimize their actions, their support, and the reactions of the world to them by addressing their own populations. The bombing of the World Trade Center should then be viewed as having had a primary target audience made up of Islamic fundamentalists worldwide instead of only Americans.

When the causes of nontraditional religious groups or cults are added to the aims of fundamentalist terrorist groups, the behavior of terrorists becomes even more confusing and unpredictable. An example of this is the 1995 Japanese subway cult attack, which should be considered a peek into the future instead of as a nonrepeatable event.

The third area of future terrorism will be *technology terror.* The information and computer highway of our future also will include a fast lane for terrorists. Modern technology makes it possible for smaller, more radical groups to access sophisticated means of destruction without significant support systems or funding. As computer systems become more powerful and cheaper, terrorists will develop a greater capability to impact resources, intelligence, and terror operations with little or no risk, depending on advances yet to be made by the antiterrorist forces.

Using information warfare tools will give terrorists access to the vast amounts of financial resources that travel the information highways. By using and attacking these financial conduits, terrorists not only can transfer funding from outside sponsors, but they can illegally tap these vulnerable conduits to obtain the required informational resources to sustain their activities. They can cripple the financial markets either by direct attacks or by instilling a credibility gap in the electronic financial world.[25] As Winn Schwartau notes in *Information Warfare,* "Money is the network that comprises hundreds of thousands of computers of every type, wired together in places as lofty as the Federal Reserve . . . and as mundane as the thousands of gas pumps around the world outfitted to take credit and debit cards."[26]

In addition to being a possible funding conduit, information warfare techniques also can provide the terrorist with an invaluable source of intelligence, ranging from sharing information on bomb making with other organizations, to targeting individual travelers through the airline reservation system, to stealing military secrets through the ever-expanding Internet presence in military organizations. Information warfare provides an invaluable aid to the intelligence-gathering ability of the modern-day, high-tech terrorist. The information highway not only allows access to this wealth of information but allows access to this information from places safely within the borders of terrorists' safe havens.

Using the information highway also can enable the terrorist to coordinate remote multiple-cell activity with little probability of discovery, and provide the terrorist with a method for attracting worldwide attention to their acts of violence almost as the events are unfolding. This information highway can make the command, control, and intelligence techniques used on the military battlefield available to terrorist groups worldwide.

Besides the support functions of managing resources, gathering intelligence, and disseminating information, information warfare techniques is to create terror or chaos and wreak havoc against a target. When considering the use of information warfare techniques by terrorists, give the first consideration to the most vulnerable target to information warfare attacks. By its very nature, information warfare attacks are most effective where the information highway has made the greatest inroads into people's everyday lives, business and governmental functions, and defense. Thus, the modern westernized societies are more vulnerable to information warfare than are third world nations. This vulnerability also corresponds to the nations most frequently targeted by terrorists.

The types of terror that can be created by astute information warfare terrorists range from targeting key individuals to influencing decisions favorable to terrorist causes to attacks that cause massive destruction and loss of life. The following examples illustrate these purposes.

On the personal level, terrorists could use the information highway to gather incriminating information on key decision-makers. Whether it is bad check-writing activity, subscribing to pornographic magazines, belonging to nonpolitically correct groups, or having a medical condition that has remained a secret, people in positions of influence sometime have material in their past that might make them vulnerable to coercion. However, if their past is not tainted, the terrorist could begin sowing the seeds of doubt along the electronic highway by altering credit history databases, banking records, mailing lists, and medical records in enough detail to compromise the individuals.

Schwartau recounts one incident about an individual being bombarded with hate mail and police inquiries due to a computer request for pedophilia information. Someone else had requested the information using his identification.[27] Thus, information warfare tools in the hands of the terrorist has the potential to either influence or discredit influential individuals.

On the corporate level, terrorists could use information warfare techniques to cripple corporations physically or economically. Using such computer techniques as trojan horses, viruses, or spoofing terrorist attacks could bring corporate information systems—including corporate research and development, financial data management, personnel information, and shipping and receiving—to a grinding halt. The cost to corporations could be millions of dollars. Even without physically crippling these systems, enough doubt could be instilled in the operators of the systems to render the systems worthless. Examples include faulty bookkeeping software, inventory control systems that generate random numbers, and shipping and invoicing systems that become so unreliable that they can no longer be trusted. With these unreliable systems, vast quantities of manpower have to be expended to ensure accuracy in the data that has become the life blood of the corporation.

Other examples of terrorism against corporations include industrial espionage, modifying tests results to give inaccurate data, and release of data that would discredit the corporation or individuals within the corporation. Thus, besides being able to hold individuals hostage, terrorists also could hold corporations hostage by using their own information systems.

On a global level, nations become vulnerable to terrorist attacks through the use of information warfare techniques. Such national infrastructure as banks switched telephone systems, power grids, and air traffic control systems are but a few examples of targets that could cause massive disruption in a developed state if attacked. Nuclear power plants with bad controller chips, jamming aircraft transponders, and theft of national security information from military networks are other examples that could cause massive destruction and loss of life.

In addition to computers, terrorist groups have moved into the technology and missile age with hardware and human intelligence. For example, in 1973 it was rare for terrorists to use missile attacks.[28] Today missile attacks are commonplace. However, the future wave of technological terrorism will include more than missiles. These new technology terrorists will be intelligent and creative, and will have learned from past terrorist activities worldwide.

In *Final Warning*, Robert Kupperman and Jeff Kamen discuss a scenario in which a Middle East terrorist group obtained nerve agents for a strike.[29] In 1995 a quasireligious cult used a similar attack in a Tokyo subway to kill 16 people and to injure over 5,000.[30] The police investigation revealed a terrorist plot aimed at international mass destruction (for as-yet-undetermined religious reasons) by members of the Aum Shinrikyo, also known as Supreme Truth Organization. Included among the cult membership are 30 chemists who worked for the cult's science and technology ministry. Police sources suspected the 30 chemists of preparing the chemical, sarin, that was used in the subway attack. A terrorist organization with a science and technology ministry may not be typical of past terrorist organizations; however, this high-technology, computer-based organization is more mainstream than the world would expect.

The fourth area of future terrorism will be what Donald Hanle refers to as "apolitical terrorism," or terrorism for nonpolitical ends.[31] This category has stirred some controversy because some experts feel all terrorist acts have a political or social foundation and therefore should fall under the political umbrella. However, recent terrorist events around the world clearly indicate that some terrorist activities do fall under the apolitical category.

The apolitical terrorist should be considered the most dangerous type. The availability of modern technology and nuclear, chemical, and biological weapons combined with someone with a criminal or unbalanced psychological mind-set—makes for an ominous concern. An individual or small group of terrorists with personal motives could carry out an event of mass destruction with relative ease and success. Additionally, such an individual or group will probably be available for hire on a national or global market. Modern technology, computers, and information resources all tend to facilitate the interaction and communication of both individuals and groups.

The recent 19 April 1995 bombing in Oklahoma City of the federal building which left 168 people dead could be considered apolitical under certain conditions. If the two indicted bombers (11 counts each with death the maximum penalty for each count),[32] Terry Nichols and Timothy McVeigh, do not represent a particular group, organization, or movement,[33] but were acting out their own antisocial and antigovernment views (both men believe they are patriots protecting the Constitution from a misguided evil government),[34] the terrorist act would not be considered exclusively politically motivated. The act could then be described as the abnormal behavior of two individuals based on either *psychotic* thinking in the gravest sense or criminal behavior in the narrowest sense. The psychotic thinking scenario is adequately described by Hanle when "estranged and fragmented individuals . . . lose self-identity and [seem] doomed by a soulless bureaucracy. . . ."[35]

Another example of apolitical terrorism is the "Unabomber" in the United States. During the Unabomber's 17-year reign of terror, three victims have been killed and twenty-three have been injured. The latest victim, a lobbyist for the timber industry, was killed by a package bomb that went off in his Sacramento, California, office. The victims represent varied backgrounds, and their particular selection for motive or orientation to the terrorist is unknown. Both the Federal Bureau of Investigation and local law enforcement agencies believe the Unabomber is brazen, typically cool, and psychologically unstable.

However, the Unabomber fully understands the value of media, fear, and intimidation. That he or she demands that two of the nation's leading newspapers print a 35,000-word manifesto against the industrial and technology complex is a classic terrorist shakedown attempt. Unlike most political terrorist groups or state-sponsored groups, the apolitical terrorist has little concern for political or economic repercussions.

What Can Be Done?

As terrorism enters the twenty-first century and impacts the global community, a limited number of options will be available to counter the new threats. One option which attained some success after the World Trade Center bombing is the utilization of economic incentives or bounties. After that World Trade Center attack, the United States government offered a reward of several million dollars for the identification of persons responsible for the attack. An informant in Pakistan provided the information that led to the arrest of Ramzi Yousef as the mastermind of the act. Yousef was arrested in Islamabad, Pakistan, and was immediately extradited to the United States (New York City), where he awaits trial. However, an unfortunate follow-up to the arrest was the speculation that the subsequent killing in Pakistan of two American embassy personnel was revenge for the Yousef extradition.

The reward program can be complicated, as in the case of Pakistan. That country is in the middle of sectarian violence between Sunni and Shiite Muslim groups. These groups are engaged not only in terrorist activity, but are involved with the country's powerful drug Mafia and the militant Muslim groups.[36] This ongoing terrorist activity complicates the bounty program but does not negate it. Thus, the United States government, to repeat the success of its original "reward program," offered two million dollars in bounty for the killers of the two United States government workers.

A second option for global nation-states against terrorism is "national resolve." It should be acknowledged that a fool-proof system against terrorism in democratic societies does not exist. In the words of terrorism expert Stephen Sloan, "There can never be a totally effective program to deter or prevent a determined adversary from seeking softer targets of opportunity in what he perceives to be a justified war against all."[37] Such simple procedures as better intelligence and improved physical security of critical sites will, in most cases, deter a particular terrorist group. However, a terrorist group deprived of a particular target typically will seek a more accessible alternative target.

A traditional limiting factor to national resolve now and in the future will be cost and politics. Using the United States as an example, 100 days after the Oklahoma City bombing, the two-billion-dollar antiterrorism bill had stalled in political debate because of opposition to the bill from both liberal and conservative lawmakers.

The key point of any nation attempting to combat terrorism, now as in the future, is that terrorist activity will take place and that casualties will occur. As was evident after the Oklahoma City bombing, additional funding and legislation will harden some targets and drive some terrorist organizations underground. The realization for a global society is that technology attacks and conventional or unconventional attacks, including hostage taking, will continue. The terrorist's requirement for media coverage typically will exceed a democratic society's inclination to control the media or the public's demand for news.

Thus, in the future our global society may expect more rather than less terrorism. Much of that terrorism will be based on religion and ethnicity. Economics, technology, and the whims of both criminal and psychotics will ensure ongoing and, at times, spectacular incidences. Terrorism has reached American interests both domestically and internationally; hence, we will see more public and political efforts to counter terrorism. Unfortunately, terrorism in the developing countries will continue almost unabated.

Notes

1. Department of State, *Patterns of Global Terrorism 1993*, April 1994, IV.
2. Ibid.
3. Grant Wardlow, *Political Terrorism* (New York: Cambridge University Press, 1982), 3.
4. Martin van Creveld, *The Transformation of War* (New York: Free Press, 1991), 225.
5. Jonathan Harris, *The New Terrorism: Politics of Violence* (New York: Julian Messaer Press, 1983), 33–37.
6. Ibid.
7. Ibid., 36.
8. David E. Long, *The Anatomy of Terrorism* (New York: Free Press, 1990), 9.
9. Ibid., 10.
10. Ibid., 4.
11. Department of Justice, *Terrorism In the United States* (Washington, D.C.: Federal Bureau of Investigation, 1993), 26–27.
12. Department of State, 22.

13. Donald J. Hanle, *Terrorism: The Newest Face of Warfare* (Washington, D.C. and Elmsford, New York: Pergammon-Brassey's, 1989), 14.

14. "Police Seeking Cult's Chemist," *Montgomery Advertiser*, 14A.

15. Robert Kupperman and Jeff Kamen, *Final Warning: Averting Disaster in the New Age of Terrorism* (New York: Doubleday Press, 1989), ix.

16. Yossef Bodansky, *Terror: The Inside Story of the Terrorist Conspiracy in America* (New York: Shapelsky Publishers, Inc., 1984), 29.

17. Trevor N. Duprey, *Future Wars* (New York: Warner Books, 1992), 158–59.

18. Bodansky, 29.

19. Department of State, 23.

20. Bodansky, 31.

21. Department of State, 22.

22. Long, 65.

23. Bill Gertz, *Washington Times*, 22 February 1995, 4.

24. Marvin J. Cetron, T*error 2000: The Future Face of Terrorism*, Prepared for Office of Special Operations and Low Intensity Conflict, Unpublished report, 1995.

25. Greg Smith, computer consultant to research coordinator, Air University, Maxwell AFB, Ala., personal notes.

26. Winn Schwartau, *Information Warfare* (New York: Thunder Mouth Press, 1994), 61.

27. Ibid.

28. Long, 92.

29. Kupperman and Kamen, 87.

30. "Police Seeking Cult's Chemist."

31. Hanle, 121.

32. Sally Burbee, "Nichols Charged," *Associated Press*, 10 May 1995, 1; and Kevin Johnson, "In Shadows of Oklahoma," *USA Today*, 16 August 1995, 5.

33. Pete Copeland, "Prosecutors In Bombing Case," *Scripps Howard News*, 10 August 1995, 8.

34. Hanle, 124.

35. Greg Myre, *Montgomery Advertiser*, 10 March 1995, 13A.

36. Stephen Sloan, *Beating International Terrorism: An Action for Preemption and Punishment* (Maxwell AFB, Ala.: Air University Press, 1986), 49.

37. David Espo, *Montgomery Advertiser*, 30 June 1995, 5A.

PART V

CONCLUSION

17

The Transmillennial World from an American Perspective

John A. Warden III

You have just completed a fascinating *tour d'horizon* of the world and the problems likely to plague it. This final chapter gives an integrated view of the world and a set of prescriptions for American success in it. Many ideas are at odds with some of the preceding chapters; when you find this to be true, use your judgment to decide which view or interpretation makes the most sense and holds something with which you can work.

We are experiencing the most revolutionary period in human history. Three revolutions of incredible magnitude and import confront us: a geopolitical revolution seeing a single power dominating the world for the first time since the height of the Roman Empire; an information revolution fostering an explosion of knowledge and giving birth to a second industrial revolution with the potential to exceed its predecessor; and a military technological revolution ushering in the first-ever conceptual change in warfare. Any one of these revolutions would be exciting on its own; when combined, however, the excitement is unparalleled.

The monumental change the world is experiencing is filled with paradoxes. We are living in the most revolutionary of times, but there is more order in the international system than the world has seen in two millennia; military weapon systems cost far more than ever, but the best of them make war extraordinarily inexpensive to execute. Rapid economic growth spurred by the information revolution is seeing more and more people able to afford houses and automobiles, and prices for raw materials are falling while their availability increases. In other words, our basic assumptions about how things work in the commercial, political, and economic spheres are undergoing as radical a change as the change from Newtonian to quantum physics. Let us now focus on the next 10 to 15 years by suggesting the general environment in which the United States will operate.

The accelerating dispersion of information will define the next decades. Far more people will be connected to each other and to sources of information than ever before. To a certain extent, information is a metaphor for wealth, and the explosion of information will be matched by a proportionate increase in world wealth. Contrary to many commentators, most areas of the world will become noticeably richer. The disparity between the richest nation—the United States—and one near the middle of a per capita wealth chart will be just as great or even greater. But the disparity will be irrelevant; what is relevant will be the realization of poorer countries that it is possible to become richer without stealing; that is, that men *create* wealth. It is not disparity of wealth that causes problems, but legal or physical bars to attaining it which will cause internal and even external conflict. Simply stated, much of the world finally will realize that wealth is not finite but infinite. As this realization grows, people around the world will devote increasing energies to working and building wealth and decrease their interests in war and violence accordingly.

Accompanying and spurring a world increase in the standard of living will be a decline in the cost of raw materials and an increase in their availability. They will have less and less relevance to standard of living and will become significantly less likely to be a cause of war. The reasons are many: technology which finds substitutes for old staples; new exploration techniques driven by the information revolution; and more efficient use and distribution. With a rapidly rising standard of living worldwide, the demand for foodstuffs beyond subsistence will increase; thus, producers of luxury items like coffee and fruits should see excellent market opportunities. The likelihood of violent conflict over natural resources will decrease because the things themselves are less valuable and seizure of them is by far the most expensive and least rewarding way to secure access. Overall, removing a traditional cause of war ought to be positive; adjustment, however, will be necessary for many. As an example, resource-rich states have been able to exchange their resources for money and political influence worldwide. As the value of raw materials recedes, some violent adaptation likely will occur.

Water is a special case in natural resources. As earlier chapters stated, many believe that water will be a source of serious conflict, especially in the Middle East. The possibility is there, but the Middle East also may have some market and technology solutions at hand. One of the primary problems with water everywhere is the way it is priced and sold. For the most part, the cost to users is a small fraction of the real costs—monetary and political. Since the user pays so little for an important product, he has virtually no incentive to find more efficient ways to use it. If water were priced at market-established rates, we can predict with certainty that usage rates per acre of agriculture, ton of steel, or merely per capita would fall quickly without decreases in the production it enables. In other words, if water-use efficiency improved by a factor of two or more, locales that now experience a critical or deficit situation suddenly would be comfortable. The United States can help to eliminate this predicament by developing the technology needed to increase water productivity and by leading the way in developing market-rate approaches to water sales.

The last few paragraphs have painted a rosy economic picture. In fact, this picture is but part of a larger mosaic (or system) which is even more optimistic. When we look at the world from a top-down perspective—where we only allow ourselves to see the first level of the world system—we are struck by how peaceful it is. For the first time in historical memory, we see a world without serious great-power competitions. Currently (at the end of the twentieth century) no significant power has extraterritorial designs for which it would go to war with another significant power. (We are deliberately excluding a handful of irredentist claims—because irredentism is simply different from the conquest and imperialism that dominated the world since at least the days of the ancient Egyptians. In addition, relatively little of the irredentist emotion extant is strong enough to propel its holders into open warfare nor does it generally pit one important power against another.)

The world at the first order of analysis is uniquely peaceful; an understanding and acceptance of this fact is essential. Failure to grasp it means that all of our decisions will be based on erroneous data. At this point, many readers will be inclined to reject this hypothesis out of hand; they will point to the many wars and conflicts currently underway, to the number of people dying as a result, and to the nightly television recaps. Everyone of these unfortunate conflicts, however, are second order and normally have no direct effect on the world system which is in a very ordered state.

Thinking about weather systems helps us to understand this unusual situation. In the United States, we frequently see long periods (days and sometimes weeks) when no big fronts move across the country and when no hurricanes strike. We then talk rightly about what great weather we are enjoying. At the same time, however, the probability is high that someplace in the nation, a thunderstorm developed, and a neighborhood experienced lightning strikes and wind damage to trees. In other words, we had a local disturbance in a system which was otherwise in a very orderly state. It is the same with the world today: the world political weather is excellent, but local disturbances exist, nonetheless.

As we know from daily and historical experience, the overwhelming majority of local disturbances—be they weather, economic, or political—remain localized. Occasionally, however, one will start to behave somewhat like a rapidly multiplying cancer cell and drive the parent system into chaotic, or disorderly, behavior. Unfortunately, we don't yet have the ability to predict which disturbances are linear and will dampen out quickly and which ones are nonlinear and will drive the parent system to chaos.

So how do we operationalize these ideas for the United States? First, we understand that the world is generally peaceful and that we can make political and economic decisions based on its continued tranquillity. To return to our weather analogy, we can plan to make a trip anywhere in the country without the need to equip ourselves with foul weather gear and emergency rations. If we get caught in a local storm, we know it will be short-lived; the low probability of getting caught justifies our decision not to spend money and effort on preparation for worst-case weather problems. Americans in business can plan on world ventures with high probability that global conditions will not change appreciably—although they must keep a weather eye out for occasional local storms.

Second, from operationalizing stability concepts, we understand that the overwhelming majority of local wars resemble local thunderstorms which pass without creating large system instabilities. Thus, we can treat each one of these events strictly on its own merits; we need not be concerned about extraterritorial consequences—because the world as a whole is stable and small disturbances will not drive it into chaos. By contrast, when the world has been unstable—that is, in most of human history—small disturbances had a high probability of creating global chaos. Consider the effects of the assassination of Archduke Francis Ferdinand in 1914. That same event today would do little more than make a small splash in the world news media.

We are driving to the idea that the United States need not worry much about small disturbances without a specific reason for doing so; on the other hand, as the dominant power in the world—and as the richest power in the world—she has an enormous interest in seeing that worldwide stability continues. Note that the majority of the remainder of the world shares the American interest because stability is good for almost everyone almost all the time.

The reasons for worldwide stability today are many and complex; the most important of these reasons, however, focuses on American dominance. In a certain sense, stability flowed to the rest of the world because of American stability and because there was no large force to resist it. Since we are forced to presume that a substantial diminution of American dominance would remove the most important underpinning of world stability, maintenance of dominance ought to become America's grand strategic goal. Success in this realm will cover a host of localized errors, whereas failure leads to global instability which is by definition highly unpredictable and dangerous.

In the past, a state wanting to maintain even local dominance felt that it needed to reduce the power of its neighbors. This was certainly a key element of Prussian and German grand strategy for nearly two hundred years (and the consequences were predictably disastrous). This kind of policy, of course, guarantees robust opposition because the neighbors cannot share either the goal or the means to it.

For the United States, there is another way, one without much precedent: maintain dominance by progressing faster than anyone else in military, economic, and political endeavors—and, simultaneously, by avoiding actions which might cause other states to form anti-American coalitions. In the military sphere, this means dominating the military technological revolution by staying one revolution ahead of all contenders. Given our current huge lead in almost every relevant military field, staying ahead need not be costly. In the economic sphere, it means aggressive pursuit of growth policies and the creation of real wealth. In the political sphere, it means accepting—humbly—the mantle of power and exercising it rarely, but always decisively and successfully. American military and political forays must be successful, because failure reduces the aura of dominance and contributes to instability.

We are now at a point in our analysis where we can move from theory to specifics and lay out some general rules for American grand strategy and operations. In the grand strategy arena, after ensuring American dominance by out-accelerating everyone else, our primary concern becomes one of quelling disturbances that portend large instabilities. Our working assumption can be that almost all internal conflicts are unlikely to have global significance and can be ignored. What can't be ignored are those conflicts which the perpetrator has undertaken to force change on a neighbor. When one state crosses a border forcefully—or threatens the use of force against a neighbor—risk to global stability goes up exponentially. Therefore, the working assumption here is that American intervention is probably justified and demanded. On further reflection, there may be something special about the situation that makes intervention unnecessary. But if we start out with the assumption that it will be needed, we are likely to be better prepared, and our potential enemies are less likely to do something out of ignorance.

Our emphasis here concerns American intervention. This does not mean that others may not help—but we must understand that as the dominant power, our interest demands that we act and to do it right and quickly. To the extent that we abdicate our responsibilities to lesser powers and groups, we reduce greatly the chance of decisive and quick action, and we raise dangerous questions about our will and capability.

Our other general rule for intervention is more traditional: if someone breaches contractual arrangements forcefully or destroys American property or kills American citizens, we must act. Why? Because we have a real interest in encouraging others to reject stealing and killing to seize power or treasure, and second, because a key function of government is protection of its citizens' lives and property. One might suggest that this is more properly a role for the United Nations or some other group. It isn't. It is quintessentially the responsibility of the world's dominant power. Failure to act when provoked in this manner is dangerous.

Likewise, asking others (North Atlantic Treaty Organization and the United Nations) to do the job reduces American prestige and America's ability to control the situation. Doing so contributes to potential world instability because it reduces America's aura of dominance. It also raises the specter of competing coalitions—something not in the dominant power's interest. Some would say that the dominant power has a moral obligation to intervene for humanitarian reasons to stop suffering, to stop killing, or to accomplish other worthy goals. To the contrary, America does not have any such obligation and should not accept a blanket responsibility for the affairs of the rest of the world. The reasons are many: first, unless the situation meets criteria stated earlier, we have no business intruding into other people's fights. We will rarely understand what they are about, and rarely will we find one side with a preponderance of right on its side. Second, the number of these local disturbances is theoretically unlimited (like the number of thunderstorms that take place even when the world's weather is generally nice). An unlimited number imposes an unlimited burden, which in turn is certain to lead quickly to fiscal and political distress if not outright bankruptcy. Third, the likely absence of a world consensus that one side or the other is right or wrong means that American intervention against one party is certain to arouse considerable resentment in other parts of the world—resentment which stresses world stability—America's number one imperative.

We live in a political world and America is ruled by politics. Consequently, it is inevitable that America's leaders will insist on interventions which are strategically dangerous and unwarranted. When this happens (as wrong as it may be) the worst way, and, unfortunately, the most likely way to address the problem is through serial, escalatory steps. Serial, escalating operations reduce the predictability of the outcome, and each one creates a new, different situation—a situation that may lead to inadvertent creations of nonlinearities, which could affect the broader system. Interventions must be fast and successful. To a certain extent, fast and successful are far more important strategically than choosing the right side.

The last few paragraphs have suggested broad operating principles to achieve important strategic objectives. The question now is how to carry out military campaigns to satisfy domestic, political, world, and local conditions in the conflict area. In general, our campaigns need to do or be the following: very fast—hours or days from decision to action until success is assured; free of unintended casualties on either side; geared to the postwar situation regarding what should or should not be functioning or easily restorable after the war; and appropriate to the desired postwar political situation. These criteria then define in broad terms the appropriate force structure for the United States for offensive purposes. Of course, defense is important, something we will come to shortly. Before addressing either offense or defense issues, however, let us first define war.

In the last 40 years, and especially in the last several, we have come close to confusing ourselves hopelessly by trying to classify military activity into a whole range of categories as though each one had its own logic and by establishing a need for a different set of theories, doctrines, and weapons. At the most important level, application of force has no boundaries. This is true at the operational and strategic levels, for only at a tactical level might we begin to see any differences from one situation to the next. We can remove much of our confusion if we simply define war as "the use of force or threat to use force to change an inimical environment to an environment which satisfies the combatant's objectives." This definition applies equally to disaster relief (changing an inimical environment created by wind or water) and to total war (colonizing the loser's territory). This definition of war relieves us of the need to invent strange terms like *military operations other than war*, *peacemaking*, *peacekeeping*, or *peace enforcement*.

The next level of analysis introduces us to the characteristics of weapon systems appropriate to American war requirements in the next 25 to 50 years. They must have the capability to:

- allow the United States to conduct parallel war—that is, to bring under attack almost simultaneously the centers of gravity needed to attain political objectives and to preclude organized repair or reaction;
- operate from strategic depths in the United States directly—without the need for intermediate basing—against the center of any opponent;
- reach any point on the globe from the United States in about an hour and return in the same time frame;
- impact to within inches or less of the desired impact point;
- destroy or affect only what they are supposed to destroy or affect;
- hit desired targets quickly enough to assure at least strategic and operational paralysis;
- do what is necessary without imposing any unintended casualties or property damage;
- allow the United States to operate with few or no casualties;
- penetrate defenses (most likely through some combination of very high speeds, radio and visual spectrum stealth, and very high altitudes, including space from near earth to deep space);
- loiter literally or figuratively for long periods (weeks or more) above the enemy for some combination of observation and lethal attack;
- and deliver any type of energy—whether lethal or nonlethal (even in the form of food)—and systems which are highly productive in terms of manning and support.

Some might call this force structure prohibitively expensive; on the contrary, it is designed to leverage the output of the information revolution. The force structure needed to carry the operations just discussed will offer far more productivity than our current force structure and will rely on fewer platforms and far fewer people for support. We saw a three-to-four order of magnitude increase in the productivity of the bomber pilot from the World War II B-17 to the Gulf War F-117 aircrafts. That increase occurred within a 50-year period only one-half of which was during the age of the doubling of computer power every 18 months or so. We can gain another similar improvement in productivity in a fraction of the time because of current technology. Smaller numbers, fewer people, and little or no requirement for en route support and refueling spell huge savings—savings sufficiently high to pay for what must be a real capital intensification of airpower providers.

Before overviewing needed defensive systems, let us examine particular threats which exist in the world, namely chemical weapons, biological weapons, nuclear weapons, and terror weapons. Chemical weapons are much overrated and are of little value beyond a tactical level. They are difficult to deploy and employ, have uncertain and unpredictable effects, are dangerous for the user as well as the target, and are easy for well-trained and equipped military forces to negate. They may have some terror value when used against civilians, but the probability of terror attacks provoking the attacked state to sue for peace quickly is small. Since a cross-border attack probably would lead the United States to intervene (if it follows the rules proposed above), any attack which does not lead to almost instant victory has little value.

Is it worthwhile to spend much time in trying to prevent countries or groups from acquiring chemical weapons? The answer is probably "no" because weapons can be easily produced with the same processes used in legitimate nonweapons manufacture. Our best counter is to advertise the problems associated with chemical war and then make clear the United States will not tolerate chemical use against extraterritorial civilians. Paradoxically, our official, public paranoia about chemical—and nuclear—weapons gives them an underserved cachet which makes it more likely that someone will use one or the other. After all, if an American administration expresses great fear about possible North Korean nuclear weapons and then agrees to negotiations previously rejected, one must assume that others will see special weapons as providing leverage against the United States. Or to use another analogy: the poker player who always folds in the face of a robust bet is begging to be bluffed. We should make clear that the United States feels fully capable of thwarting the use of chemical and nuclear weapons and imposing long-lasting paralysis on the using state.

From an American standpoint, nuclear weapons are interesting but have little utility. The United States can accomplish any military objective with nonnuclear weapons; therefore, their use embodies extreme political risk. They may have some use to opponents of the United States, but their advantage is likely to be solely in the threat of use against the United States or one of its allies or friends. The threat should be emphasized because it is highly unlikely that any state or group will employ sufficient weapons to defeat the United States. Anything less than a quick defeat would give the United States time to retaliate and shut down the nuclear user. We have a paradoxical situation: weapons that we find useless can cause us problems. A nuclear-free world (or close to it) would be ideal, and we should probably drive as far as possible in that direction with a combination of arms control initiatives, incentives for others to turn over or destroy current stockpiles, and vigorous, active measures to foil nascent plans of preemptive attack on nuclear facilities. If we fail to produce a nuclear-free world—and zero is nuclear-free—and clearly a dream—we must have the best possible defenses.

Terrorism is another unclear area to which the United States must respond; it does not constitute a real strategic threat directly to the United States, but it can destroy an already weak or unstable government. And, it can certainly be painful even if it is strategically ineffective. Our best counter to terrorism embodies a clear-cut policy which says that any sponsoring government and its people may be denied modern conveniences like electricity, gasoline, and telephones until such time the government and people agree to stop using terrorism. Finding and attacking nonstate groups can be quite difficult, but the same general policy should apply. We can do something defensively, but not much because terrorists frequently try deliberately to goad the target state to deploy defenses which the defended people will find intolerable. As in war, the best defense is a good offense.

Our final special concern focuses on biological weapons. These weapons may be the most troubling because of their capacity to damage. Chapter 12 detailed how small quantities can devastate an area. Unlike chemicals which are so difficult to deliver, biological weapons are far easier to deliver either by air platform or by infiltrator. In addition, they are ideal offensive weapons because of the difficulty of developing vaccines or antidotes in advance. A good biological weapon does its dirty work before the attacked party realizes that it is suffering from a man-made ailment. Defenses against air platforms are necessary to reduce or eliminate an attacker's ability to deliver such weapons. Defense against infiltrators is difficult and requires superb police work. Finally, the penalty for use must be swift and severe. Despite our best efforts and our strongest threats against users, our chances of total success are small. This area urgently needs a lot more thought and innovative proposals.

Although we have not mentioned information as either a weapon or war concept, let us say that it may be both and may be extraordinarily effective, because information is vital to organizational existence. Destruction, manipulation, and injection of information may be sufficient to wage and win wars. A military machine cannot function at operational or higher levels without enormous quantities of fresh information moving into, around, and out of the organization. A nation cannot function defensively or offensively without a reliable stream of information. A criminal cartel needs to move great quantities of information to remain intact. The field is fertile. Offensive information weapons range from radio and television broadcasts (the longer range and more powerful the better) to computer viruses to holograph projectors. Information weapons will play a key role in defensive and offensive operations for the foreseeable future.

We left a discussion of defenses until now, because defense is something you do because you failed to do something else right. Allowing yourself to be attacked is dangerous and something you should avoid. If proactive measures fail to prevent an attack, however, do everything possible to ensure the attack does not impose strategically or operationally significant burdens. The United States needs a good worldwide defense against ballistic missiles which almost certainly dictates a space-based system as opposed to a limited area coverage ground system, a defense against cruise missiles, and a defense against remotely piloted vehicles. These systems, and a system to detect terrorist infiltrators, should give the United States ample flexibility to conduct the only kind of operations which solve problems—offensive operations. No one has long survived with defense alone—and the rapid pace of technological development shows offense remaining dominant for the foreseeable future.

The future is brighter than ever, and the prospects for a century or more of global peace are good. America, however, must participate actively—but circumspectly—to make this future a reality. Pursuing aggressive growth and technology development policies and staying a revolution ahead of all competitors in the military sphere will allow the United States to go far to ensure the kind of stability in the world which will redound to everyone's benefit and which will allow for an unprecedented leap in the world's standard of living. The opportunity is there, but the United States must assume the mantle first donned two millennia ago and lying unworn for almost as long.

Contributors

Lt Col Mark Browne currently serves on the faculty at the Air Command and Staff College, Maxwell Air Force Base, Alabama, where he is attached to the War and Theater-Level Studies Department. He holds a BS degree in business administration from William Jewell College and an MS in operations management from the University of Arkansas. He has completed Squadron Officer School and Air Command and Staff College. Lieutenant Colonel Browne has been a missile instructor and an AFROTC and airborne missile operations instructor, and chief of the standardization/evaluation section. His most recent assignment was at Headquarters United States Air Force as budget and programming branch chief in the Force Programming Division.

Lt Col Richard W. Chavis is the director, Distance Learning Department at the Air Command and Staff College. Lieutenant Colonel Chavis received a BS degree in criminal justice administration from Middle Tennessee State University, an MA in public administration from Central Michigan University, and a MS in criminal justice from Tennessee State University. A doctoral candidate at the University of Alabama and a career security police officer, he has held various jobs at several levels of command and has joint and combined experience, including extensive duty in Southwest Asia. Lieutenant Colonel Chavis is a graduate of Squadron Officer School and Air Command and Staff College. He is also a graduate of the FBI National Academy.

Lt Col Wayne D. Davidson currently serves as the United States Air Force representative to the Royal Air Force (RAF) Command and Staff College, RAF Bracknell, United Kingdom. He formerly worked on the faculty of Air Command and Staff College and has served as a C-130 navigator with worldwide flying experience. He earned an MA degree in international relations in 1989 and is a graduate of Squadron Officer School and Air Command and Staff College.

Lt Col Bradley S. Davis is the chairman of the Command and Strategic Studies Department at the Air Command and Staff College. He holds a BA degree in history from the University of California, Los Angeles, and an MS in organizational behavior and human resource management from Chapman University. He has completed Squadron Officer School, Marine Corps Command and Staff College, Air Command and Staff College, and Air War College. A career missileer, Lieutenant Colonel Davis has been an ICBM missile instructor, a joint strategic target planning staff weapons targeting specialist, missile squadron operations officer, and chief, wing standardization/evaluation division. His most recent assignment was at Headquarters USAF, with the responsibility for the policy and implementation of arms control treaties for the Air Force. He has written numerous articles on proliferation and the perils of weapons of mass destruction.

Mr Gregory T. Frost is a State Department Foreign Service officer detailed for the 1994-95 academic year as an advisor/ instructor at the Air Command and Staff College. He has served 20 years with the State Department, including seven tours of duty at various overseas diplomatic and consular posts, mainly in Africa and Latin America. Mr. Frost's last assignment was as principal officer of the US Consulate in Hermosillo, Mexico. He holds a BA from the University of Kansas, an MA from Washington University in St. Louis, and is a graduate of the Air War College.

Col Frank L. Goldstein, PhD, is the dean of education and research at the Air Command and Staff College. He is the author of several works on psychological operations and on terrorism. He formerly worked at the US Special Operations Command and is the author of the Air Force Secretary's Gulf War Air Power Survey.

Maj Robert H. Hendricks is a faculty member at the Air Command and Staff College. He holds a BS in international affairs and history from the Air Force Academy and an MS in human relations and management from Abilene Christian University. A senior navigator, he flew in and offered instructions on the B-52 and the B-1B. He is a graduate of Squadron Officer School, Marine Corps Command and Staff College, and Air Command and Staff College.

Maj Jan Kinner is a faculty member at the Air Command and Staff College. He holds an MBA from the University of Wyoming; a MUA from Wright State University; and is currently working on his doctorate in public administration from the University of Alabama. He is an acquisition officer with numerous manufacturing, contracting, and program assignments in AFMC and DLA, his latest at HQ AFMC.

Dr Karl P. Magyar is professor of National Security Affairs at the Air Command and Staff College. He holds a BA in philosophy from Michigan State University and a PhD in political science from The Johns Hopkins University. Dr Magyar has taught at universities in the US, Japan, and South Africa. He has also served as an international trade specialist in the US Department of Commerce in Washington, D.C., and Nigeria. He was economic development advisor to an African government. His academic areas of interest include international relations, US foreign policy, third world strategic developments, and an Africa area focus.

Lt Col Maris McCrabb is professor of Politics and Economics at Air University's School of Advanced Airpower Studies. He has held department chairmanships at the Air Command and Staff College and the College for Aerospace Doctrine, Research, and Education. He earned his doctorate in public administration from the University of Alabama. He is a command pilot with 3,100 hours in F-4 and F-16 aircraft and saw combat during the Gulf War.

Maj Paul J. Moscarelli is currently chief of the Operational Structures Division at Air Command and Staff College. He holds a BS in accounting from the State University of New York at Buffalo, an MBA from Rensselaer Polytechnic Institute, and a master of political science from Auburn University at Montgomery. He received his commission in the United States Air Force through Officer Training School in 1981 and has completed Squadron Officer School and Air Command and Staff College in-residence. He has logged 3,100 hours in the B-52 and flew 27 combat missions during the Gulf War.

Mr James E. Overly is a State Department Foreign Service officer detailed for the 1994–95 academic year as an advisor and visiting instructor to the Air Command and Staff College. His 20-year career in the US Foreign Service has emphasized political-military and African and European affairs. His last assignment was as deputy political counselor at the US Embassy in Lisbon, Portugal.

Capt Vicki J. Rast is currently an academic instructor at the Air Command and Staff College. She holds a BS in history from the United States Air Force Academy, an MPA degree from Troy State University, and is currently a doctoral candidate at the University of Alabama. She has completed Squadron Officer School as a distinguished graduate. An aircraft maintenance and munitions officer, she served in the United Arab Emirates during the Gulf War and in Saudi Arabia during Operation Southern Watch.

Lt Col Michael J. Savana, Jr., currently serves as chairman of the Wargaming Department at the Air Command and Staff College. He holds an undergraduate degree in remote sensing and cartography from Southwest Texas State University, and an MS in systems management from the University of Southern California. He is a career command control officer and has completed Squadron Officer School, Air Command and Staff College, and Air War College. He is also an acquisition officer and his previous assignment was as the director of an Air Force Material Command C^4I research and development facility.

Maj Kurt A. Stonerock received his commission from the United States Air Force Academy in 1982. He has a BS degree in management and an MS in procurement and acquisition management. Major Stonerock is currently pursuing a doctorate in public administration. He has had one tour in program management of space systems and three tours in contracting to include a four-year tour as the commander of a contracting office in the Republic of Singapore. He is currently on the faculty of the Air Command and Staff College.

Lt Col Gary A. Storie is the chief, Strategic Studies Division, at the Air Command and Staff College. He holds a BS in engineering sciences from the Air Force Academy, an MA in business administration from Webster University and is working on a doctorate in public administration from the University of Alabama. He is a command pilot with approximately 3,000 hours in T-37 and T-38 aircraft.

Col John A. Warden III, USAF, Retired, is the former commandant, Air Command and Staff College. He is the author of *Air Campaign*, was a major Gulf War planner, and has been a fighter wing commander and special assistant to the vice president of the United States. In June 1995 Colonel Warden retired after a distinguished 30-year career in the service of his country.